OLYMPIC REPORT '76

OLYMPIC REPORT '76

ed. JAMES COOTE

KEMPS, BATH STREET, LONDON E.C.1.

First Published in Great Britain 1976

ISBN 0 905255 038

Kemps Group (Printers and Publishers) Ltd
1–5 Bath Street
London EC1V 9QA

Printed in Great Britain by
Richard Clay (The Chaucer Press) Ltd
Bungay, Suffolk

Illustrations and Jacket printed by
The Halesworth Press Ltd
Halesworth, Suffolk

This book is dedicated to all those journalists who had to work in real haste under difficult conditions in Montreal during the month of July 1976.
To those contributors, and especially my co-author/editor, John Goodbody . . . thanks.

James Coote,
Press Centre, Montreal,
August 1st, 1976

CONTENTS

LIST OF ILLUSTRATIONS

Section Four

Section Five

PICTURE CREDITS

Pictures supplied by: Associated Press, UPI–Popperfoto, Ed Lacey, Colorsport, Allsport and Co Jo.

1

MONTREAL BACKGROUND

"Money has been stressed too much. It is time to bring back the real truth of the Olympics." Jean Drapeau, Mayor of Montreal.

AVERY BRUNDAGE, the former President of the International Olympic Committee, warned of the dangers of "giganticism" as long ago as 1936. But it needed the killings in Munich of the Israeli competitors—something that took place because the Palestinian terrorists knew that at an Olympics there would be enormous publicity for their actions—for the rest of the world to listen seriously. The IOC, who had been examining the programme of sports, made only half-hearted attempts to make the Games smaller. The international sports federations usually agreed that the Games should be smaller but invariably resisted any attempt to reduce drastically their events or the number of competitors.

If Munich had been an Olympics when efficient opulence was deliberately aimed at (and usually achieved) then Montreal began by attempting to stage a Games that were not only self-financing but modest in its intention and execution. It failed. This was not entirely the fault of Jean Drapeau, the Mayor of Montreal, who had pleaded with the 76-member IOC in 1970 to allow his city to host the Games. It was partially the fault of the IOC and the International Federations, who both paid only lip-service to making the Games a more manageable size. It was all very well for the new President of the IOC, Lord Killanin, to announce after Munich that the only thing that worried him about Montreal was that the Games were continuing to cost too much, but the IOC itself is principally to blame for this development. The IOC had trimmed the Games when they needed a severe cut. And until they take a firm stand such as the elimination of team sports they cannot gripe if the Games can in future only be staged by totalitarian states or by countries like Iran with vast private resources. In 1948 it cost the British organisers £161 per competitor to stage the Olympics. This year the price was nearer £150,000. Even considering inflation the London Games cost £3,506,000 whereas Montreal is expected to reach £850,000,000—twice the cost of Munich. The Olympics are exorbitant.

It is consequently ironical that Drapeau had wooed the IOC at Amsterdam in 1970 with an intentionally moderate programme and budget. It contrasted significantly with the lavish promises of Los Angeles—perhaps not a very serious offer—and Moscow. Drapeau envisaged the Games as being the cheapest for sixteen years and excited IOC members with his announcement as to how revenue would be raised. He listed lotteries, the sale of coins and stamps and the hawking of the Games symbol for use in product promotion as methods of raising 400,000,000 dollars. Drapeau blandly announced that the Olympics would no more have a deficit than a man could have a baby. And he stated that it was vital for Montreal to show Moscow that state backing was not a prerequisite for staging the Games. The confidence proved eventually to have as little foundation on accurate assessment as the hyperbole might have suggested.

Yet Drapeau's own status and reputation for effectiveness must have swayed the IOC. He has always been determined and forthright: a man who carried out what he believed was right, a leader of causes rather than a mediator between different factions. In the early 1940s when Drapeau began his career by fighting conscription as a Quebec Nationalist (his campaign manager incidentally was Pierre Trudeau, now Canada's Prime Minister), Montreal was nicknamed the Tijuana of the North. He fought corruption vociferously. It made him mayor in 1954 but Drapeau was defeated three years later because the Duplessis machine beat him. As a result he established a machine of his own.

This Civic Party consists of Drapeau's nominees to the Council, himself and his uncle as treasurer. In 1960 Drapeau won 91 per cent of the votes and all fifty-five council seats. Subsequently Drapeau has carried out his grandiose ideas for Montreal. He likes grand opera . . . so the city has grand opera. There was the expensive French-built Metro. And when Moscow dropped its bid for a World's Fair, Drapeau seized the chance of staging Expo '67. Thus when the IOC met in 1970 (thirty-one of their members and wives had made an all-expenses paid trip to Montreal) they knew that there was substance in Drapeau's declaration that the "history of Montreal" was the only financial guarantee they needed that the Games would be held. They did take place—but at a cost that shocked an IOC already startled by the escalation of costs needed for Munich.

For if the IOC perceived Drapeau's ability to get things done, they should also have perceived that he got things done expensively. It is true their decision was influenced by a reluctance to get involved in the East–West conflict because the other applications to stage the 1976 Games came from Los Angeles and Moscow. Montreal seemed the sensible alternative. Nevertheless, they also hoped that the Games would be less lavish than some recent Olympics. It was a hope that was based on scanty knowledge of Drapeau's work in Montreal between 1960 and 1970.

It is worthwhile examining the statement of Nick Auf der Mauer, the Opposition leader in Montreal, and while bearing in mind the probability of political bias, wonder how valid his words are. "The Mayor had no intention of staging modest Games. Look at his record! Modesty? He consulted no one when bidding for the Games. The head of his Planning Office found out on the same day as the Press. We have managed to discuss the Olympics in Council just twice when we had to pass on appropriations. When the budget came before us it was really amazing. There was just this one line: 'Cost: 496 million dollars. Accounts receivable: 496 million dollars.'

"The turning point with Drapeau concerned Taillibert" (the French architect of the Olympic Park) "Our heads swam with a billion dollars but when we heard that an uncontracted architect had been paid 3·5 million dollars in advances and stood to make another 30 million in fees and royalties that was something different.

"But Drapeau sits in the chair. We are always overruled. Anyway what could we have done? The abuses were committed. The mafia in the unions was just one aspect. Drapeau didn't have the power to stand up to them. The Games had to go on. The unions had us over a barrel."

The Canadians themselves realised the difficulties that were bound to arise when a city commits itself to staging an Olympics. Pride overcomes rationality so that there is an unreal, disillusioned atmosphere about the whole event. This was well caught by John

Robertson, a columnist for the Montreal Star, who wrote, long before the difficulties of the winter of 1975–6 made the situation acute: "If you talk about the real cost of the Olympics I'd say maybe one billion dollars if you counted the subway extensions. But who really knows? My guess is that no one really knows, no one at all. On the other hand I, like almost everyone else here, have an incredible sense of inevitability about it all. Drapeau will bring it off somehow, and I doubt whether we ever will know what it's costing. And maybe we won't even care. That's the way it is with Drapeau's dream."

The 1972 estimate of Drapeau was that the Games would cost 310 million dollars—a total which did not include such "infra-structure" projects as the new Metro line and stations and improved roads leading to the main Olympic site. This was half what Munich cost and evidently pleased the IOC because it demonstrated that a city like Montreal could stage the Games satisfactorily without huge state support. Indeed, Trudeau repeatedly refused to budge from his stand against direct financial involvements from the national Government.

For a while it seemed as if Drapeau's meritorious policy of making the Games self-sufficient would be fulfilled. Despite increasing world inflation there were feelings in 1973 that COJO (the Comité Organisateur des Jeux de la XXI Olympiade Montreal 1976) had applied themselves to the task with inspired diligence and enterprise. They launched numerous schemes to make money but the one that received greatest publicity was the attempt to raise considerably the amount which television companies paid for screening the Games. Although a compromise was eventually reached, it was a grudging one in which the Canadian organisers had clearly been influenced by the IOC's desire that the Games should be seen by as many people as possible.

The deadline after which it would have been impossible to order the equipment to screen the Games was only three days off when the rumours, later confirmed, that an agreement had been reached filtered through to the newspapers of London, where the meeting was being secretly held. It ended months of wrangling which to many people seemed absurd because the IOC's influence was paramount in an event over which they have the ultimate control. Nevertheless, Roger Rousseau, the Olympic Commissioner General, originally asked Europe for £13 million, then dropped it to

£7,800,000. The European Broadcasting Union, under the chairmanship of Sir Charles Curran, the director-general of the BBC, refused to raise their offer of £4 million, having originally bid considerably less.

Rousseau sought an equity of payment for TV coverage from all countries and argued strongly that European television had been getting the Olympics televised far too cheaply for too long—cheaper indeed per hour than international football or, occasionally, drama. He contrasted the European figures with those of the United States, who were paying £11½ million for their TV rights. And it was pointed out that the difference between the offer of the EBU and one that was acceptable to the Canadians was the difference between each viewer in Europe paying 6p for seeing the whole of the Olympics from his armchair as opposed to 3p.

However, the EBU argued that it was unfair to compare the United States with Europe because many members of the EBU (such as the BBC) did not take advertising and so could not benefit commercially from the huge numbers who would watch the Games on TV. American companies, on the other hand, sold advertising space during the Games coverage for high sums. In addition, although the price per viewer is an intriguing statistic, there is no method of raising money for a particular programme because of its immense popularity—as the Canadian organisers were aware.

Less subjective observers could have been justified in feeling that the EBU should have anticipated the increase in the price demanded to screen what is surely one of the most popular programmes on television and adjusted their budget accordingly. After all, for the first time the Olympics were shown at peak viewing hours in Europe.

As it was, the intervention of Lord Killanin, who reminded COJO that they were only acting as agents for the IOC and hinted broadly that this arrangement might have to be reviewed, proved crucial. The London meeting produced a number of face-saving formulae that allowed the Canadians to accept the EBU's offer. The payment was to be made in American instead of Canadian dollars, thus marginally improving the value of the bid. And there were also some minor readjustments of the amounts to be paid by some countries outside the EBU.

Further reasons to believe that the EBU were not paying an appropriate share are that twenty-seven per cent of the world's TV sets are in the EBU while thirty-four per cent of the Olympic competitors came from European countries. COJO originally asked the EBU for only twenty-six per cent of the total TV costs.

But just how delighted the BBC were with the arrangement was stressed when the Independent Television companies withdrew from negotiating to screen the Games live. Sam Leitch, the BBC's leading sports executive, could scarcely conceal his enthusiasm. "It's a licence to collect 30 million viewers. When Geoff Capes putts the shot for Great Britain at 9 o'clock in the evening who will be watching the other side?" The screening of the 130 hours of the Games (seventy hours fewer than in Munich) cost the BBC about £850,000. Considering how much promotional value they got out of the exercise one wonders whether this was enough.

Indeed COJO, who had been hoping to raise 50 million dollars for televising the Games—ABC, the American Company, agreed to pay 25 million dollars—in fact will get less than 3 million dollars. Half had to go to the Canadian Broadcasting Company for the cost of production, forty per cent went to the IOC for distribution to National Olympic Committees, plus the fees to an agent. Consequently television would have raised less than one per cent of the 310 million dollars which COJO originally estimated the Games would cost.

The allocation of tickets was equally controversial. A total of eighty-five per cent of the 5,400,000 tickets available (less those for VIP's and competitors) were reserved for Canada and the USA leaving just fifteen per cent for the rest of the world. The British Olympic Association were not alone in protesting. However, COJO argued that the ticket allocation had been estimated on the population of each country, the number of competitors from that country expected to take part, and the number of tourists from each country to have visited Quebec in 1973. Inevitably, in the difficulty of obtaining tickets, the costs of seats soared in Montreal. A fifty-dollar opening ceremony seat was reaching up to ten times that amount some months before the Games began.

The most successful money-raising enterprises of the Games was the lottery. It was originally anticipated that it would raise 32 million dollars, but the response by the public was so high that the organisers expanded its ticket base and held nearly three times as many draws as at first planned. By the early summer of 1976 this had been expected to raise 230,000,000 dollars, nearly seven times

OLYMPIC GAMES 1976
MONTREAL

A fish-eye lens' view of the opening ceremony. Eventually the roof will be covered by a retractable mast.

The salute of a champion by Lasse Viren after winning the 5,000 metres, and his fourth gold medal in successive Olympics. Below (left) in the 10,000 the strain is already telling on Brendan Foster, sandwiched between the leader, Carlos Lopes of Portugal, and Viren. Tony Simmons is fourth. Right: Dick Quax agonisingly loses the 5,000 metres title to Viren. Klaus-Peter Hildenbrand dives for the bronze.

A study in finishes: only Lasse Viren (301) is driving through the line, a perfect stylist belying the effort at the end of his fourth gold medal in two Olympics. Dick Quax, the silver medallist (691) shows all the agony of the race on his face while Klaus Peter Hildenbrand is about to fall over the line for third place. Rod Dixon (689) is still sprinting but has left his effort too late, while Brendan Foster (between Dixon and Quax) expresses annoyance at his own performance. Willy Polleunis (96) is a satisfied sixth, while a fairly disgusted seventh is Ian Stewart (380) in the background.

Anders Garderud may appear to be about to fall, but it is an illusion for he went on to lower his own world record and win Sweden's first athletics gold medal since 1948. Bronislaw Malinowski (724), the leader at that point in the steeplechase, finished second with Frank Baumgartl (behind Malinowski) falling over the last hurdle to take the bronze medal.

the projected net revenue. It is quite possible that the lottery would have raised even more, but national legislation was needed and, in between Montreal winning the Games and the bill going through Parliament, Trudeau's government lost the working majority it needed to get the lottery legislation through. Therefore Drapeau's plans were held up and without the money coming in the banks were unwilling to provide the capital for the most important section of the Olympic building operation—the main stadium complex.

This had two principal effects. Firstly it took the whole programme into the worst period of world inflation since the 1930s. And, also, the need to recover lost time meant overtime payments for the site workers—a situation the unions fully exploited. Moreover, although the figures for the lottery indicate that it was a large financial success, one must bear in mind that COJO only received the share from tickets sold within the Quebec province.

The sale of coins was less successful. Simon St Pierre, COJO's vice-president who died after a riding accident during the preparation for the Games, was a voluble advocate of selling coins minted especially by the Canadian Government for the Olympics. He pointed out that Munich had raised 213 million dollars during 1972 and that Montreal hoped to improve on these figures. Twenty-eight different coins were issued on seven different occasions at six monthly intervals. Although the first issue sold out quickly (fifty per cent in Canada and twenty-five per cent in the USA) the anticipated revenue of 250 million dollars never materialised. This was partly due to the fluctuating price of silver. When the value of silver went up the price of the coins (there was three-quarters of an ounce of pure silver in the 5 dollar piece and one and a half ounces in the 10 dollar piece) had to be sold above face value. This partially affected the response. The market, too, became oversubscribed and there was even a strike at the Federal Mint in Ottawa—halting production of Olympic coins. The sale of coins also benefited the individual National Olympic Committees because three per cent of the face value of the coins sold in each country was handed over for the promotion of amateur sport. This also applied to the sale of special Olympic stamps which COJO authorised. The probable receipts from the sale of the coins will reach 125 million dollars—a commendable amount but not when set against the vast rise in the overall cost of the Games.

Although COJO could be congratulated on their zest in exploiting the potential market, there were criticisms that this was against the Olympic spirit. The official Games symbol (a beaver) was sold to firms. For instance Coca-Cola paid 1·3 million dollars for the right to use the symbol and in addition received 18,000 tickets. As Gerry Snyder, the COJO Vice-President, explained without evident remorse: "We developed sponsor, supplier, supporter programmes—the three S's. We said to people 'We'd like to take your money but we can't. But for a sponsor contribution you can have a gold beaver award, for $50,000 to $150,000 you can have a torch and hang it on the wall in the president's office.'" He concluded that "it was a soft-sell operation in good taste". Some people were not so sure that he knew what good taste was.

If Avery Brundage would have been less than enthusiastic at the encroachment of business techniques on the Olympics nevertheless he would have had difficulty in arguing that the Canadians' strategy was not the only feasible one when large government sponsorship was unavailable. What made the determination of the Canadians to make the Games pay for themselves so depressing was that despite their business enterprises they failed—and failed badly. They did not try to follow a high ethical line of which the Baron de Coubertin would have approved. They tried for the future of the Olympic movement to show that a non-totalitarian state could succeed in staging a Games without recourse to government support. So when the Quebec province took over the responsibility of all the major Olympic facilities from Drapeau on November 20th, 1975 it was an indication of how risky it will be for future cities in the Western world to stage the Games unless there is considerable state support.

Montreal, of course, had few of the advantages that other prospective candidates may have in the future. They had no main stadium which was both suitable and completed. This is in distinct contrast to Moscow which has the Lenin Stadium and surrounding complex available. In Montreal, moreover, a swimming complex had to be built, plus other major installations. In addition, the Olympic Village had to be erected. The Canadians suitably decided to follow the example of Munich and have the Village adjacent to the main sports areas. The convenience of the competitors, the Canadians plainly decided, was a prime motivating force. Thus COJO were confronted with a massive building programme of the sites which carry most prestige for the staging of the Games.

When Montreal obtained the 1976 Games in 1970 it submitted to the IOC a file in which it listed the sports facilities already in existence and which it intended to use for the Olympic competitions. Also quoted were a number of new facilities which the city planned to build. From then the initial responsibilities associated with the Games were divided between the City of Montreal, who had control of the building sites (except Kingston) and COJO for the costs connected with the preparation and presentation of the Games themselves.

There was particular difficulty about the Olympic Village because the twin eighteen storey pyramid-shaped towers were scheduled to be built on the Viau Park, one of the few verdant areas on the east side of the city. However, although critics, eager to preserve the open space, expected that 50 acres would disappear, in fact only 4 acres did. The 78-million-dollar project was given to the developers, Frank Zappia's Zarolega Company. This was raised by obtaining 18 million from the National Bank of Canada on a mortgage secured by COJO and the remainder from COJO itself. Originally the plan was for the Village to be completed in the early part of 1976.

The IOC were understandably concerned when no work had begun on the Village by the autumn of 1974. Roger Rousseau was told by the IOC that unless it did they would take the Games away from Montreal. Within three months building started. Not for the first or last time the Olympics showed that not only do they create expense but also have the capacity to generate intense activity. Within sixteen months the building was almost complete, but at a great cost both to COJO and, indirectly, to the Olympic movement. The cost of the construction tripled. Zarolega (an acronym for Zappia and his partners Robinson, Lepine and Gatty) believed that the escalation of costs was due to inflation, the expense of sub-contractors and Rousseau's decision not to start building the Village until too late.

COJO had renegotiated the contract so that it could buy the development back after 1977 for 5 million dollars. The dramatic rise in costs alerted the police who investigated the proceedings for six months. They were concerned with allegations that sub-contractors paid Zarolega money to establish long completed contracts so that they could earn the 7,500 dollars a day offered by COJO for finishing ahead of time. One sub-contractor actually managed to complete the work 100 days ahead of schedule. There were even allegations that a deported Mafioso, Gilbert Zemmour, was involved in some of the Olympic contracts.

What did occur was that the Quebec Government passed legislation ending Zarolega's ownership of the Village on the grounds that the project had been supported largely out of public funds. It became clear that little of the public investment in the site would be recovered. The Olympic Installations Board took over ownership of the Village and arranged compensation for Zarolega through a three-man board of arbitrators. In any case it was not as if the Village was ideal for athletes preparing for the most exacting physical test of their lives—an occasion when the slightest irritation puts a competitor on edge. Even before the Games began numerous people were planning to live outside the Village before their actual events. An Olympic Village is claustrophobic at the best of times but 9,500 competitors had to sleep in 980 apartments in Montreal. In Munich the Village housed the same number of athletes in 4,722 apartments. There was correspondingly less pressure on the competitors. Even Rosaire Corbin, the Village spokesman for COJO, admitted before the Olympics that the competitors would be crowded but insisted that they wouldn't be overcrowded.

A further problem was that the teams' administrative offices were separated from the athletes' living quarters thus making control awkward. Yvan Dubois, COJO's directeur general of the Olympic Village, was more concerned that the atmosphere was right rather than that the buildings were suitable, declaring two years before the Games: "Oh, I want this to be a human village, full of good spirit and fun. And that won't depend on how the buildings are built will it?" What he didn't apparently appreciate was that the construction of the Village does influence, and influence greatly, the ambience of the Games.

But if there were inconveniences about the building of the Olympic Village there was a furore about the erection of the Stadium and swimming complex—the centrepieces of the Games. There would have been less controversy if some of the other centres had not been finished but athletics and swimming are the most publicised sports internationally. Consequently when the worry about whether these facilities would be ready reached its height in the winter of 1975–76 people tended to brush aside the fact that nineteen of the twenty-one installations were completed. Even as late as February 1976, moreover, Ramirez Vasquez, the architect of the 1968 Olympics, assured a doubting world that Montreal was closer to completion than Mexico City before the 1968 Games. The 7,500 seater Velodrome, which held the cycling and judo events, was to have been completed for the World Cycling Championships in August 1974 but difficulties with the unions spoilt the ambition. It was this failure that led so many journalists to be justifiably sceptical about whether the athletics and swimming venues would be finished on time.

Their concern increased when Dr Harold Henning, the President of the International Swimming Federation, visited the swimming venue and doubted whether the work would be completed in time. But the site engineers always believed the job would be done as scheduled—and said so. It is true that there was a delay last year but this was caused by the difficulty in discovering the best way to anchor the giant tower. Once this was settled the building of the pool continued uninterrupted. By the time of his visit of March 24th the water filtration system was in place, the tiles were being laid and water was being pumped into the pool.

But by then the escalation of costs had become so alarming that Drapeau had been forced to ask for a provincial-municipal Olympic partnership which could borrow money against the provincial government's far larger resources and would be able to use the threat of tougher legislation against the unions. Drapeau had spent 400 million dollars (much of it borrowed against Olympic revenue programmes) and could not raise any more. The province decided to take complete control themselves because as Dr Victor Goldbloom, the Minister in charge of Construction, pointed out, they feared they could not curb Drapeau's extravagances.

Goldbloom headed the Olympic Installations Board, which was created by the Quebec National Assembly on November 20th, 1975. Their mandate was to build, control and operate the central Montreal Olympic facilities. They took over the responsibilities which formerly the City of Montreal had assumed: the Olympic Stadium, Mast and Pool and the Olympic Velodrome.

Drapeau sought assistance because the costs had finally become impossible for a single city to support (the Games are allotted to a city and not a country). Despite the fund-raising activities Drapeau's plans had been undermined by a huge underestimation of the costs and the activities of the construction unions who could threaten (and carry out) strikes for increased wages. A typical example was the strike of 1,200 ironworkers from November 27th, 1974 to January 20th, 1975. Time was crucial because the Games had to go on.

There was friction, too, between the French architect, Roger Taillibert and the contractors. Taillibert, the designer of the Parc des Princes Stadium in Paris, required imported staff—something that was bound to antagonise the local unions. The stadium was constructed by pre-cast concrete moulds, a practice that was unfamiliar to Montreal workers. Even the value of concrete rose to mysterious heights. It cost the Games 460 dollars a cubic yard when in 1976 it cost another construction only 80 dollars a cubic yard—an extraordinary disparity. There was surplus work on the site and Drapeau's offices authorised expensive items which had little or nothing to do with the Games—for instance a scuba diving tank, and skating and curling rinks.

The Stadium itself was designed to house the Montreal Expos baseball team, who already had a purpose-built stadium of their own in the city. Although the Montreal Expos will use the new Stadium, it is, nevertheless, hardly sound economics to have two suitable venues in the same city. Many of the new Olympic facilities are not likely to be appropriate for massive participation by the citizens of Montreal.

When the Olympic Installations Board took over the responsibilities for the buildings they decided that only facilities essential to the Games would be completed by July 17th. Anything unnecessary would be eliminated. However, some frills like the eight-million-dollar fountain in the underground parking garage had to be completed because work had progressed so far on it. But the two major buildings were not finished: the main press centre and the fifty-five-storey tower. The press centre was moved to the middle of the city—in some ways more convenient for the journalists. The tower was left 51 metres tall instead of the 168 metres that was envisaged. The abandoning of building the tower meant that the 200-ton, 18,000-square-metre rubber membrane roof which was attached to the tower by cables would not be on show to the Olympic spectators. It will be completed after the Games. In any case there was little need for the stadium to be covered in the heat of the Montreal summer.

Another effect of the original delay of building the Stadium was that the changing facilities had to be only temporary. Instead of having permanent rooms under the lower stands the athletes were accommodated in eighty large mobile rooms in the parking garage adjoining the main stadium. Larry Eldridge, the Organising Committee's track and field co-ordinator, put a brave face on the situation by describing the quality of the facilities as comparable to permanent facilities in most stadiums.

The Stadium itself had severe problems in its construction. Lord Killanin, who once described it as a "sort of squashed Japanese lantern", was perhaps correct when he explained that one of its troubles was that it was built from the sky down. After it was found that some rows of spectators could not see properly a concrete guard rail was cut away and replaced with glass. Sportswriters, too, began poring over *Construction News* when the magazine reported that there were cracks in the structure of the main stadium. It further reported that the beams were too weak and in danger of excessive deformation. However, the presence of cracks was not necessarily significant because this was commonplace in a country which had extremes of hot and cold temperatures.

There were also problems in the roofing of the Velodrome with acrylic sheets—similar material to that used in the construction of Summerland, the Isle of Man amusement centre which burnt down in 1973, killing 50 people. The Quebec Labour Department withheld approval because of the lack of independent fire testing.

The concern that the Olympics would not be staged in Montreal reached its peak in January 1976, when the lowest temperatures for ten years caused 2,000 workers on the main site to be sent home. Rumours were rife in the world's press. If the athletics could not be staged on the proposed site they might be held outside the city or even in Los Angeles. Mexico announced that if Montreal were unable to stage the Games they would be prepared to deputise as hosts; they had the facilities and expertise from the 1968 Games. However, the IOC, although unquestionably worried, had an assurance from COJO that the Games would go on. And their confidence, despite all the problems and cut-backs, was ultimately justified.

Unusually mild spring weather meant that the building could continue more easily. Perhaps an indication of how the outside world began to share Montreal's confidence was the statement of Lloyds of London, who know something about risks. On January 20th they announced that they would need a £50 premium to insure a £167 airflight to the Games. Five weeks later the premium had dropped to £20.

Even if the Games were certain to be staged at their original venue, the cost in men and money continued. Nine men had died in accidents on the Olympic site by March 26th; and when details of the security arrangements were released the costs rose once again. Montreal, mindful of Munich, employed 16,000 security men to make it Canada's biggest military operation since the Second World War.

The Canadians generally had the attitude of a drunken man at a party—the indulgence in the euphoria of the moment rather than any overt concern with the hangover the next day. Quebec residents were taxed heavily on tobacco to raise the 600,000,000 dollars needed to cover the deficit but the provincial authorities insisted that Montreal would have to raise the remaining 200,000,000 dollars through its own municipal tax system.

But if the citizens of Montreal may eventually have learnt the harsh facts of the Olympic Games because a combination of factors made them as expensive as they were, one wonders whether the IOC have learnt. Lord Killanin, usually such a perceptive and understanding man, remarked at the IOC Congress at Varna: "The IOC has the Olympic Games and the Olympic movement well in hand." After Montreal one is bound to wonder how he could be so complacent.

The one certainty of the Montreal Olympics was that the Games would not take place without them being used as a plaything by the world's politicians. After the problems over South Africa in Mexico and the exclusion of Rhodesia and the killing of the Israeli competitors at Munich it was inevitable that the final few days before the Montreal Games would be concerned with the International Olympic Committee trying to get all their members taking part in the Games despite the intervention of the politicians.

The International Olympic Committee are handicapped on these occasions. The world's politicians generally do not care about sport. The IOC do: they want the Games to go on. Demands such as those which confronted the IOC over Rhodesia in Munich have much of their impetus from the fact that they were made so near to the Games. The IOC had to make their decision in 1972 knowing that on their decision depended the ambitions of many young athletes who had already gone to Munich and that their task was to give as many competitors as possible a chance to fulfil those ambitions. They knew that the Supreme Council for Sport in Africa, prodded by the politicians of the Organisation for African Unity, had chosen to make their stand at the last moment because that was the best way of ensuring what they wanted: the banning of Rhodesia.

So it was in Montreal. The Canadian Government knew that if they had announced up to the beginning of 1976 that the participation of Taiwan under the banner of the Republic of China was not acceptable to them then the IOC would have withdrawn the Games from Montreal. And they also were aware that by making their feelings clear as late as May 28 it was impossible for the IOC to get the Summer Games staged elsewhere. Consequently they presumed—and presumed rightly—that the IOC would be forced to give way.

The reason for the Canadian Government's stance was surely the valuable grain trade with Communist China. A new contract was about to be negotiated and plainly the Canadians' negotiations would be helped if they refused to allow Taiwan to compete in the most prestigious sports event ever staged. That they couldn't do—but what they could do was to present the International Olympic Committee with a situation which made it very difficult for Taiwan to take part in the Games. The IOC did wring out of the Canadian Government the concession that the Taiwan competitors could enter the country—two yachtsmen were in Kingston while the negotiations were going on—as long as they did not use the name of the Republic of China.

It is rare that the world's media get emotional on occasions like this. But the sheer fury behind the questions to the Canadian officials as they came out of negotiating with the IOC a week before the Games were due to open was evident. So was the cheering of the speech of IOC President Lord Killanin as he publicly lambasted the Canadian Government. What was at stake was the basic principle of the Olympics: that the athletes of any country recognised by the IOC may assemble in the Olympic city to take part in the celebration of the Games without let or hindrance. But the IOC Executive Board had to recommend to the Committee that this principle had to be abandoned because the Games had to go on.

But what they also did was to set a precedent which could have the most damaging affect on international sport. Now any government may ignore earlier agreements without which the country staging the event would not have been allocated the championship or Games in the first place. This was recognised by many of the international federations as they gathered in Montreal.

These federations saw not only their participation in competitions like the Olympics and Commonwealth Games hindered but also events directly under their own control: world and continental championships. Typical of this reaction was Charles Palmer, who is not only President of the International Judo Federation but also the secretary of GAIF, the world body that represents 64 different international sports federations. "I cannot stress enough that the IOC have set an incredibly dangerous precedent for all international sport." The future may well show that the Montreal incident was just the first of a series of such dictatorial incidents.

It would be pleasant to be able to record that Taiwan behaved with dignity on this occasion. But they didn't. What was even worse than a lack of dignity was their foolishness in not agreeing to the formula that the IOC had prepared for them—competing without a flag, without a name and without an anthem. The value to Taiwan would have been enormous. Their athletes would have competed in Montreal with enormous goodwill from the other participating nations. Indeed their entry alone into the Stadium at the Opening Ceremony bearing the Olympic flag would have generated enough support for their cause to have ensured that Communist China would have had little support if they had sought to return to the Olympic movement which they left voluntarily in 1958. Taiwan would have safeguarded their presence in the Olympics for many years to come. As it is they have lost support from other countries and they have unwittingly facilitated the return of Communist China to the Games.

Although the USA scarcely showed diplomatic ingenuity by threatening to leave the Olympics if Taiwan were excluded, the President of the United States Olympic Committee, Philip Krumm, did say what many people in Montreal thought—that the decision of the IOC could be the beginning of the end of the Olympic movement. "The matter is as serious as that."

If the negotiations over Taiwan were complex, those over the boycott of the Games by the Black African nations were comparatively straightforward. The issue, too, was clearcut. Should the New Zealand Olympic Committee be responsible for the country's Rugby team playing in South Africa? A number of Black African nations believed that it was—perhaps not believing that, unlike many of their own countries, Government control over sports (in this case Rugby) in New Zealand was minimal. The New Zealand Government has a clear, unequivocal policy of non-interference in sport. Nor does the New Zealand Olympic Committee have any jurisdiction over the New Zealand Rugby Union. Although some 30 African and Arabic countries joined in the boycott of the Games, the weakness of their case was evident by the lack of support from the communist nations or indeed from the negroes in such teams as the United States. In 1972 the United States negroes in Munich had supported the cause to have Rhodesia barred from competing in the Games. This time they didn't. Although many of the track events and also the boxing competition were grievously affected by the Black African withdrawal in Montreal they have surely lost a lot of good-will over their stand. If the communist nations and the American negroes had believed that they had a valid case they would have joined in the boycott.

The Olympics went on, then, without about 700 competitors but as often occurs on these occasions, rightly or wrongly, people became more concerned as to who was competing rather than who wasn't. Nor did the statement of Lee Evans, the Nigerian coach and former Olympic 400 metres champion, elucidate: "It's all well and good to say that the Olympics are sacred and nobody should tamper with them. But life is sacred, too, and when you think of 176 people killed in South African riots, maybe you can appreciate why we felt so strongly. There seems tendency in the world to shrug it off when blacks are killed. We're people and we've decided human life is more important than winning medals." The lack of logic in his stand makes one question how the New Zealand Olympic Committee can be so associated with the killing in Soweto as to make it impossible for African athletes to compete alongside New Zealanders in Montreal. One wondered how much Evans and other African spokesmen were motivated by emotional revulsion at the killings in Soweto and how much by a distinct belief in the guilt in the New Zealand athletes. If the Black African nations felt so strongly one wondered why they didn't apply their protest to Canada because a South African cricket team was touring the host country the week the Games began.

Perhaps there was an element of truth in the feeling in Montreal that the Supreme Council for Sport in Africa had gambled that the

IOC would submit to them as they had done in 1972. And, when the IOC didn't prefer to sacrifice even a small country like New Zealand for the African nations, the National Olympic Committees of the African countries had to carry out their threat because of instructions from their individual governments.

Although one should applaud the Africans protesting on behalf of Black South Africans, a defenceless party who are oppressed in their own lands, nevertheless one questions their methods of doing so. They have done their own noble cause—the elimination of apartheid in sport in South Africa—little good by their action and spoilt the chances of many of their competitors from taking part in the Games. This is, of course, not the end of this issue. The participation of the Black African nations is more crucial to the 1978 Commonwealth Games than it is to the Olympics.

It is a pity that countries cannot leave questions like a boycott to the consciences of individual athletes. What was so disturbing about the boycott in Montreal was the distress felt by many of the competitors who had to obey instructions to leave. Nigerian 400 metre hurdler Taiwo Ogunjobi summed up many feelings when he said: "They tell me to run right I run right. They tell me to run to left I run left. They tell me to go home I go home. There's nothing we can do."

2
ATHLETICS
(*Men*)

Nine world records, 12 Olympic records; certainly the standards in Montreal did not appear to be affected materially by the absence of the black Africans. Tanzania, Uganda, Ethiopia and Kenya will be the chief to suffer, for their records will be affected in the years to come and create a depreciation in interest in their own country. It has been repeatedly proved that interest is stimulated by success and if black African athletes see that their dream of taking part in the greatest sporting festival, the Olympic Games, is affected by political decision, they will transfer their sporting interest to other ventures.

With a series of double gold medallists: Alberto Juantorena (400 metres and 800 metres), Lasse Viren (5000 metres and 10,000 metres) Baerbel Eckert (women's 200 metres and 4 × 100 metres relay), Valentina Kazankina (800 metres and 1500 metres) and some other remarkable champions—Ed Moses (400 metres hurdles, Irena Szewinska (women's 400 metres) and even some of the non winners, such as Willie Davenport, in his fourth Olympics, it is difficult to name the man and woman of the Games. So many in their own event achieved so much more than others before.

Juantorena heralded a new era in short distance racing for his double had never before been achieved and his powerful frame with its huge thighs, as opposed to the broad shouldered Dave Jenkins, might yet herald a new breed of 400 metres runner.

Moses ran a perfect 400 metres hurdles with 13 strides all the way round between each barrier while Bruce Jenner won the greatest decathlon ever seen, both in world record.

But all these must stand below the feat of Lasse Viren, who for the second time in four years took on the best distance runners in the world and beat them. Thus he became the first man in history to retain his two Olympic distance titles—in fact only Emil Zatopek and

Vladimir Kuts (1952 and 1956) and back in Olympic history the first of the Flying Finns, Hannes Kolehmainen, in 1912, had achieved the double in the same Games.

When Viren later tackled the marathon and finished a weary fifth, this set the seal on a remarkable triple and his training methods and racing style must inevitably be copied by many others.

He and many other top Olympic competitors share one feature: their ability to race often, under strange conditions, against handicaps and to reach peak form at the right time. The slavish desire of the British selectors to please their sponsors by having fully representative Olympic trials will inevitably always produce over-fit athletes early in the season and until the day that non-professional officials hand over to professional coaches or a full time professional administrator the sport will suffer.

A sign of this too-rigid policy can be seen in the decision to overlook the remarkable racing record of Ian Thompson, while allowing Alan Pascoe every possible opportunity to get fit. Each man was a reigning European and Commonwealth champion. Thompson should have been given the same opportunity as Pascoe, who fully deserved his chance.

If only the British Board would look at the records of Don Quarrie, Haseley Crawford, Alberto Juantorena and Lasse Viren and see how they scoot about from meeting to meeting, country to country, amassing defeats and victories but being able to observe and study their rivals.

Britain did worse in these Olympics than any before, whatever yardstick is taken; whether that of winning medals (one mere bronze to the great credit of Brendan Foster) or of finalists. While the men achieved fractionally more than the women neither earned much praise but the overall standard of women's athletics, which has not kept pace with the rest of the world, is a very real worry and will not improve until all those at the top give way to men and women in whom the athletes have complete confidence and can fully communicate.

100 Metres

The strict format of the American selection trials ensured that they were without their two best men, Steve Williams and Houston McTear, who were unable to make the team because of injury. The

United States athletics team can only be nominated on the results of the trials; the first three in each event automatically being selected for the Olympic Games. This rigid system has brought famous omissions in the past but there has always been such depth that the gold medals have continued to pour in.

Even before the Games, the team coach, Leroy Walker, spoke of the need to have this system altered. The Americans could not even find a place for Williams, who has broken the world 100 metres and 100 yards records on frequent occasions between 1973 and 1976.

In fact, it was the first time since 1928 they failed to win a single medal, their fastest man on the day, Harvey Glance, an indifferent fourth.

The reigning champion Valeriy Borzov of the Soviet Union, the sprint double gold medallist in Munich, attempting a repeat performance, which no other sprinter has yet achieved in the history of the Games, came into the Games with a spotty record. He did not compete in 1973, had injury problems in 1974 and 1975 and early 1976, yet in the final he repeated his 1972 performance of 10·14sec, but this time picking up the bronze medal.

The winner was the first ever for Trinidad and Tobago in any Olympic sport, when Haseley Crawford, the 6ft 1in., 165-lb athlete, who reached only the quarter finals in Munich, won by two hundredths of a second in 10·06sec from Don Quarrie, of Jamaica.

200 Metres

With the elimination of Steve Williams the way had to be open to Don Quarrie, the Munich favourite four years earlier, who registered his first Olympic victory.

Quarrie, world record holder at 200 metres, and Commonwealth champion, had only to worry about Haseley Crawford, the Trinidadian winner of the 100 metres but after 50 metres Crawford pulled up, because of a bad start which put him too far down the field.

The absence of the reigning champion, Valeriy Borzov, who withdrew to concentrate on the 4 × 100 metres relay, made the result more open, but the eventual outcome was rarely in doubt with Quarrie crossing the line ahead of two Americans, Millard Hampton and Dwayne Evans.

The only Briton entered in the event, Ainsley Bennett, finished last in his semi-final.

400 Metres

The 400–800 double of Alberto Juantorena cannot be over-emphasised for it is a double victory combining a series of talents not normally present in one runner. The 400 metres specialist is a man who has gradually moved up from 100 metres, to the 200 metres and then the 400 metres. He rarely runs over 400 metres, believing that his basic speed will suffer. An 800 metres expert is usually a man who lacks the basic 400 metres speed and moves up in due course to 1500 metres.

To have the ability to cover both spectrums takes a very special competitor. In 1974 Juantorena, at 6ft 3in, was the world's No. 1 400 metres specialist. Then a foot operation caused him to miss most of the 1975 season but he came back at the end of the year to win the Pan-American Games title. For a man who had not survived the preliminary rounds in Munich it was an eye-opening improvement.

He had a go at the 800 metres early in 1976, opening with a 1min 45·2sec, before improving down to 1min 44·9sec but there was uncertainty as to whether he would be able to risk his certain 400 metres gold medal with the 800 metres first on the programme. He might with the 800 metres and then be too tired for the 400 metres. There was no worry about this on the day. He set his world 800 metres record, and then in his seventh race of the Games (three at 800 metres and four at 400 metres) he strode away from a good field to win in 44·26sec, the fourth fastest time ever, and the best by a non-United States competitor.

Juantorena started the race slowly and only really got his huge stride working as he entered the back straight, with apparently too large a gap between him and his main rivals, of whom Fred Newhouse, the most experienced of the American pair, was most dangerous.

The Cuban can not have forgotten that in the 1972 American trials Newhouse ran a semi-final in 44·2sec, then in the final covered the first 200 metres in a suicidal 20sec before finishing on his knees in seventh place. That experience had made Newhouse vow that he would atone 100% in Montreal; although his silver medal proves this was not to be. Having closed the gap Juantorena ran an excellent final bend to enter the home straight ahead.

Dave Jenkins (European champion at nineteen, in 1971, was unable to reach the final in 1972, but, better prepared and coached by Dave Hemery, the former Olympic champion) kept British hopes alive. However, in his own words, "everything went blank after 200 metres." He had run according to orders and sat on the heels of Newhouse until 200 metres but that was the end of the race so far as British chances were concerned. He tired and finished a lonely seventh, beating only the Pole, Jan Werner, in an indifferent 45·57sec.

The irony of the race was that had Jenkins equalled his own British record (of which he was completely capable) he would have earned himself a bronze medal.

800 Metres

The "doubling-up" tradition in the Olympic Games for runners to go for the 200–400 and 800–1500 double has never been successful. Yet Alberto Juantorena, the powerful Cuban, with the huge, loping, stride and almost exaggerated back-lift, decided he would confound all the critics by attempting it. With the 800 metres first on the programme it might be thought that he would hold something back. After all, he was very inexperienced at the distance, despite a world No. 2 ranked time of 1min 44·9sec.

He gave hints of power in the preliminary rounds, the only shock of which was the disqualification of the American favourite and world 880 yards record holder Rick Wohlhuter, for barging in the back straight. In an event where bodily contact is the norm, Wohlhuter's push scarcely raised a ripple but an over-zealous Canadian ruled that he had gained an unfair advantage. Upon appeal, however, he was rightfully restored to a place in the final.

When the first lap was covered in just over 50sec it seemed that a world record must be on the cards. As it happened, this was the case. Juantorena stormed through, never really opposed, to cross the line in 1min 43·5sec, improving by one fifth of a second the previous record set by the South-African born Italian Marcello Fiasconaro three years earlier.

Ivo Van Damme, who had some excellent pre-Games marks, repeated Roger Moens' 1960 silver medal for Belgium, with Wohlhuter third.

Steve Ovett, still only 20, was drawn in lane 8, which cost him any hope he may have had of keeping up with the crowd. Unable to see the searing pace being set inside him, he went out at what he felt was an adequate speed only to find himself a long way behind when the field broke at the 300 metres mark.

Rushing to close the gap he took too much out of his legs and had no challenge later in the race. Even so, he achieved a personal record in fifth place. At his best, had he been drawn in a better lane, it was difficult to see him running better than fourth in such exalted company.

1500 Metres

The 1500 metres is the classic event that has never yet failed to arouse the greatest interest of all events in an Olympic track and field programme. Montreal proved no exception. The added spice on this occasion was that the favourite John Walker, world mile and 2000 metres record holder had surprisingly been eliminated from the 800 metres heats on the opening day due to illness and it was not known how much the attempted Black African boycott of his team had affected him.

After all, one of the highest points of these Games had originally been the prospect of a clash between him and Filbert Bayi, of Tanzania, the world 1500 metres record holder and Commonwealth gold medallist, two of the finest front runners ever seen. Alas there would be no Bayi and how Walker would fare on his own with no one to set fast pace was problematical.

The heats gave little hint of outstanding outsiders although the Irish Eamonn Coghlan, a student at Villanova University, in the United States, confirmed the speed which took him to two National Collegiate gold medals and third place behind Bayi in his world mile record breaking race the previous year. In the semi-finals Coghlan nipped through a gap on the inside to finish first and showed that not only did he have speed by a spirit of originality. Britain placed Frank Clement and Dave Moorcroft in the final—the first time Britain has done as well since the 1964 Olympics—but Steve Ovett, after a most encouraging heat, was too tired in the semi-finals to challenge for a place in the last eight.

With intermediate times of 62·48sec and 2min 3·15sec at 400 metres and 800 metres it was obvious that the final would result in a tactical race. Coghlan again attempted to force the pace and it was not until some 20 metres before the start of the final lap that Walker really came into his own.

The sight of Walker, his long blond locks flowing behind him, and dressed in the traditional New Zealand All Black running clothes, is one that cannot easily be forgotten. Steady acceleration made it impossible for his rivals to come past and although four or five men bunched up behind he was never really worried. Coghlan got left behind in the dash for the line with Ivo Van Damme taking Belgium's and his second silver medal (having already been placed runner up in the 800 metres) and Paul Wellman, of West Germany, the bronze. Frank Clement produced one of Britain's better runs of the Games to snatch fifth place and his time of 3min 39·65sec was within half a second of Walker. Dave Moorcroft finished seventh in the nine-man final.

5000 Metres

Before Lasse Viren came to Montreal he was interviewed by a journalist who asked him why he wanted to continue and attempt to defend his titles when he had already achieved more than most. His reply, after a long pause, was that he wanted his countrymen to stop always talking about Nurmi as THE Flying Finn, to stop comparing him with Paavo Nurmi and to talk about Viren. In a small country of only four and a half million, less than half the population of London, athletics is a fierce religion. Theirs is a tradition which stretches back to the first Olympics.

Never has this little country been disgraced in an Olympics; when one champion retires there is another to take his place and it is not just national pride or sporting ability that brings medals. It is that fierce Finnish spirit "*Sisu*" which made them take on the entire Soviet nation in the war and which makes them into mentally strong people able to conquer the many problems faced by their nation.

In 1972 Lasse Viren won first the 10,000 metres and then the 5000 metres. This double had only been achieved by Hannes Kolehmainen in 1912, Emil Zatopek in 1952 and Vladimir Kuts in 1956, putting him in exalted company.

When Viren came to Montreal, after an indifferent intervening four years, during which he had undergone a hamstring operation and minor nasal surgery for blocked passages, nobody really believed that he could defeat two excellent fields with men faster, and many with far better racing records—Rod Dixon, of New Zealand, Brendan Foster, of Great Britain, Carlos Lopes, of Portugal, and a number of others.

By winning the 10,000 metres he became the first man successfully to defend the title; but, by then, finishing first in the 5000 metres he set a record it is difficult to see anyone beating. And it was his hardest gold medal of the four. Everyone was determined that the Master should not be allowed to get away with another victory. But nobody knew how to combat him. Should it be a fast pace from the start and hope to tire him out, or should it be a medium pace with mid-field bursts? Or how about a slow crawl and then a dash for the line hoping to squeeze him out? It is an amazing proof of his mental power over his rivals that no-one could produce the right tactics. Even Foster, after his bronze medal in the 10,000 metres, made minor breaks, which were easily combated by half a dozen of the others, including Rod Dixon, Dick Quax and Ian Stewart.

The stomach bug, which had affected Foster in the early part of the Games, obviously affected his judgment in the 5000 metres as he was unsure how effective his breaks would be; Quax, who had been on a glucose drip to combat a severe attack of dysentry could not obviously use the speed which had taken him to a time of 13min 13·2sec—one fifth of a second off the world record—earlier in the season and it was left to Viren, himself, to command proceedings.

He made one or two little bursts towards the end after Foster had made a minor break at 3000 metres, which was reached in a slower time than in the 10,000 metres; these had the effect of tiring the field more than they imagined and from then Viren had only to use his remarkable reserves to fight off a fast finishing Quax.

At least the silver medal was some consolation for Quax who had missed the 1972 Olympics and the 1974 Commonwealth Games through injury ... and from a personal point of view especially satisfactory as it was the first time I had seen a long-time friend run a good race, free from injury.

The bronze medal was snatched from Dixon by the West German Klaus-Peter Hildenbrand, who threw himself over the line in a last desperate bid to earn himself a little glory.

10,000 Metres

The absence of the Ethiopians and Kenyans may have cut the interest of the 10,000 metres but certainly not the standard, for the first eight men were just as fast as in Munich, with the eventual winner, Lasse Viren, of Finland, retaining his title in 27min 40·4sec, only 2sec slower than the world record he set in Munich.

The race was run as never before: there were no mid-race breaks by Brendan Foster and nobody was able to crack the field wide open early on. What did happen was that an almost unknown runner from a country with no athletics tradition at all, Portugal, set a pace unique in the annals of the sport.

When he took over after three kilometres, each successive kilometre time had been faster: the first took 2min 53sec, the second 2min 15sec, the third 2min 49·4sec.

The fourth again was 2min 49·4sec, and the fifth 2min 46sec. Half way was reached in 14min 8·9sec, about half a minute slower than Dave Bedford in his world record race at the same stage. As a world record had been predicted before the race got under way, it was a trifle disappointing as was the lack of kick by Foster, Britain's hope for the first 10,000 metres medal since 1920, when James Wilson won a bronze.

The sixth kilometre took 2min 43·5sec, the seventh and eighth eased fractionally, both being covered in 2min 43·5sec but Lopes really attempted to pile on the pace in the final two kilometres covering the ninth in 2min 38·6sec the last in 2min 37·8sec. Lopes had not finished sprinting and it was the only way he knew of getting away from the clutches of the Olympic champion, who was breathing hot over his shoulder.

The inevitable happened slightly more than a lap from home, when Viren so easily sprinted by to become only the second man in Olympic history to retain his 10,000 metres crown. Foster wearily hung on for the bronze from the fast finishing Luton lecturer, Tony Simmons, who ran an underrated race throughout.

Time and again it looked as if he wanted to dash for the front, and indeed both Viren and Lopes kept glancing nervously over their shoulders wondering what the Briton was doing. They did not know that Foster had an attack of tummy trouble, which pills could not clear up, and as a result he was slightly weakened. The race soon resolved into a leading group between Lopes, with Viren on his shoulder, and with Foster falling further and further back.

Mark Smet, the Belgian, tripped over at one point, just as Viren did, in the Munich final, but unlike Viren could not find enough speed to win, although he bravely carried on and finished with a badly bruised arm in seventh place.

110 Metres Hurdles

The greatest pressure on Guy Drut to become the first Frenchman to win the Olympic high hurdles title was from his countrymen with whom he had lost a certain measure of support by joining Prime

Minister Chirac's staff, advising on sport. As Chirac only got into power on a small majority this necessarily put a large percentage against him. Indeed, French spectators had taken to booing Drut whenever he competed, an almost unheard of occurrence in a country where the sportsman is king.

As France can produce so few competitors of outstanding ability the result was that the only athlete she possessed of world class standard found himself in the invidious position of having to win two times over—for those who supported him and those who disliked his politics.

The preliminaries produced no surprises, Britain's Berwyn Price going out at the semi final stage after an appalling start, Drut hitting two hurdles and making Frenchmen's hearts stop momentarily, until he recovered his rhythm.

Lined up against Drut in the final were the Americans Charlie Foster, rated as the main danger, and the veteran Willie Davenport who had competed in every Olympics since 1964. He was a semi-finalist, but injured in 1964, won the gold medal in 1968 and placed fourth in 1972. A further danger was yet another Cuban, Alejandro Casanas, who had handed a surprise defeat to Drut earlier in the year.

In 1975 Drut forecast that he would run 13·28sec, on July 28th, the day of the Olympic final. As he had already set a (hand timed) world record of 13·0sec and run an electric 13·28sec this statement did not seem unreasonable. The one thing telling against Drut was that in 1971, at the Helsinki European Championships, he fell when a favourite and repeated this in the 1975 American Championships. However, if his training was geared correctly, anyone else in the field wanting to win would have to improve that target of 13·28sec.

Came the final ... and what time was flashed on the scoreboard? Yes, 13·28sec. An amazing coincidence. That it was amended later to 13·30sec by the timekeepers is scarcely significant, more a confirmation of an oustanding competitor's ability to size up his rivals and stay ahead of them. The Cuban took the silver medal, Davenport the bronze.

400 Metres Hurdles

Three successive Olympic finals: three world records. Dave Hemery brought the gold medal in a record to Britain in 1968 with a 48·12sec timing; John Akii-Bua took it over for Uganda in 1972 with a 47·82sec and in 1976 Ed Moses took it back to the United

States with a superlative 47·64sec. For Britain the race was not happy. No Olympic medal for the first time since 1964 and only the sight of the not-yet-fit Alan Pascoe, fighting against all the odds to force his body faster than it should go.

In 1964 John Cooper took a silver medal; in 1968 Hemery and John Sherwood the gold and bronze and in the last Olympics Hemery earned himself another bronze. There is no doubt that had Pascoe not been so long injured he could have collected at the worst a silver medal for all his training had been based on a 47·5sec winning time in the Olympics. He managed to overcome the earlier rounds well, but was obviously desperately short of races and in a race where the first man would probably be under 48sec and the next under 49sec he had only two options: to go out and settle for fifth or sixth or to run flat out from the start, dig into his reserves to the very depth and then struggle, hoping that he would not "die" too far from home.

Alas! the European and Commonwealth champion, ran to a halt at the 10th hurdle and only just managed to stagger across the line. Exhausted to a point almost of collapse. Still, no one could have asked for more.

With Akii-Bua an absentee because of Uganda's boycott of the Games, along with the other African countries, a terrific clash between him and Moses was not to be. Who would have been the winner? No one can tell. However, Moses had a more perfect stride pattern that even Akii-Bua, with 13 strides between each hurdle, compared with the Ugandan's 13 and then down to 14 in Munich. Yet the American bespectacled negro had never run a 400 metres hurdles before March 1976. He opened his account with a steady 50·1sec, by June was down to 49·8sec and then in the Olympic trials produced the third fastest time ever of 48·30sec. A real natural if ever there was one.

3000 Metres Steeplechase

When Dennis Coates, the Gateshead club colleague of Brendan Foster, improved his personal record by 8sec and the British record from 8min 22·8sec to 8min 19sec there were great hopes that he would follow in the tradition of Chris Brasher's gold medal in 1956 or Maurice Herriott's silver in 1964. Realistically there was no way he would be able to win, for Bronislaw Malinowski, Poland's European champion, born of a Scottish mother, had a remarkable big-race temperament and it would be only a matter of whether both he and Anders Garderud, Sweden's world record holder, fought out the final, or the Pole on his own.

Malinowski finished fourth in Munich when only 21. Garderud, the fastest steeplechaser in history, had successively taken the world record from 8min 14sec (by Ben Jipcho, of Kenya) to 8min 9·8sec in 1975. Before that in 1972 he knocked 1·8sec off the best time on record by Kerry O'Brian, so the Swede was fully experienced.

Both men had very fast 1500 metres times, but Garderud had the unhappy memory of Mexico where he did not survive the opening rounds of the 800 metres and 1500 metres in 1968 and of Munich where he was equally unsuccessful in the steeplechase and 5000 metres.

Garderud, Malinowski, the fastest improving East German, Frank Baumgartl, a world junior record holder, and the Finn Tapio Kantanen, third in Munich proved the significant pace setters after Coates, and others had dropped back. With a killing pace it was obvious that technique and speed across the hurdles and water jump would decide the destiny of the gold medal. And this is what happened. Malinowski set a bludgeoning example by refusing to allow anyone to make a significant impact on matters and with the water jump and one hurdle to go the race had evolved into a struggle between Poland, East Germany and Sweden.

All three men crossed the last water jump within a second of each other and sprinted for the final hurdle. Alas there, poor Baumgartl, the youngest, at 21, of all the challengers, was so exhausted that he could do no more than fall over the hurdle, flat on his face. At this point Garderud was well placed to win, Malinowski looked at the best a bronze medal prospect.

The Pole surged by the unfortunate German who picked himself up to limp wearily over the line, rewarded at least with a bronze in itself was an excellent feat for he had been seriously injured.

Garderud set yet another world record, 8min 8·02sec with Malinowski second, and Coates, producing his second fastest time ever of 8min 22·99sec was ninth with the second Briton, Tony Staynings, 11th.

Marathon

The failure of both the American and British competitors to win can fairly be laid at the door of the respective selectors. In the

United States they forced the reigning champion, Frank Shorter, and the man who ranked No. 1 in the world in 1975, to run a gruelling marathon trial slightly more than a month before the Olympic Games; in Britain the well-known controversy over the non-selection of the reigning European and Commonwealth champion, Ian Thompson, continued long after the marathon runners had crossed the line in Montreal's Olympic stadium.

The reasons: the placings of Jeff Norman (26th), Keith Angus (31st) and the English champion Barry Watson (45th). There can be no question that had Thompson, and the extremely experienced Ron Hill been selected, there is no way they could have finished so low down the field. And it is not a case of hindsight. The selectors were urged from all quarters to allow commonsense to override personal prejudices and select not just the best three men on the day but the best men for the Olympics. For a country with such a tradition of Marathon running these three poor placings is little short of disgraceful, but one cannot blame the runners who did their best on the day. They were patently not up to the requisite standard and it is interesting to note that neither the third placed finisher, Karel Lismont, nor the winner, Waldemar Cierpinski, had ever beaten Thompson.

Shorter and Thompson have never clashed over the marathon course, and it is speculative whether Cierpinski could have matched Thompson's pace throughout the latter stages, after breaking away from the Americans. An exciting entry was that of Lasse Viren, of Finland, bidding to become the second man in history and the first since Emil Zatopek's famous feat in 1952, winning the three longest distance titles. One difference between and 1952 and 1976—that in 1952 Zatopek had one fewer race, and more rest before he arrived at the marathon. Nevertheless, a significant run produced a fifth place by the Finn, who must surely have now surpassed the great feats of his fellow countryman Paavo Nurmi (whom incidentally he never met) and who, was, until Viren, surely the greatest runner the world had produced.

Shorter, Rodgers, the Canadian Jerome Drayton and Cierpinski forced the pace throughout the early stages and it was not until between the 30-35km markers that the East German, better known in the past for the steeplechasing, began to pull away. At 30km he and Shorter were level. Within 5km Cierpinksi had opened a 13sec gap. By then Viren had started to ease off fractionally, Lismont, a former European champion and silver medallist in Munich started to come through, and a third American Don Kardong had effectively worked his way through the pack.

By 40km the leader's advantage had stretched to 32sec, Kardong was third and Lismont fourth. Cierpinski kept up the killing pace and despite the rain, seized the advantage of the flattish course to set an Olympic record of 2hr 9min 55sec, fastest time in the world in 1976 by two minutes and a personal record by 2½ minutes.

A sign of the thoroughness of the East Germans is that Cierpinski was installed in the Olympic Village in early June, a full month before his rivals, was encouraged to live as "normally" as possible, not to spend time in the entertainment areas provided by the hosts but to take his own stereo and to live in his own room as if it were his home. Such thoroughness and concentration on detail could never be found in Britain.

20 Kilometre Walk

The staging of the 1976 Olympics at last brought some dividends to Mexico who won their first ever gold medal in the athletics—although Jose Pedraza had been very close in 1968, with a silver in the walk. However, nobody had really thought that the Mexican trio who had been registering some exceptionally fast times would really overcome the mighty trio from East Germany; sentiment made one hope that the 40-year-old veteran Vladimir Golubnichiy, winner of a gold medal in 1960, could pull off the impossible. The Mexicans had their tactics well thought out.

They cut out an exceptionally fast pace, attempting to break up the East Germans, Hans Reimann, Peter Frenkel and Karl Heinz Stadtmuller, all three of whom are, or have been, world record holders at one time or another. It was a suicidal gamble knowing the Germans' racing record. At 5 kms Daniel Bautista, Raul Gonzalez and Domingo Colin were together.

By 10 kms the pace had begun to tell; Colin dropped back and eventually was disqualified for "lifting", Frenkel was leading fractionally from Bautista, Reimann and Stadtmuller, in that order. Five kilometres later Bautista had forged ahead, proving that the ultra fast times he had been recording in Europe were no fluke, but at that point he still had not been able to shake off Frenkel, although the other Germans were a couple of yards adrift.

Piling on the pace, Bautista, a superb stylist who has set a world 10,000 metres track record, continued his inexorable challenge which even Reimann could not cope with. Striding in first, just over half a minute ahead of the runner up, Bautista's first action when he crossed the line was to drop to his knees, cross himself and kiss the ground which had carried him in his finest victory, in an incredible time for an Olympic race at sea-level.

High Jump

One of the most extroverted, exciting, aggravating and cussed of athletes is certainly Dwight Stones; world record breaking high jumper he has the irritating habit of wandering over to the judges and pointing out their errors, of walking over to his rivals during competition and helping their techniques. Of putting on the wrong clothes in an Olympics and getting told off by his own American officials; and even of receiving his third place medal in an old track suit.

His preparation in the few days before the Olympic competition seemed unusual, even by Stones's standards. He left Montreal saying the Olympic Village was not ideal for the build up to a gold medal, and flew back to his California home. Upon his return to Montreal five days before the competition, he held a press conference attacking the organising committee, French Canadians, certain political figures and anyone else worthwhile. The result was seen when he came out to the qualifying competition. Everytime he prepared for a jump he was heartily booed but nevertheless became one of the 14 to reach the final.

It was obvious, though, that he was worried by the cat-calls and, although it was his second Olympics, it remained to be seen whether at the age of 22 he could handle such crowd opposition.

The booing of the Canadians started to prove counter-productive when United States supporters barracked the Canadians taking part, Claude Ferragne and Greg Joy, but the latter managed to overcome the problem, eventually taking a silver medal for the hosts.

Heavy rain which left puddles on the run up area hindered Stones more than his rivals as he has an extremely sharp approach to the bar and whenever he ran up one could sense that conditions underfoot made it difficult for him to concentrate fully. After a couple of rounds, during which the field events judge made no attempt to have the rain cleared, Stones took the rubber pusher and started wiping away the puddles on his own.

With Stones's recently set world record standing at 7ft 7in combined with the early departure from the competition of the second ranked man in the world, his teammate Bill Jankunis, it seemed probable that Stones could win easily despite all his handicaps, for the next ranked man, Sergey Budalov, of the Soviet Union, was a full two inches behind. But it was not Stones's Games. He had a clear passage to 7ft 3in but then at 7ft 3$\frac{3}{4}$in came unstuck. As there were four men jumping at that point he had a guaranteed fourth place but all depended on whether those jumping after him, Jacek Wszola, of Poland, Seniukov, and Joy could clear the bar.

Wszola was over first time, placing Stones second; Joy was over on his third attempt, leaving the bronze now between Seniukov and Stones. Taking a gamble, Seniukov took only one leap at 7ft 3$\frac{3}{4}$in, reasoning that if he could clear the next height, 7ft 4$\frac{3}{4}$in, then he could snatch the silver on the fewer errors rule, pushing Joy and Stones to third and fourth. It was a good try but it did not work.

In the meantime Joy had been taking his own gamble; realising he had few good leaps left in his legs and that even if he could match Wszola's 7ft 4$\frac{3}{4}$in clearance he would not win on the count-back, elected to take one attempt at 7ft 3$\frac{3}{4}$ and the next two at 7ft 5$\frac{1}{4}$in. Another gamble which failed. Still it had produced one of the major upsets of the Games and for the 19-year-old Wszola an extraordinary gold medal.

Ironically only four days later Stones improved his world record to 7ft 7$\frac{1}{4}$in.

Long Jump

Arnie Robinson turned the tables on the Munich victor, teammate Randy Williams successfully, leaping nine inches more than the 1972 Olympic champion. Robinson was the favourite before Munich but had problems with his run up and could not make more than third place. Since then he had concentrated on that aspect of his jumping and steadily improved from 26ft 9$\frac{1}{4}$in in 1972 to 27ft 2$\frac{3}{4}$in in 1974, which he almost equalled in 1975 (27ft 2$\frac{1}{4}$in) and entered the Montreal Olympics with a best of 27ft 3$\frac{1}{2}$in, 2in ahead of Williams.

Nenad Stekic, of Yugoslavia, the No. 2 long jumper of all time with his 27ft 8$\frac{3}{4}$in, flopped miserably placing fifth with a best leap of less than 26ft while the bronze medal went most unexpectedly to Frank Wartenburg, of East Germany, who did not even rank in the world's top 10 before the Games.

Triple Jump

The triple event is one which makes more demands on athlete's legs than any other, and it is a measure of the ability of the Soviet Sports Ministry that they have allowed, and encouraged Victor Saneyev, already winner in Mexico City and Munich, to stay in the sport.

The amazing achievements of Saneyev is that he has maintained world class standards despite improving standards and intermittent injury. Three world records, two in 1968 and one in 1972, six European Indoor Championships and two outdoor European Championships (1969 and 1974).

The one interesting feature would be to see whether the mystery man of the Pan American Games, Joao Carlos Oliveira, of Brazil, who smashed the world record, would be a danger, again. On that occasion he smashed Saneyev's own record of 57ft 2½in by 17¾ inches and threatened to lead a major breakthrough of this event. However, this record was reminiscent of the Mexico Olympics when the thinner air helped five world records to be set.

Saneyev had only three valid jumps; 54ft 10in, 55ft 11¾in and finally, his best, 56ft 8¾in. This put him 4¼in ahead of the runner up James Butts of the United States.

Oliveira, who has suffered from a great deal of back trouble, managed to overcome a chronic loss of training to snatch a bronze —a minor consolation.

Britain's hope in this event, Aston Moore, failed to hit the board correctly, with three no jumps in the qualifying rounds, a sad ending for such a talented youngster.

Pole Vault

On a day when Finland had already won the 10,000 metres through Lasse Viren and the silver medal in the javelin through Hannu Siitonen, the great interest surrounding the pole vault was whether a third Finn Antii Kalliomaki would hit the medal rankings. After all the Americans had the world's greatest pair of vaulters, Dave Roberts and Earl Bell and badly wanted to regain the Olympic pole vault title they had lost for the first time since 1896, to East Germany at Munich.

Roberts had been close to 19ft in training, compared with his world record of 18ft 6½in but the consistent Polish trio Wojciech Buciarski, Tadeusz Slusarski and Wladyslaw Kozakiewicz would obviously be very difficult to defeat, all having clear the 18ft barrier.

It is usual that an Olympic pole vault competition does not set a very high standard because of the length of the competition and the weariness of the competitors. And this is how the event evolved in Montreal. Three men scraped over 18ft, three just behind on 17ft 10½in and seventh and eighth on 17ft 8½in.

Naturally the world record holder (18ft 6½in) Roberts was favourite with the danger-man Kozakiewicz, European record holder on 18ft 5¼in, and for a brief time world indoor record holder.

The field was eliminated down to three men, Slusarski, Kalliomaki and Roberts surprisingly early but there had been some clever tactics in an event where the fewer attempts taken by the competitor the better it counts at the end of the day.

For example at 17ft 8½in nine men were left in. Of those only five attempted the height, eliminating one, Vladmir Kishkun, of the Soviet Union. The remaining four cleared, Slusarski, Kalliomaki and Michel Bellot, of France at the first attempt, Itsuo Takanezawa at his third.

The bar was then raised to 17ft 10½in: Slusarski passed, Kalliomaki cleared first time round, Patrick Abada, of France, and Buciarski, on the second trial, and Earl Bell at his final try. At that point Tanakezawa was eliminated, leaving the competition graciously, bowing to all four corners of the stadium, a gesture which won him great applause from the packed stadium.

Up went the bar another 5cms to 18ft 0½in, Slusarski, Kalliomaki and Roberts all clearing on their first, Buciarski and Bellot failing every time.

At this point with the bar raised to 18ft 2½in Roberts took a gamble which could have cost him the gold medal for, fearing that Kalliomaki and Slusarski would clear this, he passed and elected to go for 18ft 4½in. Unluckily for him both the Pole and the Finn failed to clear 18ft 2½in leaving him to have the bar raised needlessly another two inches. Ironically on his last try he came so close to clearing the bar ... had it been two inches lower the result would have been different: instead of Slusarski 1, Kalliomaki 2, Roberts 3, it would have been Roberts 1, Slusarski 2, Kalliomaki 3.

Shot Putt

With nearly all the top men some three feet down on their best there had to be a reason and one can only put it down to the statement by Britain's former hammer throwing record holder Barry Williams that many of the world's heavy men take weight inducing steroids to build up their strength. As these steroids are strictly forbidden under both IOC and International Amateur Athletic Federation rules the athletes stop taking them a few weeks before competition, with the inevitable result: their performances suffer. This is not to say of course that *all* shot putter, discus, hammer and javelin throwers use these drugs. One must realise that big men suffer just as much from nerves as anything else and therefore a below-standard shot putter can just as easily be suffering from butterflies in the stomach.

Britain had high hopes of a medal from Geoff Capes who opened his account in the qualifying round with an easy toss of just under 67ft. Alas, come the final neither he nor, incidentally, the new world record holder Alexander Barisnikov, were able to match their own qualifying round results.

In the final Barisnikov opened with 67ft 4¼in to lead from Udo Beyer, an East German with a hitherto inconsistent record, on 66ft 10½in and Capes with 66ft 1¼in. The American Al Feuerbach took over the second round lead with a 67ft 5in result, Beyer improved to 67ft 3in and Capes, fractionally, to 66ft 3¾in. At the half way stage, the order changed again with Barisnikov, the Russian with a unique discus style of throwing, went ahead with the first 21 metres result of the competition, which converts to 68ft 10¾in. A good throw but still not to be compared with his recent world record of 72ft 2¼in. A second East German, Hans Peter Gies, moved into contention with 67ft 2in and Capes again went up to 66ft 9½in. Thus at half way the Cambridgeshire policeman was sixth.

There was little significance in the fourth round but the fifth decided the destiny of the gold medal. Beyer, who back in 1973 added 9ft to the European junior record, suddenly blasted out a 69ft 0¾in putt ... and that was it. The No. 2 Russian Evgeni Mironov, who last year had thrown no more than 64ft 11½in, approached his pre-Games best with a 69ft to clinch the silver medal and Capes finished on a lower note than he had started. It had been his worst competition of the year and a bitter disappointment to a man who has brought so much pleasure to British crowds highlighting an event not previously considered.

The Americans, who had left off their former world record holder Terry Albritton, because of a loss of form and poor showing in the trials, were out of the medals lists for the first time since 1936.

Discus

"The gold medal is for me, not for the United States" declared the bearded Mac Wilkins after winning the discus title by a 4ft margin from the East German Wolfgang Schmidt—221ft 5in to 217ft 3in.

Always an extrovert Wilkins first came to real prominence when on April 24th he set a world record of 226ft 11in. But he really shot to fame with an astonishing series of throws, on the same day, at San Jose, on June 1st. There in one competition he improved the world record three times to become the first 230ft and 70 metres thrower in history.

On that June day he improved his April record of 226ft 11in first to 229ft, then to 230ft 5in and finally to 232ft 6in. An astonishing competition. However, there were fears that he may have reached his peak too early in the year and that the technically brilliant East Germans Wolfgang Schmidt, Nirbert Thiede and Siegfried Pachale would come through in the way the Germans always do at major Games.

This fears were not allayed until Wilkins took the lead and the gold medal with his sixth and final throw. Ludvik Danek, of Czechoslovakia who had won silver, bronze and gold at the last three Olympics was out of the hunt and another long time thrower, Jay Silvester, just made the final eight.

Hammer

The world hammer throwing record has been broken nine times in the past seven years by seven throwers, three West Germans, three Russians and one East German; the world rankings, before the Games were headed by five Russians in the first six placings, but of course only three could be selected. It is a sign of ability of the Soviet selectors that with all these facts they produced the three men who won gold, silver and bronze—the first time it has

Two of Montreal's double Olympic champions: (top) Tatiana Kazankina, first in the women's 800 metres and 1,500 metres, and (below) Alberto Juantorena, the first athlete to win both the 400 metres and 800 metres in the same Games as he crosses ahead of Herman Frazier, who finished third for the United States.

The world's greatest woman athlete, Irena Szewinska, winner of the 400 metres in a world record to add to Olympic medals won as far back as 1964.

A contrast in high jumping: Rosemarie Ackermann, the world record holder (top) displays the finish of her straddle style to add the Olympic title to the European gold she already holds, while (below) 19-year-old Jacek Wszola uses the Fosbury Flop, not seen in an Olympics until 1968, to give Poland her first Olympic title in this event. Right: the excitement of winning second place in the high jump is clear to see on Greg Joy's face as he brings to Canada a final, surprise, silver medal.

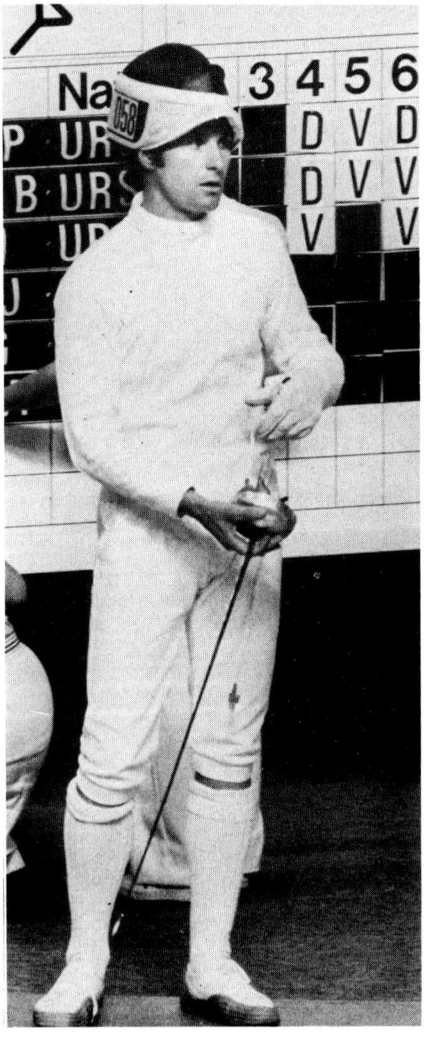

The jury of appeal (top) discuss the "bugging" of Boris Onischenko's epee with a forthright Jim Fox (right) explaining how he had realised what was happening and watched (second from right) by a pensive Mike Proudfoot, the British team manager. The moment of truth (left) as Boris Onischenko disconnects his sword from the registering equipment. Already can be seen on his face the anguish and disgrace that is to follow. With the affair behind him, Fox fought back bravely to overcome mental pressures, and his cross country run, which clinched the gold medal for Britain, ended in his being helped (above) after he has run himself to the point of exhaustion. Britain's three modern pentathlon gold medallists (left to right), Danny Nightingale, Adrian Parker and Jim Fox.

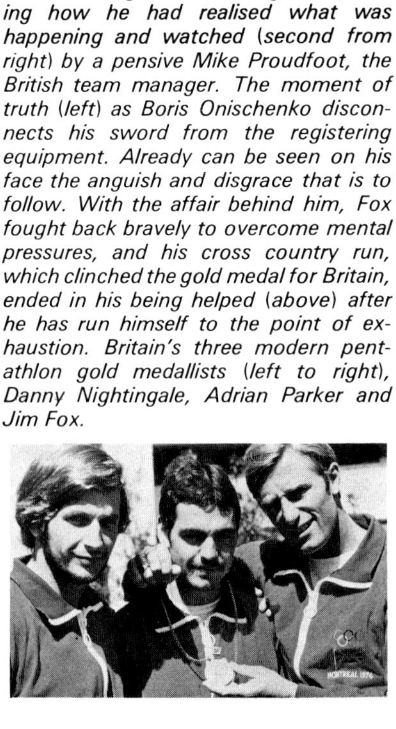

happened in the event since 1908, when, of course, standards were far lower and the event less practised.

And in fact the finishing order was exactly the same as the world rankings: Yuriy Sedyh, who made an opening throw of the year of an astonishing 253ft 5in improving to 258ft 9in in May, the second best throw in history, won with 254ft 4in. And he is only 20 years old.

The runner up was Alexei Spiridinov who held the world record briefly with 251ft 6in in 1974, which gave him the European title at the time, and third the "veteran" defending champion Anatoliy Bondarchuk, who despite being ranked only 10th in the USSR last year, came back better than ever this season with a personal record of 254ft. A remarkable achievement at 36.

Chris Black, Britain's new record holder, was by no means disgraced with his seventh place, for throughout the competition he approached his recently set British record 241ft 5in. It was the best placing by a Briton for more than 50 years. Within a week of the Games finishing he improved again to 243ft, a 13ft improvement over the season.

Javelin

The dream of every sporting champion is to have a son or daughter able to emulate your own feats. However, the pressures placed on children often proves counter-productive, so that they leave the sport or rebel by simply not training hard enough. There is also the point that they may not be good enough. And this is what everyone thought about Miklos Nemeth, son of Imre Nemeth, Olympic hammer throwing champion in 1948 and three times world record holder in the 40's.

True as a junior Miklos threw well, but his graduation to the senior ranks had never been particularly successful. Back in 1967 ranked No. 2 in the world, in 1975 No. 1 with a personal best 299ft 10in. But competitively his best performance was a seventh in Munich (he failed to qualify for the final pool in Mexico City) while in three European championships his best position was merely fifth.

But with his very first throw in the final of the event Nemeth jnr, now 29, realised that potential and justified his father's faith. He unleashed a fantastic 310ft 4in, compared with the existing world record of 308ft 8in by the reigning Olympic champion Klaus Wolfermann, of West Germany.

That was enough to cow the opposition into complete submission, even Finn Hannu Siitonen, who has thrown over 308ft, finishing some 22ft down on the eventual winner. This was the first world record in the event by a Hungarian.

Wolfermann was not in the competition, having been affected by the injury hoodoo which struck so many world class competitors in Olympic year. Janis Lusis, the Soviet thrower with the greatest record in history still managed an eighth place with 263ft 4in to culminate a career which started significantly in 1963, 13 years earlier.

Decathlon

The forecast was that this decathlon would prove to be the greatest contest ever; a classic 10-event haul between the reigning Olympic champion Nikolay Avilov, from the Soviet Union, and Bruce Jenner, the world record holder from the United States.

Jenner has been in the news for the past three years, improving from 7533 in 1971, 7806 in 1973, 8308 in 1974 to the world record 8524 earlier this season.

By contrast Avilov, a superb technician who won seven of the 10 individual events in Munich, in the intervening years had rested from competition, taking part only casually in 1973 and not at all in 1974. Obviously though he had been working on his weaker events for he started off 1976 with a 8336pts total.

However, he was destined to finish third, to Jenner and the West German Guido Kratschmer in a competition which produced a world record 8618pts total, a masterpiece of all round ability. In only one event did Jenner fall below 819pts, and that in the killing final event of the day, the 1500 metres where he scored 714pts. His individual performances make classic reading: a 10·94 100 metres, followed by a 23ft $8\frac{1}{4}$in long jump, 50ft $4\frac{1}{4}$in shot putt, 6ft 8in high jump and at the end of the opening day a 47·51 400 metres.

Jenner started the second day with a high hurdles of 14·84sec, 164ft 2in discus, 15ft 9in pole vault, 224ft 9in javelin, and finally a 4min 12·61sec 1500 metres. The total improved his own world record by 76pts, and show him to be a master of all events.

Daley Thompson, Britain's sole hope (Mike Corden was injured and could not start), had the following marks: 10·79sec 100 metres, 23ft 7in long jump, 42ft $11\frac{3}{4}$in shot putt, 6ft $3\frac{1}{4}$in high jump, 48·15sec 400 metres, 15·98sec 110 metres hurdles, 119ft 3in discus, 13ft $9\frac{1}{2}$in pole vault, 148ft 3in javelin and finally 4min 29·55sec 1500 metres.

His final total of 7434pts placed him 18th, not a bad position at all for a teenager in his first major competition and he must be good for over 8,000pts within a year.

4 × 100 metres

The advantage of using Lee Calhoun, 110 metres hurdles champion in 1956 and 1960 as relay coach certainly paid off, for with a reserve squad, the Americans still gained an overwhelming victory in the sprint relay, by a clear three tenths of a second. The success is all the more enhanced when it is realised that Steve Williams, the world's fastest man, was not in the American team and that for the first time since 1928 they had failed to gain an individual 100 metres medal.

The final saw Harvey Glance, John Stones, Millard Hampton and Steve Riddick click sweetly into place and run an excellent 38·33sec. A surprise was the mere fifth place of Cuba who had finished runner up to the United States in the Pan American Games the previous year. Valeriy Borzov earned himself another bronze medal when he anchored the Soviet Union to third place behind those masters of relay running, East Germany.

4 × 400 metres

A rare and hotly disputed error of judgement cost Britain a place in the final for the first time since the war. Britain has always had a proud record at 4 × 400 metres racing in the Olympics, finishing fifth, third, fifth, second, fifth and second since 1952 and although the British four were not as good either as in Munich or in the 1974 European championships a final place was never in doubt—especially when the draw was revealed.

For with the first three qualifying and the two fastest losers also going into the final it looked easy. Britain's rivals were the United States, West Germany, Jamaica, Canada, Finland, Puerto Rico, and Saudi Arabia. No way could Britain finish behind Puerto Rico and Saudi Arabia and as the heat appeared faster than the other one Britain could possibly go as low as fifth and still get through.

Ainsley Bennet started off well, but Glen Cohen handed over to Alan Pascoe some way down the field. However, with Dave Jenkins on the final leg Pascoe only had to finish to guarantee Britain that final berth. Fifty metres from the change over a Jamaican jostled Pascoe and the baton fell, bouncing on to the infield. Pascoe stopped, hesitated, looked at the baton and ... gave up. His claim is that even had he picked up the baton the team would have been disqualified as it had fallen off the track but there is no doubt that the jury would have applied the advantage rule and told Britain that they could go through to the final—possibly even disqualifying Jamaica, *had Pascoe continued.* That he did not carry on was purely voluntary and the jury could not possibly reinstate the British team, as they had failed to finish. Had Pascoe even fallen over and pleaded injury they would have stood a chance but despite a wonderful career, including an MBE and European and Commonwealth gold medals, Pascoe must accept on this occasion that his was a serious error of judgment and one he will never erase from his memory.

With Britain out, interest in the race suddenly waned and when it was seen that the minor placings were considerably slower than in Munich the heartache became ever greater. Cuba, again an expected contender, gave their double Olympic champion Alberto Juantorena too much to do on the last leg and he finished seventh, but at least the United States regained the title they had lost to the Kenyans in Munich, with an excellent 2min 58·65sec.

3

ATHLETICS
(Women)

100 Metres

The first world record in the athletics competition came not in a final but in the semi finals of the women's 100 metres where the new breed of West German girls continued to challenge the long standing supremacy of the East Germans. Renate Stecher, who has set half a dozen world records during a long career which has taken in European and Olympic sprint double crowns, not to mention the many relay gold medals, was inevitably due to come to the close of an exciting career in sport. At 25 she had spent nearly 10 years near the top.

The world record came not from Inge Helten who had posted a 11·04sec world record in Furth the previous month but from her teammate Annegret Richter, who was fifth in Munich and who entered the betting stakes as an outsider. In fact her best pre-Olympic time was 11·17sec, excellent, but she had little course record or recent form to justify such an achievement as her 11·01sec.

Richter took off to a perfect start, holding off the powerful Stecher all the way with her teammate, Helten third, probably as a result of her reaching a peak too early in the season.

With Sonia Lannaman out of action with a pulled hamstring received during relay training our medal hopes were non existent but the memorable feat of Andrea Lynch, who had been hit with sciatic trouble at a crucial point, in reaching the last eight should not be overlooked. It further confirms that had she been fully fit she could have been in the first three without much trouble.

200 Metres

The disqualification of Raelene Boyle, the Australian medal hope, in the semi finals due to two false starts, and the absence through injury did not hclp the final as a spectacle. Moreover Irena Szewinska, who could probably have brought home a gold medal for

Poland in this event decided to stick to the 400 metres as a 200-400 double was impossible with the programme arranged as it was.

Annegret Richter, the West German winner of the 100 metres, lacked the strength to combat the East Germans, who would dominate procedings with Carla Bodendorf, Renate Stecher and the lowest ranked, Barbel Eckert.

Renate Stecher, winner in Munich was patently past her best, having won a bronze in the 100 metres, but it was thought that her inherent strength might just be enough to carry her first past the line. Thus it was a great surprise to see Miss Eckert, finish first in an Olympic record 22·37sec with Richter splitting the East Germans in second place and Stecher snatching the bronze.

400 Metres

Even Fanny Blankers-Koen, winner of four gold medals in the 1948 Olympics would agree that Irena Szewinska could lay claim to being the greatest woman athlete ever. A winner of medals in every Olympics since 1964, world record breaker on frequent occasions, the first girl to run under 50sec for 400 metres—once considered impossible—and also the recorder of a 48·5sec relay clocking in a relay leg, she was so far ahead of the rest of the field, including the 18-year-old East German Christina Brehmer that it was only a matter of how fast she would run and by how great a margin she would win by.

In the end she beat the second girl Brehmer by 1·22sec, compared with a ·47sec margin between the silver medallist and the seventh placed Riitta Salin, of Finland. Although 30 years old when she won the title, the oldest of all the women gold medallists she could inevitably win more medals in Moscow.

800 Metres

One of the biggest break-throughs in any event in Montreal, came in the woman's 800 metres. Two minutes was not broken until 1971 when Hildegard Falck, the 1972 Olympic champion ran 1min 58·5sec. This record stayed until 1973 when the Bulgarian Svetlana Zlateva lowered it to 1min 57·5sec. Another three years passed until June 1976 when the Soviet speedstress, Vera Gerasimova chipped another 1½sec off the record with a shattering 1min 56sec in Moscow.

The heats showed that the pace would be frightening, under two minutes being generally needed to rate a place in the last eight. Once in the final it was certain there would be no tactical racing, only a two-lap dash for the line. Gerasimova had already been eliminated in the semi-finals, so fierce were the early rounds and if it was thought that she would be missed this was not the case.

At no time were there fewer than seven runners in contention. And when the runners crossed the line, headed by Tatiana Kazankina, the second Russian, who was primarily the Soviet 1500 metres hope with her shattering world record of 3min 56sec at Podolsk, it was seen that the slowest of the first seven had run inside 1min 59sec. The fastest 1min 54·9sec.

But more significantly the first four girls, Kazankina, Nikolina Chtereva, Elfi Zinn and Anita Weiss had all run inside Gerasimova's previous world record. What an event ... a highlight which will never be forgotten.

Britain's three girls failed to survive the opening round. They were Liz Barnes, Angela Creamer and Christine McMeekin, although Miss Barnes was unlucky to be drawn in the fastest heat and still ran 2min 1·7sec.

1500 Metres

Had Mary Stewart been able to find that little extra edge and advance to the final she could well have ended up near the top of the world. In contrast to the super fast preliminaries it was obvious from the start that tactics and a fast finish would be the norm in the final.

With no girl willing to take up the pace, the first 2½ laps were taken at a steady trot, before the speed intensified on the last lap, the winner, Tatiana Kazankina, the 800 metres gold medallist, emerging from the pack to sprint home in relaxed style in 4min 5·48sec, compared with the 1972 Ludmilla Bragina's world record setting victory of 4min 1·4sec in Munich.

Bragina who was only included as a late selection finished fifth and it is noteworthy that the slim Kazankina, originally named only for this event was actually put into the 800 metres team on the very last date of entry. An example of British officialdom who feel duty bound to select the team too early and are unable to take into account up to date form. Here the real culprits are more the British Olympic Association who are more concerned with kitting out and fitting clothes than giving guidance which will ensure the *best* possible team.

100 Metres Hurdles

With the world record holder and reigning Olympic champion, Annelie Ehrhardt obviously injured it was not in the least surprising that she did not win. What was more sad was that she failed even to make the final despite the advantage of a re-run semi final after Tatiana Anasimova, of the Soviet Union had been knocked out of her lane by the Rumanian Viorica Enescu.

But so great is the depth of the East German athletic machine that they had a deputy ready to fill the gap, in Johanna Schaller, who ran far and away a personal record of 12·77sec to take the gold medal from the two Soviet hurdlers, Tatiana Anasimova and Natalia Lebedeva.

A noteworthy performance was scored by Esther Rot, who became the first Israeli athlete to reach an Olympic final; in Munich Esther had been poised for a place in the last eight of the 100 metres but the tragic shooting of the Israeli team members resulted in her withdrawal from the Olympics—and competition of all type for a year. Yet despite a lack of good competition and facilities in her country she found remarkable form again.

High Jump

Rosemarie Ackermann, three times world record breaker, has, since her disappointing seventh place in Munich, dominated competitions around the world. A straddler with an impeccable technique she never looked shaken even when the Italian girl, Sara Simeoni carried through almost the entire competition without knocking off the bar.

It even got to the state that had Ackermann not cleared the bar at 6ft 4in, the gold medal would have gone for the first time to Italy. Recalling the appalling behaviour of the Italian crowd at the European Championships in Rome two years ago when every jumper was religiously booed, while silence reigned when Simeoni leaped (she finished third in the end), Ackermann although winner on that occasion, too, had an old score to settle.

Having won the gold medal easily with 6ft 4in, she then had the bar raised to 6ft 5¾, ½inch above her own world record, but three times failed narrowly. Simeoni took the silver, the only non-East European in the first four.

Women's Long Jump

The women's long jump was one event where standards did not come up to expectations with the eventual winner, Angela Voigt, the former world record holder, from East Germany, clearing a distance of 22ft $0\frac{1}{2}$in, not even as good as that achieved by Mary Rand in the Tokyo Olympics 12 years earlier. It seemed before the Games that the competition would be fought out between Angela Voigt, her teammate, Sigrun Siegl, the current world record holder—who was anyway more interested in the pentathlon—the Russian Lidiya Alfeeva, world's No. 1 in 1975, and the young, 18-year-old American, Kathy McMillan.

This is how it proved and although the competition was tucked away along the back straight the enthusiastic crowd of 59,000 gave the girls every encouragement, especially young Kathy, who was cheered even as she was running up to jump.

After the first round Angela Voigt, who has a reputation for making a mess of the important competitions, produced a great leap of 22ft $0\frac{1}{2}$in. As it happens she could have stopped there as no other girl came within a couple of inches of her throughout the long afternoon's competition.

Siegrun was joint second with 21ft $7\frac{1}{2}$in at this point with the Hungarian Ildiko Szabo. Sue Reeve, Britain's remaining entry (Myra Nimmo having failed to qualify), jumped an average 20ft 7in, which was to prove her best of the day.

The second round produced no change in the order but on the third, Kathy McMillan started her break-through with an improved 21ft $1\frac{1}{4}$in, which as she became increasingly confident improved to 21ft $2\frac{3}{4}$in on the fourth round, and then a marvellous 21ft $10\frac{3}{4}$in on the fifth.

Likiya Alfeeva scored her best leap, 21ft $7\frac{3}{4}$in, on her third while Siegl improved, but not quite enough, to be pushed out of the bronze medal by $\frac{1}{4}$in. Not a classic, but a good afternoon's entertainment.

Women's Shot

Four women who have received world record plaques contested the final of the women's shot: Nadejda Chijova, of the Soviet

Union, who has set 10 world records between 1958 and 1973, Helena Fibingerova, of Czechoslovakia, who set a record of 70ft 9¼in in 1974, Marianne Adam, of East Germany, who improved the record on two occasions in 1975 and 1976, the last to 71ft 1¼in and finally the Bulgarian Ivanka Christova, who threw 71ft 9¾in early in July, making her the effective favourite to win the Olympic gold medal, despite being at 34 the oldest of the contenders, and taking part in her fourth Games.

Chijova, four years younger, was third in the Mexico Games, and first at Munich (where Christova took third place), but missed 1975 because of a back injury, giving her rivals the opportunity to catch up.

With the last two Olympics producing world records, 62ft 6¾in by Margitta Gummel in 1968 and Chijova's 69ft in Munich it seemed that the first 22 metres (72ft 2¼in) throw would be produced. This did not happen although the first girl, Christova did improve the Olympic record of 69ft by 5 inches. In fact there were only five girls over the 20 metres (65ft 7½in barrier) compared with eight in the world ranking lists.

This is yet further evidence that the world's top throwers are using artificial means to raise their standard where dope tests are not in force but cannot take the steroids during major championships fearing risk of disqualification.

Christova was second from the second to fourth rounds. On the fifth she produced her best throw, with Chijova, who had only two worthwhile throws, second, and the other former world record holders Fibingerova and Adam third and fourth.

Discus

In one of the more unusual incidents in the Games, Faina Melnik, the defending Olympic champion and 11 times world record setter had a mental collapse and could not get her technique going properly. Although more than 5ft ahead of the second ranked girl Carmen Romero, of Cuba, it seemed impossible for her to be beaten. Nevertheless when in the fifth round she threw 225ft 1in to take the runner's up place to the East German Evelyn Schlaak, still only 20, it seemed that she had gained a consolation prize at least.

But it was seen that judges and IAAF were arguing and gesticulating angrily. Apparently Melnik had walked into the circle to throw but then walked out of the front of the circle and then walked back in again before taking her turn. The action of walking out of the circle had in effect nullified the throw but no doubt under pressure Melnik had forgotten.

An IAAF official Leonid Khomenkov, of the Soviet Union ruled that the field events judge had been incorrect to disqualify Melnik's throw and her performance stood. However, upon appeal by the field events referee and meeting judge, the jury of appeal studied the incident and decided that there was no way Melnik's throw could stand and cancelled out her throw.

As her next best performance was a mere 217ft 10in, she was relegated to fourth place and no medal.

The first Olympic athlete to be disqualified for taking drugs was a discus thrower, the Polish girl, Danuta Rosani. It was found by the Medical Commission that she had taken steroids, traces of which were found in her blood stream after random tests had been taken, from three competitors. The drugs cannot have helped much as she had failed to qualify for the final pool of 13.

Women's Javelin

When Marion Becker set an Olympic record in the qualifying round of the women's javelin it looked at first as if the reign of the Olympic champion Ruth Fuchs was over. When Becker competed for Rumania in the Munich Olympics she failed even to qualify for the final stages but with a pre-Games record of high standard to her credit obviously had improved greatly.

However, when the tall East German girl, who had recently improved her own world record, had just one throw in the final it was obvious that she would retain her title—barring an extraordinary performance, possibly from the American Kathy Schmidt. This was not to be.

Fuchs threw 216ft 4in, which in turn improved Becker's Olympic record with ease; Becker failed to match her qualifying throw with a third round 212ft 3in while Kathy Schmidt just managed to pull out the big one on the final and sixth throw of 209ft 10in.

Tessa Sanderson, who performed with distinction, improved her own British record by more than 3ft to 187ft 7in and almost matched this in the final with a 187ft effort to place her 10th, therefore justifying her selection.

Pentathlon

East Germany dominated a surprisingly flat pentathlon competition taking all the medals. Coincidentally Siegrun Siegl, the world long jump record holder and runner up in the long jump finished with the same points total as Christine Lasar. As Siegl had better individual placing she took the gold medal.

Burglinde Pollak who has set world records on three occasions since the Munich Olympics, where she placed third behind Mary Peters, Britain's only 1972 athletics champion, had a bad competition and had to be content with yet another third place with a points total nearly 200pts below her latest world record set some three years ago.

Britain's Sue Longdon was 12th with 4276pts, some places higher than her world rankings. Her total was made up of a 13·91sec 100 metres hurdles, 35ft 8in shot putt, 5ft 7¼in high jump, 19ft 5in long jump and 24·20 200 metres.

This may well be the last pentathlon in this form in the Olympics as there is talk of switching the 200 metres into an 800 metres to make the event more of an all-round test, an intelligent move to shift the tendency from the bulky explosive girls to allow the lighter ones to have a chance.

4 × 100 Metres

Short of dropping the baton or injury nothing was expected to halt the exceptionally well-drilled East German squad with their galaxy of medallists and although the West Germans, perhaps more talented individually with Inge Helten and Annegret Richter as their spearhead, ran them close, the gold medal went—for the first time—to East Germany.

The British team, without the injured Sonia Lannaman and with Andrea Lynch not at full fitness, despite her reaching the 100 metres final, scraped into the final but once there finished eighth. At their best they would have been unlikely to finish higher than sixth.

4 × 400 Metres

One country has dominated women's 4 × 400 metres relay racing since the early '70s, East Germany. They arrived in Montreal without one of their four runners from the 1972 Olympic gold medal team yet still looked unbeatable. In fact they proved so outstanding that they cracked by 3·73sec the world record they set in Munich and probably could have fielded another team which could have taken a silver medal, too.

It is fantastic to consider that the first sub 50sec 400 metres was only run by Irena Szewinska, in 1974, yet here in a relay four girls *averaged* under 50sec for the four legs, and with one reserve after their No. 3 girl Marita Koch, injured, had to pull out of the individual 400 metres semi finals.

Ellen Streidt and Christina Brehmer, on the third and fourth legs were timed at 49·51 and 49·79sec respectively but it should be remembered that neither had any opposition to worry about and the actual times could have been faster when line-to-line timing is taken into account.

Britain could hardly fail to reach the final considering that their opposition included Canada, Bulgaria and Belgium, but once there, the best they could do was seventh out of eight, in a time only fractionally faster than that they achieved before coming to Montreal. As a comparison the team with three of the four girls running in Montreal ran last year 3min 26·6sec, for a United Kingdom and Commonwealth record.

4

SWIMMING, DIVING AND WATER-POLO

BETWEEN the Munich and Montreal Olympics East Germany had unquestionably become the new dominant force in swimming. If the USA had held on to their leadership of the men's events they had lost their supremacy of the women's. In 1972 the East German girls took only two individual and two relay silver medals. It was the tip of the iceberg that was to be revealed when the 1973 World Swimming Championships were held in Yugoslavia. They won eight of the 12 titles and both relays, a feat repeated at the 1975 World Championships. In between these competitions they swam away with every individual title except one at the 1974 European Championships in Vienna and were first in both relays. Nor had they lost their momentum. The East German Championships in June 1976, produced a host of world records which overshadowed the fine performances of the American girls at the USA Trials the same month.

The predominant figure in East Germany's breakthrough was Kornelia Ender, who in Munich as a tiny 13 year-old girl was the winner of one of East Germany's two silvers. By Montreal she had grown to 5ft 10in tall and 11 stone and was the greatest female swimmer of the era. Her all-round technical proficiency was demonstrated in Munich when she was second in the individual medley. And on her flawless style, based on a long, reaching stroke and tremendous flexibility, she developed the stamina and strength which brought her four gold medals in the Montreal Games—one more than any other female competitor in the history of the Olympics. In 1968 the USA's Debbie Meyer finished first in the three freestyle events in Mexico City and four years later Shane Gould equalled it with two freestyle titles and the gold medal in the 200 metres individual medley. Miss Ender's superiority was not unexpected. In the 1973 and 1975 World Championships and the 1974 European

Championships she had taken four titles. Montreal was par for the course for Miss Ender.

Her performances at the East German Championships showed that she was still improving. She established five individual world records—the 100 and 200 metres freestyle, the 100 metres backstroke, the 100 metres butterfly and the 200 metres individual medley. She is in many ways a typical product of East Germany's meticulous system for producing champions in any sport. "Scientific preparation" she said in Montreal "has helped our girls a great deal but in the first place there had to be exceptional talent. Greatness cannot come in sport without talent." Miss Ender has this ability although interestingly enough she only took up swimming as a precaution against developing a carriage defect. And it was not until she started to enjoy holidays on the Baltic with her parents who live in Plauen that she felt at home in the water.

But once she began swimming she got caught up in the detailed organisation which distinguishes the East German sport. When the country began to take the sport seriously in the 1950's there were about 20,000 registered competitors using 20 full-sized pools. By 1976 this had grown to 85,000 registered swimmers and 130 pools. Yet it is noticeable that the consequences of East Germany's emphasis on swimming has largely been felt in the female side of the sport. Only Roland Matthes, winner of both backstroke titles in Mexico and Munich, has been as consistently successful as the women have been. Matthes may have lost his crowns in Montreal but he had a particular interest in the womens' swimming because he is engaged to Miss Ender. The sport is more popular among women than men in East Germany, admitted Professor Rudolf Schramme, a product of the famous Institute of Physical Culture in Leipzig and the head coach of the East German swimming association in Montreal.

It was Schramme, who led the other East German coaches to accept the principle that women can be subjected to almost as much stress in training as the men. The East German coaches are themselves the products of a five year course which has made them familiar with the latest researches in the physiology of exercise. Although there is always a doctor on the pool-side to assist the coach, what makes the relationship between the two supervisors sometimes so different from Western countries is that the coach is sufficiently versed in the principles of physiology to understand the reasons behind the doctors' recommendations. Their emphasis on weight-training has been a feature of their recent success. In 1973 it was learned that they spent two hours in the gymnasium to every three in the water. This has subsequently been adjusted to four hours of swimming to one hour of weight-training. In recent years many Western coaches have regarded weight-training as only a minor part of a swimmer's training and much of that on pulleys, duplicating the competitor's stroke against increasing resistance. Now some of them will think again.

Yet despite this emphasis on stamina and speed, what impressed David Wilkie, Britain's first male swimming gold medallist for 68 years, was the smoothness of their technique. "When I look at them what strikes me is the beautiful flexibility of their strokes." Considering that came from someone whose own movement through the water is so refined that it is praise indeed.

If Wilkie expressed his pleasure at the technique of the East Germans, another men's gold medallist Rod Strachan, first in the men's 400 metres individual medley, was less circumspect about their appearance. He said what a lot of spectators felt: that the East Germans were "not exactly like girls" because of the weight-training they do and the anabolic steroid drugs that they were rumoured to be taking. None of the East German girls incidentally was tested for steroids in the pre-Games examinations. None was picked by the random testing method.

Miss Ender, who certainly is not unattractive, was understandably embarrassed by the allegations and replied that there was a "femininity controller here", referring to the proof required that an individual is female before taking part in the womens' events at the Games. Dr. Schramme appealed to everyone's sense of decency. "Whoever said that was not a chivalrous man. If you were to line up the American and German girls in a row I would defy you to say 'this is a girl' or 'this is not a girl'. It's Strachan's bad luck if he doesn't know our girls."

The Americans, and in particular Shirley Babashoff, their big, blonde and beautiful freestyler, declared that they did little weight-training compared to the East Germans and together with the other American girls would be unwilling to do a great deal more. This suggests that if the Americans are to recover their status in the women's branch of the sport they will have to find some other way of defeating the East Germans. Dr Schramme is convinced of its value: "Without a comprehensive programme of weight-training no swimmer is going to achieve big results in modern swimming."

Miss Babashoff, who won two silver medals in individual events at the Munich Olympics, finished behind Miss Ender in the Montreal Olympics. But she announced after being asked by an American journalist what the USA were going to do about the East Germans' formidable progress: "We're having fun". The American reporter replied with notable indiscretion and exaggeration—traits which are common in many reporters: "The Americans are having fun, and the Germans are doing all the work". Miss Babashoff had expected to defeat Miss Ender in the 200 metres after winning the world title from the East German the previous year. The American also lost the 400 and 800 metres.

Three individual silver medals would please most people in the Olympics and perhaps it would have been better if she had said straight out that she wasn't quite good enough on the day. This, however, would not have pleased the American reporters, who seemed to view her defeats as a national disaster which had to be explained away to their readers in terms of a lack of seriousness on the part of the American team rather than lack of talent. Miss Babashoff supplied them with the perfect words. "I took up swimming because I love the water. Nobody picked me out of kindergarten and put me into a ten year programme. That's what happens with these East German girls. When our team have a warm-up it is fun. We play around in the water. With them it is work, work, work and nothing else."

What she omitted to say was that her life had been principally work, work, work and little else because if it hadn't she would not have had the superb career that she has done. Her collection of medals is astonishing particularly as she has done what few female swimmers have ever done—won them at two Olympics. Perhaps she reached her peak in comparison with the rest of the world a year too early for the Games for she was a confident winner of the 400 metres at the 1975 World Championships as well as her gold medal in the 200 metres. Probably the race in the Games which she was expected to win was the 800 metres in which she set a world record of 8min 38·63sec at the American Trials. But the fact that two other competitors had broken the world record in the three week period leading up to the American Trials at Long Beach stressed that there was plenty of improvement possible in the Olympics. This is exactly what happened.

East Germany's Petra Thumer, trailed Canada's Shannon Smith over the opening 300 metres but was ahead by the half-way mark, although closely followed by Miss Babashoff. The American girl has always admitted that her biggest weakness was a poor sense of pace and clearly felt that her most sensible strategy was to follow the East German and try to outsprint her. But Miss Thumer, who had done 8min 40·68sec during the East German trials, was equal to anything that Miss Babashoff could produce. The pair accelerated up the last length but Miss Thumer was always just ahead, touching first in a world record 8min 37·14sec with the American 0·45 seconds behind. The surprise of the event was the unexceptional showing of Australia's Jenny Turrall who was slower than her old world record of 8min 50·43sec—a time that was subsequently beaten by eight people in the six weeks before the Games. Miss Turrall could not improve her performance as the others had done and finshed last. Miss Turrall's problem was to keep her weight down to her normal poundage of 8st 5lb. Sometimes she had exceeded 9 stone. The famous Australian coach, Forbes Carlile, said that he had persuaded Jenny's mother to cook less fattening foods. "But everybody in the family lost weight except Jenny."

In the 400 metres East Germany were without Barbara Krause, who had made her impact on the swimming world in Cali when, swimming the second leg, she helped her country to the gold medal and record at the World Championships. And in the East German Championships she had set new world figures of 4min 11·69sec. But East Germany were unperturbed. Miss Thumer was ready for a world record at this distance as well as the 800 metres and this was enough to defeat Miss Babashoff.

If the individual freestyle events were the prerogative of the East Germans they did not win the last event—the womens 4 × 100 metres freestyle relay. Miss Ender sent her colleagues away with an opening stage of 55·79 seconds and then watched with mounting dismay as the Americans whittled down the lead. Kim Peyton (56·95 sec), Wendy Boglioli (55·81sec), Jill Sterkel (55·78sec) and Shirley Babashoff (56·28sec) brought America home to their only women's swimming gold medal of the Games. Miss Ender was so disgusted that she flung her cap on the floor. Even a champion like her has to lose sometimes.

The Americans, encouraged by the capacity crowd, simulated election night for the American Presidency, cavorting in and out of the pool. But Miss Ender had recovered her temper by the time of the awards of medals to announce that she was looking forward to meeting her grandmother who had left East Germany 15 years previously and has been living in Kansas. A number of American coaches were surely wishing that the grandmother would have been doing her adopted country a favour if she had packed the three year old Kornelia for the voyage.

The joy which greeted the Americans' victory in this last event emphasised through its intensity and note of relief that Miss Ender was the finest female swimmer of the Games—a person whom Australia's famous coach Don Talbot described without hyperbole as "a person ahead of her time". Perhaps the evening which emphasised her quality was when she took the 100 metres butterfly by a full arm stroke and, one race later, the 200 metres freestyle by three metres. On both occasions she set a world record. It was a double without precedent in the Olympics. No one, not Dawn Fraser, Chris von Saltza, Debbie Meyer nor Shane Gould has been able to match that feat. And probably only the arrangement of the programme prevented her from challenging even more closely Mark Spitz's total of seven gold medals.

Ulrike Richter, who took the women's 100 and 200 metres backstroke titles in Montreal, was only slightly less successful. She was not ranked in the top 50 for either distance in 1972, but by August 1973, she had become world record-holder and champion for the 100 metres at the Belgrade meeting. Altogether she broke the world sprint best eight times, reducing it from 1min 5·39sec in August 1973 to 1min 1·51sec in June 1976. She was followed home by her compatriot Birgit Treiber, who has been almost as prolific a record-breaker, in both backstroke races.

Although East Germany took the 100 metres breaststroke through Hannelore Anke, they were convincingly beaten in the longer race. Here three Russians led by Marina Koshevaia took the medals with Miss Anke fourth. After such a cavalcade of East German triumphs it was a delightful change for the East German world champion (Miss Anke) and the world record-holder (Carola Nitschke) to be defeated—and in a world best.

If East Germany were triumphant in the women's events then the American men were also usually supreme. Their collegiate competition has always been the foundation of their success and it was perhaps significant that one of the few people to interrupt their cascade of successes was a Briton, who admitted that he owed his gold medal to spending the last four years at an American University.

During the Games seven Britons announced that they would be going to American colleges on scholarships. Four of them—Kevin Burns (Sheffield), Duncan Cleworth (Manchester), Peter Lerpiniere (Tidworth) and Gary Abrahams (Southampton) are going to the University of Miami where Wilkie has been studying and training. European silver medallist Jimmy Carter and world bronze medallist David Parker have accepted places in California and Gordon Hewitt at the University of North Carolina.

Under international rules it is illegal to accept scholarships based on athletic ability. But when the ASA protested in 1976 Miami claimed that their scholarships were based on academic ability as well as swimming talent. Burns, a determined but pleasant man, pointed out why he has gone to America. "Why shouldn't we accept the scholarships? I gave up a £4,000-a-year job in computers to go on the dole because I needed the time for training. Now I'll be getting further education and good swimming."

David Haller, the team coach and a man whose contribution to the success of British swimming in recent years has been enormous, believes that these people are right to go to America because there is not enough good competition in Britain to force them to raise their sights. And this applies to many other countries. They know that the gold medal that Wilkie won in Montreal partially resulted from his spell at Miami.

Although Wilkie had finished second in the 200 metres breaststroke in Munich he believes that he would not have gone on to take world titles and ultimately the Olympic title unless he had had the intensive pressure of American collegiate competition plus the high quality training partners which he was able to enjoy. Although Wilkie was a member of Warrender Baths Club in Edinburgh where he was able to train in the Commonwealth Pool there was neither the warm weather, which makes training a pleasure rather than a penance, nor a college who would take him and allow him time off to train satisfactorily. Consequently he moved to Miami.

His rivalry with his conqueror in Munich, John Hencken, spread out over four years—a series of tussles which caused Wilkie to say to his opponent: "It's been a good four years, John. Thanks a lot". To which Hencken rather abruptly replied: "It has been."

Wilkie, seven weeks older than Hencken and 23 by the time of the Montreal Games, had been superior to Hencken over 200 metres since 1972. Although Hencken, known as "Rocket Man" because he qualified as an engineer at Stanford University and makes solid fuel missiles as a hobby, won the 100 metres at the 1973 World Championships, Wilkie finished first in the 200 metres. Wilkie's smooth long stroke was better suited to the longer race whereas Hencken's short, fast pull gave him the advantage over the sprint. Hencken, however, set world records for both distances during the USA v East Germany meeting in 1974—a year in which Wilkie took the Commonwealth and European gold medals at the longer distance. Hencken decided not to enter the World Championships in 1975 and Wilkie promptly took both events, clocking the second fastest times in history. Thus the pair went to the Games with Hencken marginally the favourite for the 100 metres in which only a second covered the first eight men in the race, and Wilkie the fancied swimmer for the longer race because he had not lost to the American over this distance since the 1972 Olympics.

One person who had few doubts was John Devitt, Australia's Olympic 100 metres freestyle champion in 1960 and a man whose job marketing swimming costumes means that he is always an acute student of form. Before the Games he said: "There is no doubt about Wilkie in the 200 metres. His wins in the American winter championships at Long Beach in April following his two gold medals at last year's world championships all point to it." Britons, who were anxiously optimistic, looked at the figures and results and hoped that a more objective observer like Devitt was right.

They should have had more confidence in the Scot. He was born to be close to the water. When he was in Miami he often spent evenings fishing off Key Biscayne or simply dangling his feet in the sea. A favourite week-end recreation for him was to go surfing. His birth sign predictably is . . . Pisces.

At Miami much of the early part of his course was spent studying marine biology and a favourite restaurant of his in Miami is Stone Crab Joe's, where among the wharves of the port, people enjoy the produce of the sea. It is this attachment to the water and his enjoyment of being by himself that has enabled him to survive so long in international swimming. His girl friend, Kate Kewley, admits:

"David is a loner." When they have been together in her flat often he has spent a lot of his time alone rather than with her, plainly something that she has come to accept. With the British team in Montreal he seemed a man apart sometimes, silently mouthing the teams' songs instead of vociferously leading them. But the quiet confidence of Wilkie struck even the non-British observers as more prepossessing than Hencken's coldness. The bitterness of their rivalry was built up by the Press but not without some degree of truth. "I wouldn't talk to John about swimming. It would be like talking to myself," David said before the Games and Hencken's behaviour both in victory and defeat scarcely took the antagonism out of the situation. But Wilkie did not wilt. Despite being well beaten by Hencken in the 100 metres when the American showed that he was in the finest form of his life (an impression later confirmed by his time in the 200 metres final) the Scot recovered both physically and mentally. And mentally was more important during the days of the Games. He was probably right when he said: "At Miami I have achieved a sense of mental greatness."

Wilkie and his British colleague Duncan Goodhew both comfortably qualified for the final of the 100 metres. They finished first and third in a closely-fought semi-final. Wilkie was only 300th of a second outside his own European record with 1min 4·29secs. Goodhew touched home in 1min 4·59secs.

The surprise of this heat was the elimination of Japan's defending champion Nobutaka Taguchi who made two false starts and then finished sixth. In the other semi-final Hencken won decisively with a world record of 1min 3·62sec and Canada's Graham Smith clocked 1min 3·92sec for a Commonwealth best. Wilkie was honest afterwards: "Obviously Hencken is now the favourite but you can never tell in a final. It's going to be a hell of a race." It was. Wilkie shaved his body hair to reduce the water resistance, a common practice in swimming, and hoped to swim a faster opening length in order to reduce the advantage that Hencken had at the turn. The American's shorter body enabled him to somersault more dexterously and his powerful legs allowed him to butt through the water. Although he expended a lot of energy with this style he was fit enough to hold it for the two lengths of the pool. Wilkie said that he "had deliberately done bad things before the final. I didn't do a grab start in the heats and I was slow in the semi-final. I was making everything count for the race that mattered."

But in the final Wilkie turned in sixth place—a second behind the American—and although he came nobly through, as one expected on the second lap, he finished 0·32 seconds behind Hencken's world best of 1min 3·11sec. Goodhew was seventh. Wilkie's second place indicated that he still had his competitive edge in a race that was not his favourite. The fact that he had got so close to the American gave him confidence for the 200 metres. In the heats of the longer race Wilkie reassured everyone as to his invincibility at the 200 metres. He set an Olympic record of 2min 18·29sec—only eight hundredths of a second slower than Hencken's world best. Hencken himself looked less assured in 2min 21·23sec.

In the final Hencken must have done everything that he had hoped to do. He went out fast, leading at 100 metres and finally clocked a personal best by almost a second, over a metre quicker than his world record. It was just that Wilkie had what the distinguished American coach Peter Daland described as "the greatest swim of the Games." He finished in 2min 15·11sec—over a body length clear. He had experimented in the morning to see if an opening 100 metres in 1min 6sec would hurt him. As it did not he repeated it in the final and this time held on to the pace as much as possible, gliding away from Hencken on the third lap. And on the fourth with Hencken visibly tiring and the stadium applauding the first defeat of the American men Wilkie pulled away for victory. "Winning meant," he said tritely but accurately "that all the hard work has paid off. When I do it it gives me a big thrill. I always like to push the third length and after that the fourth length comes easily because you're going for home and being in the lead makes it so much easier."

He also said that he felt happy at the thought of never having to swim another stroke of training in his life. He knew he would not miss training but he would miss competing, although he did swim in Italy a fortnight after the Games. Paul Naisby, and David Leigh, Britain's other leading breast-strokers, failed to reach the final although Naisby was disqualified for taking dolphin kicks after his turn. Britain's protest to FINA was turned down.

Wilkie's victory stopped America from winning all 13 titles just as the USA's womens relay victory and Russia's breaststroke triumph prevented East Germany from taking all 13 of the titles. But the solitary wins meant much to the countries concerned and gave heart to other nations.

For elsewhere in the mens' events it was a flow of American triumphs with the Hungarians, East Germans and Australians rarely showing the form of which previous results suggested they were capable. One cornerstone on which this success was built was the lanky figure of John Naber, a third year student of psychology at the University of Southern California—the college which attracted such famous Australians of the 1950's as Jon Konrads and Murray Rose. He got gold medals in both backstroke events including becoming the first man to duck under two minutes for the 200 metres with 1min 59·19sec. He also got relay golds in the medley and freestyle and was only slightly less than triumphant in the 200 metres freestyle when he finished second. He wore a woollen torque decorated with badges on the back of his head ("It was knitted by my grandfather's secretary. She is a sweet lady and I call her Aunt Maud"). In a sport that seemed a succession of records and times he became one of the few personalities of the swimming events. It is not that one would have missed him easily. He stood 6ft 6in tall. He was known as "Fruit Cake" by his team-mates because he was so eager to clown around the poolside. "They are probably right" admitted Naber "I am emotional and I show it. Besides at the prices people have been paying this week for seats they deserve a bit of fun."

Another individual who gave some individuality to the sport was Gary Hall, a former rival and fellow university student at Indiana of Mark Spitz. But, while Spitz won seven titles in Munich, Hall, the favourite for two individual medley titles, failed to get in the first three. Haunted by his disappointment he decided to try again. Although in his third year at medical school and recently married he found the incentive to be selected for the 100 metres butterfly. "It would have been hard to live with myself if I hadn't at least tried." Few swimming medals were more popular than his bronze.

In the 200 metres butterfly, East Germany's Roger Pyttel was expected to be in the first three. But three Americans led by Mike Bruner collected the medals with Pyttel finishing outside his world record time of 1min 59·63sec which would have got him the bronze medal. Just how swiftly swimming changes can be shown by the 1500 metres. A year before the Games it seemed to be a clear-cut duel between the USA's Tim Shaw and Australia's Steve Holland. In the 1975 World Championships Shaw won the 200 metres, 400 metres and 1500 metres—no swimmer since Jon Konrads had possessed such a range of freestyle performances among his contemporaries. But he lost form and only made the 400 metres for Montreal where he finished second.

Holland, who relaxes by eating gallons of ice-cream and playing with a yo-yo, missed the World Championships because he was concentrating on building up a new technique for the Games. He moved from Australia to Mission Viejo Nadadores, a Californian Swimming Club centred between Los Angeles and San Diego. Here Holland, accompanied by such people as Shirley Babashoff and Britain's Jimmy Carter, altered his stroke under the guidance of Mark Schubert. He took fewer strokes but his abnormally big hands and feet were able to propel him even more quickly. The only trouble was that other people were passing him. One of them was another member of Mission Viejo—Brian Goodell, who beat Holland's world record in winning the US Trials in 15min 6·6sec. Holland set the pace valiantly at the Games and beat Goodell's previous best time. But Goodell and his team-mate Bobby Hackett clung on and sprinted home over the last two lengths to clock 15min 2·40sec and 15min 3·90sec respectively. Holland, like so many runners-up in the Games, had seen the title pass him by because he was the best in the world in the year (1974) when the Games weren't being held.

Goodell also took the 400 metres title in 3min 51·93sec. His speed and capacity for fast finishes meant that since he was able to keep close to Shaw over the opening 100 metres, join in the pace-making in the middle part of the race and because of his resources of stamina, he still had the energy to clock 58sec for the last lap. As records, even world records, become meaningless one time still stood out although it was intrinsically less exciting than many of those set. Jim Montgomery's gold medal in the 100 metres freestyle was won in 49·99sec, the first time a swimmer had ever gone under 50 seconds for the shortest race in the pool. For many years people believed that this time would never be beaten. Certainly that feeling must have been prevalent 54 years previously when Johnny Weissmuller went faster than 60 seconds for the first time. Tarzan would have had his leg bitten off by a crocodile if he'd swum that slowly in 1976.

Britain's performances were overshadowed by Wilkie's 200 metres breaststroke win. Although the rest of the team did not repeat the success at the 1975 World Championships, when they were the most successful men's team after the Americans, nevertheless they were still always challenging for places in the finals. Their third medal came in the men's 4 × 200 metres freestyle relay. It was Brian Brinkley, the team captain, who missed a possible medal in the men's 200 metres butterfly, who brought the quartet home. After Alan McClatchey, David Dunne and Gordon Downie had swum the opening three legs. Dunne, who had never before appeared in a major meeting pulled Britain up from sixth to fourth place, a position which Downie maintained magnificently. Brinkley plunged into the water a body length down on his West German rival ... but he produced the fastest race of his life.

He clocked 1min 51·25sec, overhauled the West German on the second half of the race to bring him the Olympic medal he so deserved. Although he never won the Olympic gold medal he craved, Brinkley still broke British records in every race in Montreal. And no one deserved his collection of one Commonwealth gold, two silvers and two bronzes, a World Championship silver and three bronzes and two European silvers more than Brinkley. Montreal was his last big event before retiring at the end of the 1976 season. British swimming will miss him.

Perhaps the most suitable epilogue on the Games comes from David Haller, the team coach: "Experts were surprised at the performance of the British team here. They had not expected that we would hold on to what we did at the World Championships last year. But we're still breaking records even in the face of the most awesome swimming I have ever seen in my life."

If swimming attracted most of the attention in the pool there was one diving performance which forced spectators to linger in their seats after the swimming had stopped—the victory of Klaus Dibiasi in the mens' highboard diving. The 28 year-old Italian did what no diver had ever done before (and only Dawn Fraser among swimmers)—win an Olympic gold medal in three successive Games. Dibiasi overcame tendonitis of both heels to produce a triple twist with one and a half somersaults in the fifth round to take him into the lead. Although California's Greg Louganis had a forward one and a half somersault with triple twist on his last attempt (an effort that brought him 76·56pts, the highest score of the competition for a single dive) it was not enough to overhaul Dibiasi.

Dibiasi is enormously popular in his hometown of Bolzano

where local citizens were so pleased with his Tokyo performances (he got a silver) that they built him a diving tank just for him to practise in. He is also admired internationally and received the tribute from one American during the Games who said publicly and amid applause: "I should like to thank you for all the pleasure you have given us these past years." The USA's Phil Boggs took the springboard diving. Another American Jenny Chandler won the women's springboard and Russia's Elena Vaytsekhovskaia the women's highboard.

Hungary won the water-polo as they have done on three other occasions since the Second World War. They drew 5-5 with Yugoslavia in their final match but already had an unbeatable lead. They finished with nine points out of ten in the final five matches. Italy, who last took the title at the Rome Games, were the silver medallists and Holland third.

5

MODERN PENTATHLON

THE modern pentathlon competition provided two sensations and brought the sport to the attention of millions who had hitherto considered this gruelling five event stint to be the property of the military and the Eastern bloc.

The greatest sensation was the shock disqualification of that outstanding competitor Boris Onishenko, from Dynamo Kiev, a major in the Red Army, who had won every major honour in the sport with the exception of the Olympic individual gold medal.

Holder of a world individual championship gold medal, three team world championship gold medals, second in the last two Olympics in Mexico City and Munich, he was about to close his international career after more than a decade. Close it he did, but the wildest fantasy could not have conceived that it would end in his being sent home in disgrace, disqualified from the Olympic tournament for cheating; a crime more serious in the eyes of his countrymen than in the rest of the world. In a country where the sportsman reigns supreme and has such advantages, whether in social status, guaranteed good employment, better food and higher quality living conditions, not cramped like the normal Soviet Union Citizen, to cheat is unthinkable. Alas, this is exactly what happened. In the fencing his epee was found to be bugged with a device which would make the registering equipment flash as if he had scored a genuine hit against an opponent.

The second sensation was Britain's unbelievable gold medal, their first medal of any sort in the team event. The culmination of years of hard work by one of Britain's finest sportsmen in the widest sense was perhaps the most satisfactory aspect of it all. Jim Fox, competing at 34 in his fourth and last Olympics, had so often come so near to the supreme awards, only to lose them for some unlucky reason or other. Thus when he narrowly missed the bronze medal in the last Olympics everyone thought he had passed his peak, but a third place in last year's world championships in Mexico City proved he had not.

As always the modern pentathlon competition opened, on July 20th, with the riding. There had earlier been protests by the British team manager, Mike Proudfoot, that the course was too easy but in a sport where ridership is often not of the highest standard it is extremely difficult to design a course which is easy enough without giving everyone maximum points. A time is set for the course, realising 1000pts, anything faster gains appropriately more, with deductions for obstacles hit, or slower rounds. As it happened 35 of the 47 riders gained more than 1000 pts with 13 gaining the maximum 1100 pts, including Fox, an Army sergeant, and Adrian Parker, Britain's brilliant No. 2, who had recently inflicted a rare defeat on Fox, proving that at last the nursery of British talent was beginning to make itself felt.

Danny Nightingale, the third member of the British squad amassed a few penalties but was still able to earn himself 1012 pts. All the expected people succeeded, with the Russian Pavel Lednev, the reigning world and Olympic champion, who had been unbeaten for the last five years, totalling 1032 pts, with Onishenko earning 1068 pts and the third Russian, the young Boris Mosolov, 1036 pts.

Thus after the first day the British trio were third, with 3212 pts, behind Sweden (3267) and France (3236), although there was not too much significance in these figures so early in the competition. From the British angle the vital importance was that all our men had gone round without creating any problems for the next four days, as a frolicsome horse could have ruined everything.

After 24 hours rest came the fencing: a gruelling day long competition in which every competitor fences the other, one hit only to count, with a time limit, placing the onus on concentration and stamina. In the opening competition of the day Britain were drawn against the Soviet Union, and the scene was set unknowingly for a drama, unique in the annals of Olympic history. Onishenko faced Parker first. Suddenly the recording equipment registered a hit to the Russian's credit. Parker protested and the judge came over, checked the electrical circuits, the piste, but not of course the swords. Having declared himself satisfied that Onishenko, known to be a superb swordsman, had recorded his one hit, Parker left the arena to be replaced by Fox.

As the fencers lined up, the recording device suddenly lit, as if Onishenko had hit Fox. The Russian left the stage, saying "Excuse me, there has been an accident", and was about to change weapons when Fox demanded that the epee be examined believing it to be short-circuiting, but not thinking that it was tampered with. Then the awful truth came out. It was found that clever engineering had been effected, bringing two open wires into the palm of the fencer. These, when wired to a device controlled by Onishenko, had the desired effect of giving him hits to which he was not entitled. At first no one could really believe what had happened. It was known that this could have been no accident since the weapons were subjected to rigorous control, 13 of the 16 offered by Britain were rejected, albeit for minor points, and the three fencing masks bought only that morning were found not to be fit for use for various reasons.

The jury of appeal met and even before Proudfoot had a chance to protest officially on behalf of the British squad they had expelled Onishenko. As he left the stadium he muttered only to Fox "I'm sorry. I'm sorry." The Briton, a friend and rival in international competition for more than 10 years, was deeply shocked, more at the knowledge of what would happen to the Russian than at the incident itself. Here was a man he had spent happy times with all over the world, and would never see again under the same circumstances of comradeship and friendly rivalry. Why did Onishenko do this? In my opinion it was because he wanted to defeat not the other pentathletes from Poland, Great Britain or Czechoslovakia, for instance, but to end a glorious career as the Olympic champion, which would bring its own dividends in the years to come.

There was no appeal and even the Russian authorities did not attempt to minimize the terrible deed, contenting themselves with sending him home immediately and announcing from Moscow that he was hitherto banned for life from all competition. No doubt there would be other sanctions. Loss of certain privileges and certainly the promotion to lieutenant-colonel which he had been told he could expect after his return home.

This disqualification had its side effects. It upset Fox to a degree which made his entire participation in the competition somewhat doubtful and there is no doubt that he would have thrown it in had he been able. But having managed to pull himself together he fought on, only to be shaken immediately by an extremely poor decision against the Finn, Heikki Hulkkonen, which, when combined with the Onishenko affair, had the accumulative effect of knocking him right off balance. Ironically Onishenko, who had been allowed to fence on after the incident until he was officially disqualified by the jury of appeal, had an 8–1 win-loss record and probably could have gone through the entire competition with a record at least as good as that of Lednev who finished with a 36–9 score, for the maximum points of the day, 1096.

Fox, naturally, finished with the best score of the day among the Britons with his 23–22 for 784 pts but this was at least 150 pts below what had been expected and was his lowest fencing score in a major competition for quite some time. Parker and Nightingale were given 712 and 760 pts respectively putting the British squad down to sixth overall with 5468 pts, now 277 pts behind the leaders; a not too significant margin, especially knowing that the Soviet team chances had been entirely eliminated, since with two men they could not defend their Olympic title.

In the individual competition Fox was the best placed Briton, 11th with 1884 pts. Parker was 22nd and Nightingale 29th. At this point the leaders were Lednev with 2128, Jan Bartu, of Czechoslovakia, 2076 and Janusz Pyciak-Peciak (the eventual individaul champion), 1994.

Shooting was another competition where Fox's concentration slipped at the last minute and in his fourth and last round, with a pistol, in which he had been expected to score at least an overall 195 out of 200, he finished up with a poor 187 for 846 pts. His individual round scores were a maximum 50 to start with, 46·47 and then finally an upsetting 44. Parker totalled 188, an excellent performance, while Nightingale proved his increasing maturity with the best among the Britons of 191 for 934 pts. So at the end of the third day Britain was down to eighth, 352 behind the leaders, Czechoslovakia, with a combined figure of 2648, and although the individual position did not look good there seemed to be a fair chance that a bronze team medal could be in the offing as the running and swimming were the best disciplines of the British squad.

In the overall competition Lednev still led from Bartu and Pyciak-Peciak with Fox 18th, Nightingale 21st and Parker 23rd, all within 50 pts of each other.

The 300 metres swimming brought a radical change in British

fortunes, for all members of the team swam faster than at any time in their careers; Parker the fastest with 3min 24·3sec for 1240 pts, Nightingale 3min 32·7sec for 1172 and Fox 3min 44·2sec for 1080. With only the running to come Britain was in a steady fifth position and the bronze medal looked guaranteed—there was even a tinge of silver about it. Czechoslovakia led with 12,145 pts, followed by Hungary 11,831, Poland 11,758, United States 11,739 and Great Britain 11,608. Now it was known that the Americans and, almost certainly the Hungarians, could be beaten, what about the Poles and Czechs who were making such excellent progress and who looked so powerful throughout? The change at the top of the individual competition had changed again with Bartu now leading from Lednev and Pyciak-Peciak fifth.

The 4000 metres cross country course was a tough one for the big men, such as Fox and Lednev and a hard one for anyone else. But it was essential that if Great Britain were to keep in the medal hunt the three men were to run the 26 hills faster than all other teams. Fox, for instance, was the speediest of all the runners in the Munich Olympics, but how would he stand in Montreal four years later with the eager youngsters snapping at his heels? Parker was reckoned to be the best swim/runner in the world, with Nightingale not far behind.

Parker was drawn first, with the runners going off at one minute intervals. He came home in an amazing 12min 9sec, for a fantastic 1378 pts which, as it proved, was never even approached by one single opponent. In fact the next fastest was the American Michael Burley with 12min 26sec. Nightingale was equally magnificent with a time of 12min 32sec to place fourth among the runners while Fox ran himself to utter collapse with his 12min 47sec. Then followed a period of acute anxiety as time and again figures were checked. We knew Great Britain had beaten the Americans, putting them fourth, then the Hungarians, for third and finally, it seemed, joy of joys, the Poles, guaranteeing a silver.

Counting, recounting . . . and then it was announced. Great Britain first with 15,559 pts, Czechoslovakia second with 15,451 and when all the counting was over it was seen that Parker had finished an excellent fifth, Nightingale 10th and Fox 15th, lower than in Mexico (8th) and Munich (4th) but better than in Tokyo in 1964. As he said "it took an experienced idiot like myself nearly to lose the gold

Britain's Debbie Johnsey (top), who came so close to winning a medal, in action during the team grand prix on Moxy and (below) Tad Coffin takes Bally-Cor over a fence during the cross country stage of the Three-Day Event. He went on to take the individual gold medal for the United States.

Princess Anne, the first member of the Royal Family to represent Britain at an Olympics, during the dressage section of the Three-Day Event, riding Goodwill.

Reg White and John Osborne, gold medallists for Britain in the Tornado class, in action during their remarkable series at Kingston, Ontario.

Chris Baillieu and Michael Hart, two Cambridge University oarsmen who proved that true amateurs can still compete alongside state-aided competitors and still perform with credit — they took a silver medal in the double sculls and (below) for the second Olympics running Teofilo Stevenson brings Cuba the heavyweight gold medal in the boxing.

medal!" But the pressures he had been under were so great that many a lesser man would have crumbled under them.

Modern pentathletes are always the most popular of all amateur sportsmen; never selfish or grabbing, in contrast to competitors in other more popular sports who time and again receive heavy sponsorships which so often prove to be wasted money. Theirs is a shoestring sport which makes them appreciate more than any the help they can get. But in praising the individuals one should not forget the team coach, Ron Bright, a former Army colleague of Fox and now in charge of a sports centre in Farnborough.

It is forgotten that it was Bright who persuaded Fox to return to the sport after the 1968 Olympics and who begged him to stay on after Munich when he would have prepared to retire. Now he can, but Bright wants him to hang on just that little bit longer and help guide the talented youngsters Britain possesses in major competitions. The flood of applicants the sport will receive after this success will be reward indeed for the dedication and sportsmanship of Fox, Nightingale, Parker, the reserve Andy Archibald, the coach Bright, the hard working team manager Mike Proudfoot, and many others behind the scenes.

As a postscript to the gold medal, even before the victory ceremony, Fox had said that he would like to organise a letter to be signed by all the world's top pentathletes to be sent to the Soviet Sports Ministry pleading for clemency for the disgraced Onishenko. So even in his moment of triumph he could still remember a comrade.

6

EQUESTRIANISM

It is all too easy to blame lack of success on sheer bad luck, but there is no doubt that it played an important part in the British equestrian team's failure to bring back a medal for the first time since before the Berlin Games in 1936. The teams themselves, or at least their leaders, were making no excuses. Said Lord Hugh Russell, chairman of selectors for the three-day event team; "Luck has been with us for the past few Games, now it is not. We cannot complain." While Colonel Harry Llewellyn, who fills the equivalent show jumping position, made his attitude clear when he said: "I feel we should make our own luck." Yet it would have taken only a few smiles of fortune to have given Lucinda Prior-Palmer and Be Fair and the event team a brace of silvers, and Debbie Johnsey and Moxy looked sure to win a medal of some sort everywhere except on the finishing post.

Considering the vast amount of research that had been put into the organisation of the three-day event it has to be admitted that the end-product was disappointing. The cross-country course was a step backwards from what we saw in Munich, which was generally conducive to bold jumping, did not overface the least-equipped of horses and yet still brought the class animals, and riders, out on top. In Montreal it was small and trappy, not especially pleasant either to watch nor, apparently, to ride over and produced more exhausted and injured horses than anyone would wish for. The steeplechase was run on a dirt track, because those who thought they knew better refused course-builder Barbara Kemp's advice to turf it long enough in advance, and as a result of a torrential downpour the night before the speed and endurance phase—which nearly brought about its postponement—was so hard to get through that Bertie Hill, former gold medallist and now trainer, described it as "going two steps forward and one back". It must have added to the exhausting effect of the entire phase.

The bad luck was certainly not all confined to the British, and Germany's Otto Ammerman, with Volturno, who were lying third after the dressage were eliminated when, after missing the timing gate at the finish of the steeplechase—it was not well marked and the visibility was poor—they turned back when the shouts of the crowd made Ammerman realise the error of his ways. But he was disqualified for "outside assistance". World champion Bruce Davidson and Irish Cap, on whom he won the title at Burghley, finished the dressage in second place, but had a fall in the lake.

Both the United States and German teams kept going in sufficient numbers however to be able to take the first two places eventually. A double blow put the British right out of it. Lucinda Prior-Palmer and Be Fair, the European champions, gave a particularly delightful dressage test which left them fifth, and then the chestnut galloped round the cross-country course with his own particular brand of gaiety and was one of the least tired as he came up the finishing straight. But as he came to the finish disaster struck, he went dead lame, Lucinda dismounted and poor Be Fair was found to have slipped his achilles tendon from his near hind hock, the same injury that put Columbus out in the 1974 World Championship and allowed Davidson and Irish Cap through to win.

There was no question of Be Fair continuing—nor will he ever compete again—and although Hugh Thomas and Playamar, despite an unfortunate fall also at the lake, finished strongly, the horse had also injured a tendon, on the same leg but not the same tendon which he was operated on in 1975. It was soon clear that he, too, was out of the running, and as a minimum of three horses are needed for a team result that put paid to Britain's attempt to win a third successive Olympic gold. To add to the gloom, Princess Anne and Goodwill had a fall at the 19th when the horse slipped in bad ground just before take-off.

Although slightly concussed, Princess Anne remounted to finish the course, but clearly with no further chance of any sort of medal. Only Munich winner Richard Meade gave the British something to cheer about, with a brilliant ride on Jacob Jones, who has improved to an almost unbelievable degree since the beginning of the season. Much of the credit for this must go to Meade, who was completing a clear cross-country round for the fourth Olympic Games in a row, all on different horses.

This left them fourth at the end of the day, with Karl Schultz and Madrigal, who had been ahead after the dressage, still in the lead, despite nearly up-ending at the fence in the middle of the lake, from which they made a quite acrobatic recovery. They had only a minimum amount to spare, less than the cost of one show jumping fence, over two Americans, Tad Coffin with Bally Cor and the veteran Michael Plumb, now in his fifth Olympic Games, on the seven-year-old Better and Better. Plumb had had the alternative of riding the vastly experienced Good Mixture, but wisely decided to opt for the younger, sounder horse, relying on his own experience to make up the difference.

Bally Cor, on whom Coffin, 22, won the Pan American Gold Medal in Mexico in 1975, was eleven years old in Montreal, not a great age, but she had had fitness problems and this was scheduled as her last event before retiring to stud. She was fastest of all across country and was an ominous threat to Schultz, who had given Madrigal a hard ride across country and is notably vulnerable in the show jumping ring, as he had proved in the European Championships in Luhmuhlen. The two Americans went first, Bally Cor well clear and then Better and Better just dropped a toe in the water. So Schultz knew exactly what he had to do when he came, but this did not help him to do it.

A pole off the first fence gave Coffin and Bally Cor the gold, and another presented the silver to Plumb. The German pair just managed to avoid making two more mistakes, and letting Meade and Jacob Jones take the bronze, but it was an unhappy ending for them, after leading all the way until then.

"Might have beens" cut no ice in the Olympic record books, but had Be Fair stayed sound and gone clear in the show jumping, he would have taken the silver, but Lucinda found even more comfort in the quick way he came to terms with his injury, so that even before they returned to England he was at least able to walk around his stable.

Although second to the United States—winning at last after being silver medallists in three successive Olympics—Germany were a long way in arrears, 143·6 penalties, and only just held the Australians who took the bronze, led by that leather-bound veteran Bill Roycroft, gold medallist in Rome and still going strong at 61 in

Montreal. His son Wayne was also in the three-day team and another son, Barry, in the show jumping.

The Americans were not winning out of turn in the event, and a consensus of the riders would almost certainly have chosen Alwin Schockemohle for the Individual show jumping. Yet when the German team arrived in Montreal Alwin was not even among the trio chosen to represent them in the Individual; Warwick Rex, on which he won the 1975 European Amateur Championship, had been suffering from a virus disease early in 1976 and showed up very poorly in the pre-Olympic trials the German selectors organised. But in training at Bromont Warwick showed signs of being completely revived, and, much to the disappointment of Sonke Sonksen, who had to be dropped to make way for him, Alwin and Warwick came in.

A huge course was built in the Bromont dirt arena for the Individual, ending with a treble of silver birch which especially caused problems, though the faults were generally shared around at quite a few fences, which is a sign of a fair course, allbeit tough. Merely four horses were eliminated in the first round, but only one of the others could go clear, Schockemohle's Warwick, in a quite majestic way. No fewer than seven others shared second place at that stage, including Debbie Johnsey, at 19 the youngest competitor in the competition as well as the only one of her sex, on Moxy, the Irish-bred horse, which she bought in Scotland, where he had raced, less than 12 months earlier, and with which she had formed a tremendous partnership. The one major flaw in their armoury is a difficulty with water jumps, but for which they would easily have taken the silver medal. Over all the other fences Moxy was almost as impressive as Warwick, giving them inches to spare.

Peter Robeson and Law Court, which he rode for the first time in competition at the final British trial, at Hickstead on July 3, were also among the four-faulters. Robeson, winner of an individual bronze in Tokyo and a team bronze in 1956, usually takes a long time to get horses going as he likes them, but now he gave Law Court a superb ride, making their one mistake at the triple bar, one of the easiest fences on the course, which Law Court just caught behind. Michael Vaillancourt, a French Canadian from just 20 miles north of Montreal, who rides for Pierre Delancourt, brother of the assistant course-builder, and the inexperienced Branch County, was also sharing second place, but Francois Mathy, the Belgian horse dealer, who was to fight his way into the shake-up for the minor medals, was back among those on eight-faults, with Gai Luron, at this stage.

The second round was confined to the top twenty from the first, thus going back only to those with eight faults, and once again there was only one clear round—and again it came from Alwin Schockemohle and Warwick Rex. Their round was not without its drama however, for as they came in the weather, which we had been told beforehand was liable to be oppressively hot and humid but in fact was generally wet and cool, let loose one of its periodic thunder storms, lightning flashed, crashes filled the sky and the rain began to fall in torrents. But apart from a tap at the fourth fence Warwick was clearly unperturbed, and ensured victory in the most convincing way.

Peter Robeson lost his chance of a third Olympic medal quite painfully, when Law Court could not quite manage the third element of the treble and crashed through it. Moxy again went in the water—looking indeed as though he were determined to do so—and then he too clipped the last element of the treble, and so lost his silver at the last fence on the course. Vaillancourt and Branch County hit the first part of the double, number five, and went in the water, and Gai Luron, determinedly ridden by Mathy, was clear until the final element of the treble. So these three, Moxy, Branch County and Gai Luron, with twelve fault totals each, had to jump off for the silver and bronze medals.

The jump-off was held up while the storm went on, and at the end of it the ground was a boggy mess. Branch County hit only the middle of the treble, but that was enough, for Moxy, unsettled by the delay, hit the first fence, failed to cope with the double and let Gai Luron, who had two down, in for the bronze.

If Schockemohle's victory was predictable, few would have expected the French to outstay the Germans for the team title, but that was exactly what happened, after they had been level in the lead at the end of the first round.

Another fall for Robeson when Law Court needed a clear to keep his team in the running, put Britain out of court, but the team event was a close-run thing, and at halfway Germany and France were only a fence ahead of Canada. There were no clears throughout the competition, and in the first round only Warwick and Canada's Jimmy Day, who had also been in their three-day event team, on Sympatico, were round for four faults.

The French, trained by former Olympic medal winner Jean d'Orgeix, were consistent from beginning to end, and although the irrepressible Hubert Parot, with Rivage, and his brother-in-law Marcel Rozier, on Bayard de Maupas, were slightly to the fore, especially with their four-fault rounds second time—both in the water which, in the heavy ground took a lot of jumping—their compatriots Michel Roche on Un Espoir— a most courageous and agile little roan—and Marc Roguet with Belle de Mars gave full support.

Hans Gunter Winkler, who was trying to win his sixth Olympic gold—five is a record unlikely to be beaten for a long time—had Torphy jumping out of his skin to get round from four second time, and when Schockemohle and Warwick came in, last for their team, a clear would have given the Germans victory, four faults a jump off. They hit the eleventh of the fourteen fences, but defeat still looked unlikely as they rattled, but did not lower the thirteenth; but Warwick was wrong coming into the final double, somehow cleared the first part, but could not manage the second.

There was a somewhat surprising battle for the bronze; Canada were unable quite to hang on to their half-way position, dropped half a fault behind the United States, who were then themselves passed by one fault by the Belgians.

If the jumping was something of a surprise, there can have been no more foreseeable result than that of the dressage, especially the team which went to West Germany, with the rest "nowhere".

More of a battle was expected in the Individual, between the reigning European champions, Christine Stuckelberger and Granat, of Switzerland, and the top German, Harry Boldt with Woycek. In the team event there was not a great deal between them, though the Swiss girl was clearly the better, but in the individual the margin was increased.

The Germans again proved their all-round supremacy by taking the next three places, the bronze going to Rainer Klimke and Mehmed, who are no longer the force they were when winning the World championship, in 1974.

7

YACHTING

Laughing Off Failure

Alan Warren and David Hunt, twice members of Britain's yachting team, were regarded as the Morecambe and Wise of the sport long before they staged the jape of the 1976 Games by impersonating Special Branch detectives and wearing Naval uniform "screened" Canadian police for the Queen's visit to the Olympic sailing centre at Kingston, on Lake Ontario. They had earned the tag of a comic duo even before they laughed off an almost certain gold medal at the previous Games at Kiel.

Weed on the rudder of their boat in one race; being badly caught out by a change of wind direction when they were far ahead of their rivals in another, and the escape without penalty from a situation which should have brought disqualification for the Russian who eventually deprived them of victory, was the bitter disappointment of the 1972 Games that Warren and Hunt treated as a huge joke.

The disaster that overtook them at Kingston, where their boat almost literally fell to pieces and was finally ceremonially burned at sea, was similarly treated with total disdain and a great deal of amusement by these two world-class yachtsmen who had underlined with pre-Games performances their impressive medal prospects.

Their non-conformist approach; total disregard for squad training and their unwavering decisions to do things their way in all matters relating to yacht racing, does not always make them favourites with team officials, though there is instant acknowledgement of their value to team morale. Who can fail to be amused when it is discovered that Warren and Hunt have been taking bets that they will appear on the watch tower of the prison adjacent to the Olympic harbour?

They came together by chance: Warren, a funeral director at Worthing, had made his name as a Merlin-Rocket helmsman, while

Hunt, a structural engineer who runs a thriving mast-making firm at Hamble, was a former world-champion crew in the Flying Dutchman class. Hunt was a yachting reserve for the 1968 Games in Acapulco, where officials first had a taste of the independent ways of this 6ft 4in giant.

After Mexico '68, the Royal Yachting Association ran a series of races to find talented crews for Tempest keel-boats—granted Olympic status for the 1972 Games. Warren and Hunt won the "talent-spotting" event and went on to gain Olympic selection in their boat, then named "Seeker 1". They performed so well in Kiel that at one stage it seemed they might be sure of a gold medal before any other crew at the Olympics. Fate decided otherwise and they returned home as silver medallists.

When they bought the boat, allegedly for a "knock-down" price, they called it "Gift 'Orse"—to the chagrin, it is claimed, of some of those R.Y.A. officials who had helped to make the craft available. But although the old " 'Orse" was to become the source of countless jokes, she regularly kicked up her heels when it mattered and won.

By finishing third—behind a Swede and the Russian who had beaten them in Kiel—in the European Championship of the Tempest class in Italy shortly before the Olympics, the British pair had shown that they were still strong Olympic contenders. Furthermore, they might even have won in Italy but for again being caught out, at the front, by a shift of wind.

Though they did not then know it, the chances of the six-year-old "Gift 'Orse" to continue to hold her own with younger "fillies" were ended before the boat had arrived at Kingston. During severe atlantic storms as she was shipped to Canada, the Tempest broke loose in her container and was badly damaged. Her rudder assembly, unique in the world fleet, had to be totally rebuilt and scratches and gouges on her hull filled in and polished over.

Alas, there was no inkling of the extent of the damage until the racing had begun. "Gift 'Orse" could barely canter, let alone gallop as of old. It became clear that the frames of the boat had cracked and so the " 'Orse" was put down in flames. A sad end to an amusing saga of the sea: another bitter disappointment for Warren and Hunt to swallow. But would it be that all Olympians were this charming in defeat.

Indeed, there is much to be learned, it can be argued, from the

Olympic style of Britain's yachting Morcambe and Wise. They take competition as it comes; they spurn the advice of coaches and the advantages of grant aid. They go their own way and accept defeats without rancour—infinitely better prepared for the battles afloat than is often acknowledged. Fortunately, although there are no other Warrens and Hunts, there is seldom the intensity of emotion among yachtsmen that is apparent from their Olympic counterparts in other sports. Nor, were there any of the formalities associated with the main Montreal Games at Kingston—where competitors could mingle with supporters and journalists and attend late-night parties given by many of the forty-one nations for the crews of the one hundred and thirty boats to relieve the tension of competition.

The Yachting Olympics, always a fun and informal Games, were no exception at the sprawling Ontario township of 60,000 in 1976. There was security—tight security—but few complaints, and the tall, refined policewomen were among the most admired "personalities" of the Games. Yachtsmen have other things about which to worry: wind, or lack of it; damage to boats and sails; perhaps, in Kingston, the strictest attention to the measuring of boats at any Games and, despite the smallest Olympic fleets since the Melbourne Games, probably the toughest competition ever.

This was especially so in the Flying Dutchman class in which another Briton, Rodney Pattisson, was attempting to win a hat-trick of gold-medals. Quiet and reserved, detesting publicity and certainly without the humour of his Tempest team-mates, Pattisson arrived at Kingston with a new boat and a new crew in Julian Brooke-Houghton—though they had won the world championship of the class together in 1969 before they parted as "temperamentally incompatable".

Pattisson, who had won in 1968 with Iain Macdonald-Smith—the skipper of the British Soling in Kingston—and with Chris Davies in the 1972 Games, faced perhaps his toughest test. There were at least six crews capable of beating Pattisson in the fleet of Flying Dutchmen—a thoroughbred racing dinghy and the greyhound of the Yachting Olympic before the introduction for the 1976 Games of the Tornado catamaran.

The fancied helmsmen were Yves Pajot of France, the silver medallist in 1972; Jock Bilger, an evergreen New Zealander; the Canadian Hans Fogh, also for long a leading competitor; Erik Vollebregt, a young and promising sailor from Holland; the East

German Uwe Steingross and, above all, the West German Joerg Diesch, tipped by many as the man most likely to bring to an end the Pattisson era of world domination of the Dutchman class.

Pattisson began in the best possible way with a convincing victory and although in the second heat of the seven-race series which all six classes sail—discarding their worst result from the fifth race—he was second, he was ahead of the West German. Indeed, until the fifth race, when uncertain and light winds made a lottery of the day's sailing, Pattisson always had an edge over Diesch. But, in that fifth race, the West German was sixteenth to the Briton's eighteenth and when Pattisson struggled to twelfth in the penultimate heat Diesch was fifth and then well clear of the man who had for so long dominated Flying Dutchmen fleets worldwide.

Taking delivery of a new boat only 10 weeks before the start of the Games, it proved that for once Pattisson was not prepared. In the last race, in which he had to finish several places ahead of the West Germans to win overall, he was always behind them. Pattisson finished eleventh, and the fifth placing of the West Germans gave their country the first of two gold medals which, with a bronze, made it the most successful nation in Kingston.

Britain won their only yachting gold in the Tornado catamaran class—new to the Olympics, like the 470, in 1976. This went to Reg White and John Osborn, brothers-in-law from Brightlingsea who won with a race to spare. When two others with hopes of medals for Britain were coming to grief in the fickle winds of the fifth races, the Tornado race was abandoned, leaving the class a race behind the rest. White and Osborn won their gold medal on the same day as the victors in the other five classes and did not need to sail again on the final day of the regatta. It was arguably the outstanding performance of the Games, for White and Osborn were the only crew to win four races.

But perhaps the Olympic champion who had to work hardest for his gold medal at Kingston was the Danish Soling sailor Paul Jensen, competing in the toughest Olympic class. It included half-a-dozen outstanding international helmsmen, four gold medallists of previous Games, and the best in the world of some former Olympic classes such as the Dragon and 5·5 metre. The Dragon gold medallist of 1972, David Forbes, one of the pre-Games favourites, finished eleventh overall.

Jensen, who finished ahead of the American Jon Kolius, who beat the Soling gold medallist of 1972 in the United States selection series to earn the right to race at Kingston, had placings during the seven-race contest of 2, 2, 13, 6, 13, 1, 5 and beginning the last race was one of six boats still in the running for a gold. The Swede John Albrechtson won the Tempest series without too much trouble in the convincing style expected of him, while the East German Finn winner, Jochen Schumann and the 470 winners from East Germany, Frank Huebner and Harro Bode, both came through with high-scoring results.

The conditions were difficult; the competition was tough and some yachtsmen were just not good enough in the end to win the medals about which they dreamed. But there is one element of sailing which should not intrude too much at an Olympics, and that is unfairness. This occured on the course, in the case of the fluky conditions for the fifth races of the regatta, in some of the courses, and at the starting lines, especially, it is maintained, that for the Finns and 470s. And it was in these classes that British hopes really crashed. Phil Crebbin in the 470 was disqualified for being over the line in the second race, which he led from the start to finish. He protested but did not call as witness the American crew who would have borne out the facts in his favour, believing that the international jury had themselves witnessed his plight. David Howlett in the Finn, and Crebbin and Pattisson were all among the crews most seriously caught out in the bad conditions of the fifth race.

Pattisson insisted that the race committees should have abandoned the heats and had them re-sailed. A mistake on the Tornado course, where a mark was missing as the boats approach led to that race being called off for the day. It does seem unfortunate that the long preparations by sailors can be rendered meaningless by race committees who do not apply the rules to ensure the fairest possible conditions for all.

Of course, no man can make things fair to all sailors when they rely on the wind. But they should surely, be competent enough to use the rules that exist to see there is not the nonsense that there was at Kingston on the Sunday of the regatta. It is to be hoped that the Russians in Estonia in 1980 will do more than the Canadians did to bring greater efficiency to yacht racing. Also, let it be emphasised, the International Yacht Racing Union, the world governing body of the sport, should make sure there are adequate rules and the proper people available to enforce them.

8

ROWING AND CANOEING

East Germany, who won a medal in every rowing event at the Munich Games, remained paramount in Montreal. They took five gold medals in eight finals but here and there one saw dents in their authority. Not surprisingly Russia were their most consistent challengers, taking the coxed fours, but there were also prominent challenges by Norway, winners of the double sculls, and more surprisingly by Finland in the single sculls when Perrti Karppinen swept through in the final few metres for victory. Britain, too, enjoyed their most successful Olympic regatta since 1948, which was staged at Henley, and deservedly so. Their epic performance in the eights—when they were barely overhauled by East Germany for the gold medal in the closing stages—and the second place in the double sculls of Chris Baillieu and Mike Hart was the climax of dedicated training and technical proficiency.

Behind the performance of the British eight was the analysis and inspiration of Bob Janousek, a bronze medallist himself in the Olympics when rowing for a Czech eight. He had come to Britain in 1969 after three years of being National Coach in his native country. He found no established system of building a national squad simply because the club tradition was so strong that it smothered any attempt to bring the best oarsmen together in one crew for long periods of training. Men like Jim Railton, who had been appointed Director of Training to the Amateur Rowing Association in 1964, had tried in subsequent years to persuade everyone in the sport that if Britain wanted world-class crews there had to be co-operation between clubs, to encourage the leading oarsmen to join a National Squad. But schemes like Nautilus foundered. It was only a series of defeats at the Mexico and Munich Games (when no medals were won) that turned the rowing world towards Janousek, who plainly was feeling frustrated in a country where his ability was not being used.

Janousek himself summed up the situation without malice. "Before the 1972 Olympics, we had about eight international class oarsmen in this country but there would be three in this club, two in that and the others out in the country training alone, and all would be in club crews with people weaker than them, and they would perform to the level of the weakest." The situation was particularly ripe for exploitation because the oarsmen, who were potential Olympic medallists were beginning to feel frustrated themselves. A typical example was Hugh Matheson, a member of the coxed fours which was unplaced in 1972. He was annoyed because he felt that Britain's talent and his own had not been fulfilled. "I was so bloody humiliated. Everyone said it was par for the course for Britain, and to others that seemed fine. They'd walked round the Village, seen Jim Ryun, enjoyed themselves. Me? I felt terrible. We were massacred. My reaction was to say 'I will row for two years, and nothing else in my life will interfere!' "

Janousek picked his men and the crew finished second in the 1974 World Championships. But afterwards members of the crew said that they wanted a break from the intensive daily training and constant competition. But they promised to return to prepare for the Olympics—and so they did. They were so eager for success this time that they asked Janousek for an extra session at 7.30 A.M. during the spring of 1976. Only one change in the eight was made—the lightweight Bill Mason at stroke being replaced by Dick Lester. But with Janousek to coax them and with the ARA possessing its own well-equipped Boat House at Hammersmith, the crew were ready to challenge the East Germans.

The victories in the summer regattas demonstrated to the Continental crews and to the British eight themselves that they were unusually gifted. Their chief concern was not over their own form—although they knew that they would probably be the lightest crew in the final—but in the choice of boat. John Vigurs, an ex-international oarsman, had built a revolutionary new lightweight carbon-fibre boat, the Carbon Tiger. The makers claimed that seconds would be saved over the 2000 metre course. But in the final build-up to the Games in St. Catharine's, Ontario, the craft had broken under the severe strain. Janousek admitted that the carbon boat was lighter—and faster—but there was difficulty in getting the fittings right. In pushing the carbon-fibre boat to its maximum, a stress fracture had been caused in a rigger plate. In the event Janousek decided not to risk losing the silver medal by gambling on using a boat that might help them to be even closer to the East Germans, but also might leave them shipwrecked half-way along the course.

In the early rounds Britain rowed with quiet confidence in their Empacher boat, a West German shell. Although they lost to East Germany in the first round they were clear winners of the repechage. They led all the way and although Czechoslovakia clung on to half-way, Britain were able to relax and finished with clear water. The USA never threatened them and faded to finish third. New Zealand, the 1972 champions, were the other repechage winners.

In the final the eight faced a difficulty which they had not met in their earlier races—a headwind—which was expected to affect them particularly, because they were the lightest crew. But they did not seem excessively dismayed by this or by the furious start of the New Zealanders, who exhausted themselves in the early stages. The emotion of being the defending champions affected their judgement.

They contained the pressure which the New Zealanders exerted and saved their own attack for just after 750 metres of the 2000 metres course. They raised their rating to 38, overhauled the New Zealanders within a few smooth strokes and almost dropped the East Germans too. But the East Germans were content to bide their time. They tried once more at 1200 metres but still the British eight kept clear. But in the final 200 metres the East Germans came again, raised their rate to over 40 and with magnificent power pulled back the lead of a canvas and as the British crew lost some of their momentum went on to win by a length. It was one of the most heartening performances of the entire Games by British competitors and was only tarnished by the news that Janousek, the architect of the success, was to resign as national coach. He decided before the Games that he would accept an appointment with Carbocraft Ltd., the company involved in building boats using new materials and techniques.

A pleasant postcript to the performance and the resignation of Janousek was that of Fred Smallbone, a member of the crew. 'It is a sad day for British rowing but it is understandable that a man of his great all-round qualifications needs wider fields to work in. He has taken us to the top but it took him seven days a week and like all of us he needs more time of his own."

If the eight was a triumph for the sensitive blending of different oarsmen, particularly from the Thames Tradesmen and Leander clubs, in a way that had never been done successfully before in Britain at this level, then the silver medal of Baillieu and Hart was a reminder that Cambridge, the cradle of so many excellent oarsmen, can still furnish Britain with superb individuals.

The pair, who met while they were undergraduates at Cambridge, regarded their second place behind the Norwegian Hansen brothers as a victory for amateurism by defeating the disciplined East German and Russian crews. The pair have continued their careers—Baillieu is a barrister and Hart a civil engineer—and yet upset the full-time oarsmen of the communist countries. It was so engaging and refreshing to hear the words of Baillieu afterwards: "I've got a thing about the East Germans. They are so professional and their machinery of sport is so elaborate that it seems so odd that they get involved in a supposedly amateur event like the Olympics. We thought that they might have done too much training for us to compete with them. We hung on to the early pace and are both tremendously satisfied."

The pair had won bronze medals in the previous three years' major events—European and World Championship—and were expected to be in the forefront of the race. In qualifying for the final they did not look impressive although they were using their carbon-fibre boat. But they were just rehearsing their rhythm for the final. In the opening 500 metres the British were the slowest crew except for the French. Hart had expected that the Norwegians and East Germans would be swift at the start but the acceleration of the Russians startled them. The Norwegians took over the lead at 1500 metres but by that time Baillieu and Hart were within a few feet of the Russians, who could not raise their striking to match the Britons' 35. Neither the Russians nor the East Germans could react to the burst which the British produced. And indeed they were the fastest crew across the finishing line. Hart was eminently realistic: "We knew that the Norwegians would have to crack or something extraordinary happen to us to get the gold." But they can go back to their careers content.

In the single sculls West Germany's Peter Kolbe, the reigning world champion, was expected to be an easy winner. Although his defeats in 1975 (to Ireland's Sean Drea) and in 1976 to East Germany's Joachim Dreifke had demonstrated that he was not invincible these were his only defeats in the two seasons up to Montreal. He was European champion in 1973 and world champion in 1975 and was clearly in fine form in Montreal. In the final he began about three lengths clear of the rest and although this position allowed him to see what the others were doing he miscalculated his own resources and he had no answer to Karppinen's surge opposite the grandstand. The Finn first drew level and then after a pause escalated the rate again and went on to a clear victory. Dreifke finished seconds behind Kolbe. Perhaps the West German's cold affected him in the final stages. In any case it was the biggest upset of the regatta. Karppinen's previous best performance was to come fourth in the 1975 World Championships.

In the coxed fours, the Russians, who had taken the title at the Nottingham World Championships the previous year, had three furious bursts of energetic rowing to bring them the gold medal. The West Germans were ahead for the opening 500 metres but then the Russians inserted a 20 stroke spurt which took them almost a length clear. Although the East Germans counter-attacked, the Russians held them and then, as they weakened, attacked themselves. They won by two seconds.

For the first time at an Olympics there were women's events. East Germany and Russia predictably dominated the finals with a crew in each of the six events. Since the introduction of the first Women's European Championships in 1954 only Holland and West Germany have scored rare victories against the communist bloc in which, as in so many sports, East Germany have done increasingly well in recent years.

But their most distinguished competitor, Christine Scheiblich, the world champion in 1974 and 1975, had to struggle against America's Joan Lind, rowing in an outside lane to win the single sculls. She finished barely half a second ahead after a tortuous race. The Bulgarians won both the double sculls and the coxless pairs, the East Germans both fours races and also the eights.

Britain reached none of the finals—they only sent a team of seven—and simply lacked weight for this class of rowing. Their best performance probably came in the fours when in the repechage they pulled their way past both Russia and America but then faded. In the pairs Linda Clark and Beryl Mitchell finished fourth in their repechage.

The Canoeing events also took place at the Notre Dame Island where the Olympic basin was an impeccably equipped arena. The scoreboard provided an accurate representation of the race and there were ample boat houses and seats. From Britain's point of view it was a pity that there were no slalom events (such a spectacular sport at Augsburg in 1972). Britain's women had won the Women's World Wild Water Championships in Yugoslavia in 1975 but their successful competitors then had to enter the still water races in Montreal. Britain, in common with so many other Western European countries, were little match for the communist nations who took all 10 titles for men and women.

Canada, the only host nation in the history of the Games who did not win a title, could not even finish first in the Canadian Canoe 500 metres singles event. Russia's Aleksandr Rogov just skimmed home ahead of Canada's John Wood by 0·35sec. Britain certainly seemed to have a chance of a medal in Doug Parnham in the K1 500 and 1000 metre races.

He had finished third in the World Championships. But he was eighth in the final of the K1 500 metres—an event won by Rumania's Vasile Dira. Poland's Grzegorz Sledziewski, whom Parnham had defeated in Nottingham earlier in 1976, was fifth. In the longer race Parnham was seventh. No other Briton reached the finals.

9

JUDO, WEIGHT-LIFTING AND WRESTLING

Judo

The perennial question in judo is how many gold medals the Japanese win. As inventors of the sport and still with about 8 million people actively practising it they have regarded the efforts of the rest of the world with patronising scorn. Gradually over the last fifteen years the gap between Japan and the European countries, in general, and Russia, in particular, has got closer. In Munich four years ago they took only half the titles—a performance which would have been regarded as a triumph by most countries but as a disaster for the Japanese. Fortunately they appointed as team trainer Isao Okano, probably the most skilful technician of the 1960's and a man dedicated to restore Japan's prestige in the sport. At the 1973 World Championships they took all the gold medals but a dispute between the Kodokan, the Tokyo headquarters of the sport, and Okano resulted in him being gently but firmly ignored when the 1975 World Championships took place. Japan lost two of the six titles they had so painfully taken in 1973.

Again Okano was given the task of training the Japanese team. But the Kodokan with their customary short-sightedness did not give him the powers of selection. Instead they made the All-Japan Weight Category Championships the sole method of selection. The winners went—irrespective of their records internationally. Thus we had the distressing example of the great Shozo Fujii, three times World Champion, being omitted from the middleweight division because he had lost on a decision to Isamu Sonoda. Fujii's record in domestic competitions is not as impeccable as his international performances. His style is particularly suited for fighting foreigners whereas the Japanese are better equipped to deal with Fujii's fluent style.

Fujii's absence robbed the Olympics of much of the skill which has attracted one over the years. And in retrospect this is what the judo tournament lacked—memorable throws and excitement. It was, indeed, a lacklustre competition which was not helped by the fact that the Velodrome was not the suitable place to stage it. The nearest spectators were about 60 yards away from the mat edge, separated from the action by a cycling track and rows of officials. Even the scoreboard was difficult to read. There was little atmosphere, a point cogently made by Britain's Dave Starbrook who said that the event did not seem like an Olympics.

Okano said before the event that he expected Japan to take all six titles, something that was surely designed to maintain the confidence of his squad. The Japanese feel greater pressure at the Games than they do at the World Championships when they have two fighters in each category. In the Olympics each country is only permitted one for the five weight divisions and the Open (unlimited weight) class. In addition the fortunes of the draw can often give the Japanese representative two or three hard bouts before the final. The International Judo Federation are always mindful of the need to present judo as an international sport rather than as one in which Japan have such a strong pool of competitors that they are bound to dominate the event.

What we learnt in Montreal is what we suspected from the results of the 1975 World Championships—namely that with the exception of the lightweight class the two best fighters in every category were the Japanese and Russian selections. It is true that they did not always meet in the final—although on three occasions they did—because of the vagaries of the draw.

Fortunately the International Judo Federation are considering changing the system of competition. A proposal for seeding is to be introduced. It is only a pity that no one thought of this earlier—there are a few fighters wandering round the world who have demonstrably been deprived of Olympic medals. If this is a sound move the decision by the International Judo Federation Congress to raise the number of classes to eight (seven weight categories and an Open division) is less satisfactory. They are scarcely assisting the International Olympic Committee to keep the size of the Games within reasonable bounds. As has become common with the other international sports federations everyone is eager to pay lip-service to having a smaller Games but no one is prepared to do anything about it.

Nor am I enthusiastic about the possibility of having women's judo in Moscow. I am not convinced that there is a genuine demand for it in sufficient countries to warrant it being included in a Games when so many other sports (for example Karate) are still excluded. Judo having rightly got a foot through the Olympic door is now trying to get its whole body in as well.

The tone for the whole competition, which originally attracted 54 nations, was set in the opening bout which pitted Sumio Endo, the All-Japan champion in the Open Class, against Russia's Sergei Novikov in the heavyweight class. It was a perfect instance of the foolishness of not having seeding. The pair had met in the final of the World Championships the previous year. Both must have realised the importance of the bout because the Japanese are at their best when they believe they are invincible. Once that confidence is gone they wilt.

Their demise in Munich stemmed from losing the heavyweight class on the opening day. And this is what occurred in Montreal. Endo, who at 5ft 6½in tall and 18½ stone is awkward to shift off-balance, was fortunate to win the world title. Only a refereeing mistake gave him the bout. This time Novikov's victory followed a sterile contest in which neither fighter achieved a decisive throw but the Russian was judged to have come closer to scoring. Endo was not disgruntled at the decision but he realised the effect that it would have on his country's morale. He sought out the Japanese journalists to apologise, as profusely as only a distressed Tokyo policeman can, for letting down his country.

Novikov went on carefully to get the gold medal. He hurled to the mat Gil Pak Jong, the most extraordinary figure in a Games of bizarre sights because he was officially listed as being 7ft tall and weighing 25 stone. Britain's Keith Remfry was his most stubborn opponent. Remfry, who had recovered from a back injury which he suffered a few months after throwing Novikov in the final of the European Team championships in 1974, had been expected to do well. The British Squad confided that he was even stronger for these Olympics than he was in 1971 and 1973 when he took bronze medals in the World Championships.

Remfry invariably has been better against outstanding competitors rather than competitors whom he had been expected to beat. But he was fighting with shrewd strategy and beat three communist competitors in a row before facing Novikov. He conceded an early knockdown but subsequently fought with more persistence and skill than at any time since the 1971 World Championships. In the repechage Remfry was dumped twice by Endo but he still showed himself to be the third best heavyweight in the world—a rating which was to be confirmed in the Open category.

In the final Novikov swept in to throw West Germany's Gunther Neureuther flat on his back. The West German simply had no right to be there. He was only in the class because he wasn't good enough for the light-heavyweight division and here he was as Olympic silver medallist because the draw had been so uneven.

In the light-heavyweight class a similar situation prevailed. Britain's Dave Starbrook, whom Okano named with Novikov as the two men whom the Japanese feared, was drawn the same pool as Jean-Luc Rougé, France's world light-heavyweight champion. Starbrook had never beaten Rougé in their four meetings and was believed to have lost some of his sharpness in training after losing the world title to Rougé the previous year. But he roused himself with zestful enterprise to lead Rougé on knockdowns and although Starbrook was himself knocked down in turn the Briton probably deserved the decision for being the more aggressive. Rougé had been suffering from a series of injuries but nevertheless it was a satisfactory moment for the Briton.

In his attempt to reach the final for the second successive Olympics Starbrook was overwhelmed by the Russian Ramaz Harschiladze, who was stubborn on the mat in groundwork, avoiding every attempt of the Briton to lure him into a hold-down or armlock. And he twice scooped up Starbrook's leg to tumble him to the mat with scoring throws. Finally he swung under Starbrook with a firm hip throw which made his victory inevitable.

In the bout for the bronze medal in the repechage Starbrook showed his familiar shrewdness. Because was was stiff after the rest between sessions he lured his opponent, the Korean Jeaki Cho, into groundwork to loosen himself up.

Then, when the pair rose, Starbrook swept in for his favourite throw (taiotosh—body drop) and Cho was catapulted over the Briton's outstretched leg for an ippon, the sport's equivalent of a knock-out. Starbrook was so pleased with his win that he said he felt tempted to kiss his opponent on the forehead, but one look at the unprepossessing scars and mat burns restrained him. Instead he patted him on the cheeks. Only the Koreans seemed distressed at the result as former opponents, whom Starbrook had met in his last

11 years of international fighting, came to congratulate him on his last medal. At 30 Starbrook had decided to retire from the sport after the Games.

His medal brought tears to his own eyes and to those of Ray Ross, the team manager, who trained Starbrook at the Renshuden Club in London before being appointed to his position with the National Squad. Their partnership had been perfect and it was the most suitable and emotional of ends to their careers. Even Charles Palmer, the President of the International Judo Federation and Chairman of the British Judo Association, admitted that he felt his own eyes were tingling.

In the final Kazuhiro Ninomiya took Japan's first judo gold medal of the Games. He was perhaps a shade lucky to be in the Japanese team at all. He was thrown superbly in the opening seconds of the semi-final of the All-Japan Championships Open category by the magnificent Ueguchi, one of Okano's protégés. But he beat Ueguchi in the All Japan Weight Category Finals and consequently was picked for the squad.

The final was a stultifying contest in which both fighters were warned for passivity. Ninomiya was content to keep ahead on points after bowling over his opponent early in the bout. The Russian tried to dive at Ninomiya's legs occasionally but never looked like upsetting the Japanese who won the World Open class in 1973 and lost two stone to make the light-heavyweight limit of 14 stone 9lb.

In the middleweight class, Brian Jacks, Starbrook's colleague in so many of Britain's judo successes of recent years, had a vexing finale to his international career. He was expected to be prominent because he had received a draw that seemed to give him an excellent chance of a medal. He began brightly enough, winning his first two bouts carefully but then met Slavko Obadov, a Yugoslavian who had dislocated Brian's back when the pair had last met at the 1975 European Championships in Lyons. Jacks seemed to be ahead when he was given a knockdown but this was taken away by the referee. And in the turmoil of the bout the referee warned Obadov for passivity. A fighter is permitted one reprimand without receiving a penalty point, but the recorder mistakenly signalled the infringement on the board. The referee did not notice this action and the bout continued with Jacks believing he was ahead. At the end he was confidently looking forward to his contest with Valery Dvoinikov for a place in the final.

But after consultation with the judges the referee ordered the penalty point to be cancelled and awarded the contest to Obadov. The British team's protest was only token and the competition continued with Jacks understandably irked at the way he had lost. Like most judo fighters Jacks paces a day's event by keeping ahead of the points which are registered on the scoreboard.

Jacks was clearly doing this and in addition most observers agreed that Obadov should have received the penalty point for passivity. But despite this defeat nothing can tarnish Jacks' record. He has won more European Championship medals than anyone in the history of the sport except the Dutchman Anton Geesink, the 1964 Olympic champion. In addition he took the World Championship bronze medal in 1967 and the Olympic bronze in 1972. He has pioneered Britain's recent eminence in judo.

Although he deserved to defeat Obadov one could not see him upsetting Dvoinikov, who was runner-up in the welterweight division at the 1975 World Championships and subsequently moved up to middleweight. Dvoinikov threw Obadov all over the mat and Jacks' style would have been better suited to the Japanese Sonoda, whom Jacks would have disturbed with his shoulder throw. Dvoinikov would have been too short and dexterous for the Briton to have used his favourite technique.

Sonoda had little trouble in finishing first in the other pool. His progress was assisted by the defeat of France's Jean-Paul Coche, who as European champion in 1972, 1974 and 1976 and the Munich bronze medallist, was expected to dent the hopes of the Japanese as he has done in the past. The pair never met. Coche lost on a decision to West Germany's Fred Marhenke, the winner of the pre-Olympic tournament and a stubborn if unexciting fighter. Sonoda twice threw Marhenke with superb inner thigh throws, tipping his opponent on to his back. And in the final he kept away from Dvoinikov's quick techniques—as a Japanese he must have been used to practising with someone of the Russian's dexterity—to take a clear-cut decision with his deft leg throws and fewer penalty points.

Youngchul Park and Marhenke took the bronze medals in a category that plainly needed the sparkle of a Fujii to bring it alive. The Japanese must at this stage of the tournament have been reasonably satisfied with their performances. Traditionally, because they are a nation generally of small men, they are almost always supreme in the lighter divisions. With two gold medals and a bronze at the halfway stage only the most fastidious of their supporters could have been dismayed. But their nemesis was to come in the lighter divisions. Always the Japanese have been deferential at the performances of the rest of the world. Sometimes an Anton Geesink or Willem Ruske, both Olympic Open champions, would come along but the Japanese might dismiss their victories as a triumph for strength and size over skill. Look, they would say, at the technical ability of our lighter judo men. That is real judo—not the mauling stuff with which the Westerners win their bouts. That fallacy was exposed in Montreal.

In the welterweights, Vladimir Nevzorov not only took the title with consummate ease but he showed himself to be the most proficient technician of the whole competition. The Russian had given everyone a glimpse of his ability in the 1975 European and World Championships when he took the gold medals. And he was to stress his quality in the Olympic tournament. He beat the Japanese Koji Kuramoto, who had been third in the World Championships, with a neatly-timed hand throw, bowling over his opponent for waza-ari. Earlier he had swept to three ippon victories in a tournament where ippons were rare. The inner thigh throw of Kuramoto looked cumbersome and ineffective by comparison with the smooth efficiency of Nevzorov.

Kuramoto was not impressive in the early bouts. He had only one ippon victory—the sport's equivalent to a knock-out and struggled to defeat Antonio Roquete Andrade. The days of the superb Japanese Hiroshi Minatoya, who won the 1967 world title with an ippon in every contest, were nostalgically recalled by onlookers. Marian Talay, one of the hyper-fit Polish squad and a European bronze medallist, affixed an unbreakable hold-down on Changsun Lee (Korea) to take one bronze medal. The other contest for the bronze medal pitted France's Patrick Vial against Britain's Vass Morrison, who only lost a close decision to Kuramoto.

Morrison had lost his previous four bouts to the Frenchman and never looked like improving on this record. He was frequently knocked down by the awkward Frenchman and Vass, as is his wont, hugged the edge of the mat, looking irritated when he threw Vial off the mat or separated by the referee as he threatened danger. In the final minute of the contest he did not attack as he ought to have done in a bout that was deciding the bronze medal. Still France got themselves their only medal of the judo tournament—scant reward for a country with 200,000 registered members and enormous financial resources. This support enabled them to bring over nine members of the French National Squad for the team to practice with in Montreal. This group included Angelo Parisi, who had won a bronze medal for Britain at the 1972 Olympics and was now a French citizen. The British Judo Association simply did not have the money for such an enterprising idea.

If the welterweight division was a disappointment—but at least a predictable one—for the Japanese, the lightweight class turned out to be a disaster and one that certainly was not expected. Yoshiharu Minami was not only the favourite he was the man whom the Japanese regarded as a certainty of the title. This was based on rational grounds. In both the 1973 and 1975 World Championships Minami had never looked flurried in taking the titles, throwing with astonishing power for a man so small. He had convincingly taken the All-Japan Weight Category title, and at 24 he was still improving.

But he never looked as formidable as he had done in the past and in his opening bout against Yves Delvingt (France), a gifted but not exceptional competitor, he lacked penetration. Delvingt seemed to be ahead although no score had been recorded, but he made certain of reaching the next round by tumbling his opponent to the mat just before the end of their six minute contest. Okano was so disgusted at the result that he walked off the mat at the end without speaking to the shaken Japanese.

Delvingt was, in turn, beaten by Italy's Felice Mariani, a bronze medallist at the 1975 World Championships, and a narrow winner over Britain's Constantine Alexander, known as "clunk-click" because of his remorseless gripping power. Mariani himself lost to Korea's Eunkyung Chang, the eventual finalist. It was tough getting through that pool.

The final brought Chang against the effervescent Hector Rodriguez, a bronze medallist at the 1973 World Championships, who began judo, he says, because he wanted to protect himself from his older brothers. It was a fascinating contest with the taller Cuban trying smooth ankle sweeps and the Korean replying stoutly with hand throws.

Both fighters scored knock-downs and both received penalty points and things became so complicated that the audience, the fighters and even the referee did not know at the end who was in the lead. With penalty points being marginally more important than the equivalent positive point everyone was confused—an indictment on the sport. George Kerr, formerly a magnificent fighter of the 1960's and now a distinguished referee, awarded the contest to Chang. Then as the judges came across to correct him he realised his mistake and gave the gold medal to the Cuban. As in so many other sports in the Games, Cuba were upsetting the calculations of the experts.

The Open category followed the lightweights on the next day and this gave the heavyweights, who inevitably dominate the division which is open to men of all sizes, only five days rest. In Munich they had over a week. Both Russia and Japan decided to field fresh heavyweights—Shoto Chochoschvilli and Haruki Uemura. They met in the same pool in the bout that really settled who would get the gold medal. In the 1975 World Championships Chochoschvilli had countered the Japanese with a magnificent effort receiving a waza-ari but in the action of falling to the ground, his arms clasped round his opponent, he hit his head on the mat, knocking himself semi-conscious. Uemura gratefully clamped on a hold-down for 30 seconds, and went on to win the title.

The Olympic contest was less dramatic. Chochoschvilli, who beat Starbrook for the light-heavyweight gold medal in 1972, has lost much of his aggression. He has relied increasingly on counter-throws and Uemura was the more positive in an unexciting bout.

In the other pool Britain's Keith Remfry finally came into his own. He had a consistent if unspectacular day's fighting. His tactical acumen brought him a safe victory over Gunther Neureuther, the heavyweight silver medallist earlier in the week. But he was more offensive against Jeaki Cho, the Korean who had shaved his head as a penance after being beaten by Starbrook. Remfry scored three knock-downs and never looked anxious. Against the more bulky Argentinian, Jorge Portelli, Remfry was the more aggressive of the pair to make certain of at least the silver medal.

In the final against Uemura, Remfry often fought with shrewd persistence and at moments looked the more dominating competitor. But after 6¾ minutes he was tumbled to the mat by the Japanese who cunningly trapped Remfry's left arm, and then using the climb as a purchase, secured a solid hold-down for the necessary 30 seconds.

But over the week's fighting the standard of the rest of the world had crept closer to Japan although Russia were clearly the most prominent rivals. Japan's total of medals—three gold, a silver and a bronze kept them ahead—but by precious little. By the time of the Moscow Games it would not be surprising if Russia are the leading nation at the sport.

It is not being excessively chauvinistic to point out that Britain once again were a significant factor in the distribution of the medals. The retiring team manager Ray Ross had predicted that if Britain didn't get many medals at least his competitors would only lose to medallists—and he was proved absolutely correct. The two medals and two fifth places showed that the financial support from such organisations as the British Olympic Association, the Sports Aid Foundation and Joseph Sanders, the Investment Advisors, has not been ill-spent.

But compared to many sports in Britain judo is still given scanty support. As Ray Ross remarked: "We give value for no money." It is a tribute to the persistence of the fighters themselves and to Ross and Dr. Ken Kingsbury, whose worth to the squad has been quite incalculable, that they have been so successful over the last six years. Perhaps the best epitaph that can be given to the finest judo team Britain has ever had was that given by Tony MacConnell, for many years a member of the Squad and now the Swedish National Team trainer. He said: "This team go out as the second best in Europe. There's no doubt about that. But the rest of the world have also looked at Britain in another way. When they're looking for guts and sportsmanship they know it lies in the British camp. That's what they're respected for." We shall always remember them.

Weight-lifting

For the second successive Games the weight-lifting events lacked the tension and colour of which they are capable. Perhaps it was because there were few world records, a significant contrast to May's European Championships which had produced a cavalcade of best performances. But principally it was because too many of the classes had definite pre-event favourites who did not fail. There were few of the enthralling battles of the 1960's—the mid-heavyweight clash at the Mexico Games being an excellent example—in which a number of men were grouped together with only a few pounds between them. Except for the purist weight-lifting enthusiasts, who appreciate the smaller men with better strength/weight ratios than the bigger competitors, the ordinary public watch the sport to see the heavy men lift heavy weights, intense competition with each other.

In the three heaviest divisions all the favourites won conclusively —mid-heavyweight David Rigert by 44lb, heavyweight Valentin Khristov by 33lb and super-heavyweight Vasily Alexeev by the gigantic amount of 77lb. It was Alexeev, who was expected to be most closely challenged in his bid to retain the Olympic title. Unbeaten since 1970, the 25 stone Russian declined to compete in the "World's Strongest Man" competition in London last October, announcing at the last moment that he had sustained a leg injury. Oscar State, the secretary of the International Weight-lifting Federation, declared that he believed that the Russian had withdrawn because he knew he might lose to Bulgaria's Khristo Plachkov. Both Plachkov and East Germany's Gerd Bonk maintained their assault on Alexeev in the build-up to the Montreal Games.

Plachkov set a world record snatch of 440$\frac{3}{4}$lb and at May's European Championship Bonk took the title (in the absence of Alexeev) completing a world record clean and jerk of 556$\frac{1}{2}$lb. Yet the Russian showed that he was still improving, taking the Russian Championships with a world record 959lb total. A fortnight later Plachkov added a further 16lb in finishing first at the Bulgarian Championships. All seemed set for a titanic climax to the nine days' weightlifting events.

One had suspected that Alexeev, a worthy successor to the great champions of the past—John Davis, Paul Anderson, Vlasov and Leonid Zhabotinsky—would have something in reserve. And indeed he did although it was not needed as the opposition melted away. Plachkov withdrew announcing that he had lost 24lb in bodyweight and could not be expected to challenge the Russian. Gerd Bonk was off-form, never looking like upsetting Alexeev.

Alexeev was 33lb ahead on the snatch and then raised a world record 562lb in the clean and jerk. The concern of the Russian officials before the contest had been apparent—but unnecessary. As Alexeev says: "Only I understand what is good for me. I never know when I will train. Sometimes deep in the night, sometimes in the morning. Sometimes several times a day. Sometimes I don't train at all. But I never repeat myself." Alexeev is not coached usually. After six years of weight-lifting supremacy he can train without constant supervision. He is truly the greatest lifter of our generation.

Rigert's victory was less comfortable but equally satisfying. In Munich four years previously he had three times failed to fix a 352$\frac{1}{2}$lb snatch overhead compared to his world record at the time of 368lb. As the World and European champion he was expected to be a certain gold medallist. But he went quite berserk after his failure, literally tearing his hair out in great tufts and beating his head against the wall. It took all the might of the Russian coaches and trainers to subdue him and give him a sedative. But when he woke up the next day in the Olympic Village he went berserk again. Finally with the other Russians who had missed their lifts earlier in the competition he was sent home.

Over the last four years he has trained conscientiously and lifted sensibly. Still his memories of Munich must have affected his concentration in his struggle with the USA's James Lee, the Pan American champion. Despite this he settled in with a 374$\frac{3}{4}$lb snatch to give him an 11lb lead over Lee and then went clear on the clean and jerk with an effort of 468$\frac{1}{4}$lb. The result was a delightful compensation for 1972.

The lighter divisions were more even as Russia struggled to regain their Olympic supremacy in the sport, something which they had conceded to Bulgaria in 1972. It was the Bulgarians who had discovered the revolutionary principle in the sport: that it is perfectly possible to train two or three times a day. Until 1972 it was widely believed that the body needed 48 hours recuperation between heavy lifting sessions. But the Bulgarians discovered the vital rule of so many sports—that the body can adapt itself to any strain placed on it provided the strain is increased gradually and that consequently the body becomes stronger—also applied to weight-lifting. The other communist countries and, subsequently, the rest of the world changed their training methods.

In the light heavyweight division, Valery Shary, the 1975 world and European champion, took 446$\frac{1}{4}$lb on his last clean and jerk to take the title from Bulgaria's Blagoi Blagoev. Bulgaria's Trendafil Stoichev tried the same poundage, failed and had to be content with the bronze medal. But in the middleweight class, Bulgaria's Yordan Mitkov just captured the gold medal. He missed his second clean and jerk with 418$\frac{3}{4}$lb but succeeded with his third on the same poundage to win by 11lb. Russia's Vartan Militosyan was second.

Poland's Zbigniew Kaczmarek showed that he is a worthy successor to the great Waldemar Baszonowski by taking the lightweights from the Russian Poitr Korol. Both missed their last clean and jerks with $385\frac{3}{4}$lb. In the featherweights Bulgaria's Todor Todorov missed all his snatches and this gave Russia's Nikolai Kolenskov an easier victory than he might have expected; he succeeded on a fourth clean and jerk attempt with a world record 355lb.

Bulgaria's Norair Nurikyan and Russia's Alexander Voronin respectively won the bantam and flyweight categories. The greatest interest in the flyweights was whether Mohammed Nassiri, the 1968 Olympic bantamweight champion, could take the gold medal again after his near-miss at Munich. Another nostalgic moment came with the fifth place of the astonishing Hungarian Imre Foldi in the bantamweights—17 years after he was third in the World Championships in Warsaw. He is truly a link with the past—an era when heavyweights were lifting poundages which middleweights exceed nowadays and Louis Martin won his first world title. Two weight-lifters were disqualified from future Games after the tests for anabolic steroids had proved positive.

The Communist countries, who had taken 26 out of the 27 medals available at the 1975 World Championships, were expected to be dominant in Montreal—and indeed they were, winning all nine titles. Britain in contrast were not expected to shine and again the predictions were accurate. Despite the efforts of such men as Wally Holland and John Lear, the two officials of the team, British weight-lifting lags behind the rest of the world—none of the competitors looked like finishing in the first six. Another disappointment for the British party was the failure of Oscar State to be re-elected as secretary of the International Weight-lifting Federation, a position he has held with energy and excellent organising ability for 16 years. Although many of his opponents disliked his tendency to try to control every facet of the sport—his secretaryship earned him the nickname of "state control"—he nevertheless transformed the sport. He increased the membership of the International Federation from 62 countries in 1960 to 105 in 1976 and the turnover from £360 to £48,000 in the same period. Suitably enough for a sport dominated by the Communists, he has been succeeded by one—Tomas Ajan (Hungary).

Wrestling

The Communist countries' domination of wrestling did not weaken between 1972, when they took 15 of the 20 classes in the two styles of Freestyle and Greco-Roman, and the Montreal Games. Russia, in particular, seemed to shrug off the loss of the great Alexander Medved, winner of three gold medals at successive Olympics. They were prominent in most of the divisions and their sternest opponents were invariably other communist competitors. Bert Jacob, the Chairman of the British Amateur Wrestling Association, was explicit as to the reasons why the Iron Curtain nations are so successful. "While the West are running sports as a hobby, we can't compete with the Eastern European nations."

Even the superb Adolf Seger, West Germany's world and European middleweight champion, was unable to stem the flow of communist victories in Montreal. He was only able to add a bronze medal to the one he took in Munich. A masterly freestyle technician his variety of moves included deft dives to the leg and sudden explosive throws. His work on opponents' legs, using them as levers to contrive the situation that he is seeking, was admirable. But he lost both to the USA's John Peterson, the eventual gold medallist, and Russia's Victor Novojilov. Although he was not pinned Seger was decisively defeated.

John's brother Ben was the closest challenger to Russia's Levan "Teddy" Tediashvili in the light-heavyweight category. Tediashvili has probably the finest record of any competitor at the moment. Unbeaten since 1971 he beat John in the middleweight class at the Munich Olympics and then completed the double over the family by scoring an 11–5 victory in the final bout of the Montreal light-heavyweight class. Now 28, he seems to be untouchable in international wrestling.

One of Tediashvili's earlier victories was against Britain's Maurice Allan, who in 1975 became Britain's first world wrestling champion since 1908. But this was in sambo—the Russian form of jacket wrestling—and Maurice, who is less adept at freestyle, was quickly pinned by the Russian. Tediashvili swept Maurice's legs from underneath him with an outside clip and completed the fall. The real truth was that Allan, who is also a judo international should not have been wrestling in this class at all. His normal bodyweight was far better suited to competing in the middleweight division. He retired after the Games.

In the heavyweight class the defending champion Ivan Yarygin only conceded two penalty points and had a 19–13 victory over another American Russ Hellickson, twice Pan American champion, for the gold medal. Hellickson had moved up a class to avoid Tediashvilli but came up against almost as distinguished wrestler in Yarygin. In the 100 kilo plus class (over 15 stone 10lb) the Russian produced an able successor to Medved—Soslan Andiev. Built on similar lines to Medved, he moved with neat mobility, often eluding his more ponderous opponents. In his last contest he magnificently pinned East Germany's roly-poly Roland Gehrke.

Japan took two gold medals in the lighter divisions—Yuji Takada in the light flyweights and Jichiro Date in the welterweights.

The one Russian disappointment of the Games came in the welterweights when Ruslan Ashuraliev (USSR) came fourth. Four years earlier in the lightweight class he had only got the bronze medal behind the amazingly dedicated American Dan Gable. Despite taking two world titles in the intervening years he was again outmanoeuvred by an American in the Games. In Montreal Stanley Dziedzic won a thrilling 9–6 bout which had the American spectators in ecstasy. Dziedzic took the bronze.

The Communist countries were even more prominent in the Greco-Roman with Russia taking seven titles. The biggest upset was the defeat of super-heavyweight Alexander Tomov, winner of four world titles. He lost to Russia's Alexander Kolchinski in the last bout but had suffered a shock pin at the hands of William "Pete" Lee which must have shaken his confidence. Valery Rezantsev retained his light-heavyweight crown but Nelson Davidian lost the 62 kilo class despite being world champion of 1974 and 1975. Although he defeated the eventual winner Kazimir Lipien (Poland) he conceded more penalty points. He had lost clearly to Hungary's Lazlo Reczi earlier in the competition.

A rare breakthrough by the West came from Finland's Pertti Ukkola in the bantamweights. The Scandinavian countries have always had a tradition in Greco-Roman but in recent years this has been smothered by the strength of the communist nations, who altogether took nine of the ten titles.

Britain made little impression on the tournament. Nor does one expect them to—until the sport is administered on far more sensible lines. Although there are not the resources for massive financial assistance far more could be done with the people available. Elementary mistakes were made with the British team—Allan's selection at light-heavyweight was inexcusable as was the move to bring out the team so long before they competed. The popularity of wrestling scarcely warrants as much aid being spent on it as on most other Olympic sports but until the British Amateur Wrestling Association do something to aid themselves they cannot complain if the Sports Council do not look on them with a kindly eye. The use of people like Dicky Barraclough, a former British champion and PE lecturer, in a more major role is surely long overdue.

Two gold medallists Khristov and Kaczmavek and the light-heavyweight silver medallist Blagoi Blagoev (Bulgaria) were among several weight-lifters whose samples were re-tested for positive drug traces, more than three weeks after the Games had ended.

10

BASKETBALL, HANDBALL AND VOLLEYBALL

In the early hours of the morning of September 10th 1972 basketball history was created. FIBA (the International Amateur Basketball Federation) confirmed that the result from the previous evening's final game between USSR and the United States of America would stand. The Soviet Union had dented the pride of America, the country that produced the game back in 1891, and hitherto had won every previous Olympic title without even losing a single game. Their run of sixty consecutive victories which started in Berlin in 1936 came to a halt as Alexander Belov the 6ft 6in forward from Leningrad scored the winning basket in the dying seconds, as the Russians won 51–50.

However, controversy surrounded the result, and not merely because the Americans had suffered a defeat. The final three seconds of this match had been replayed three times during a whole series of bizarre events which was contested most bitterly by the losers.

For four years America waited for revenge: defeats sustained by the Russian national team against American College teams last autumn meant very little. July 27th 1976 in Montreal was the date earmarked for the clash of these two nations.

The early matches went according to the form book: on the first day (18th) the Americans met Italy, the winners of the European Qualification Tournament, and Dean Smith the coach from the University of North Carolina, with seven of his twelve players from the Atlantic Coast Conference, but took this game comfortably by 106–86. Delle Fiori's 100% outside shooting, and the game's top scorer with 21 points had kept Italy in contention, but to no avail. Meanwhile the Russians cantered home against the Mexicans, 120–77.

On the second day the Americans had a day off whilst the Russians disposed of Austraila, but not without some difficulty, especially in trying to contain Eddie Palubinskas, known curiously enough as "The Pride of Louisiana", but born in Australia, who was to become the Game's top scorer with 219 points, an average of 31·3 per match. Somewhat surprisingly Canada defeated Cuba, the bronze medallists from Munich, in front of the Queen witnessing her first basketball match. This result later ensured a place in the semi final for the hosts.

July 20th gave the Soviets a break with the USA taking on Puerto Rico. The Caribbean island had hosted the World Championships in 1974 finishing seventh and although ranking sixth in Munich qualified as the representative from the Amercan continent when they finished second to USA in the 1975 Pan American Games. Inspired by a truly outstanding display from junior guard Alf "Butch" Lee of Marquette University, who totalled 35 points in this game, and ably assisted by Neftali Rivera with 26, Puerto Rico surprised everyone including USA. At half time the scores were tied 51–51, and late into the second half Puerto Rico actually led by 7 points. Their coach, Tom Nissalke, coach to Houston Rockets in the USA, tried to cool things down as the Americans inevitably pressed, who by their own high standards displayed against Italy on the opening day had seemed very flat. Into the last minute Puerto Rico still led, but at the final buzzer in a highly charged atmosphere, it was USA who edged home 95–94.

The next day (21st) produced a high scoring game between Mexico and Australia. Inevitably that man Palubinskas was in the act again, this time with 48 points, with his team also taking the honours 120–117, but only after extra time.

However, that was only a foretaste of what was to come. The last two games of the day featured the four undefeated teams in action against each other. Needless to say the ticket scalpers made capital outside and a packed audience saw Yugoslavia, the reigning European Champions pitched into battle against the USA. A battle it turned out to be: no less than 40 fouls were called in the first half, and once again the Americans found themselves in trouble. Yugoslavia led at half time 55–51 with Drazen Dalipagic scoring well, and Zoran Slavnic proving an inspiration with his magical passes. At half time the Americans changed their defence which proved effective, and took control of the game. Adrian Dantley of Notre Dame, and Scott May from Indiana, the reigning NCAA Champions showed their true class, and although Yugoslavia closed to within one point halfway through the second half, the USA proved too strong, 112–93.

This was immediately followed by Canada in action against USSR. Questions, of just how good the Russians were, were soon answered as they started their match with their strongest line up for the first time. The Olympic Champions had produced a 19-year-old player Vladimir Tkachenko at 7ft 2in and 25 stones affectionately known as "Lurch" by the North Americans. Canada had no answer to him and the match went very easily to the Soviet Union 108–85.

July 23rd, the penultimate day of the pool games saw USSR defeat Japan 129–63, and as Egypt had already withdrawn from the competition in support of the African action, USA automatically won 2–0. However, the second semi finalists from Group B had to be found, and saw Italy and Yugoslavia in confrontation once again. Earlier in the year at Meadowbank in May, Italy had qualified for Montreal by defeating Yugoslavia 84–79, which meant that the European Champions from 1973 and 1975 and runners up in the World Championships in 1974 had to travel to Hamilton, Ontario, in late June to qualify in one of the three remaining berths. As at Meadowbank, Italy started off like a house on fire. Luciano Vendemini, Italy's tallest man, proved difficult to stop, and Marzorati contained Slavnic, but it was really Renzo Bariviera who was the inspiration. He effectively prevented Dalipagic from scoring, whilst he himself was in superb form at the other end of the court. By half time the game seemed over, as Italy led 57–41. The second half was a different story: Yugoslavia kept their opponents to 30 points, who were not helped by an injury to Giulio Iellini, the guard-forward from the European Cup holders Mobil Girgi of Varese. Into the last twenty seconds Yugoslavia trailed by just one point as they took control of the ball. Calmly and confidently they took their time until five seconds remained when Zoran Slavnic received the ball from 20 feet. He shot . . . scored and Yugoslavia had made it to the semi-finals.

The pairings in the semi finals guaranteed a final the next day between a North American country and an Eastern European representative. Yugoslavia the underdogs in most people's minds, took on the Soviet Union. Coach Mirko Novosel from Lokomotiva Zagreb clearly had his team fired up for the occasion. Slavnic, Dragon Kincanovic who was to emerge as the game's top scorer with 27 points, and Kresimir Cosic, at 6ft 11in who had previously studied at Brigham Young University in Utah, were all oustanding as Yugoslavia raced away to an early 19–4 lead. The Russians were committing many turnovers, most untypically, and coach Kondrashin was certainly a very unhappy man. Gradually though, the Soviets came back, with both Sergei Belov and Alexander Belov (no relation) playing well, and as the half time buzzer sounded the scores were tied 42–42. Tkachenko was having a difficult time, and in fact took only one shot in the whole game, and that with only two minutes to play. Yugoslavia took command of the game in the last quarter, finally edging out USSR 89–84, ending the Soviet's hopes of retaining the title and providing the biggest upset of the tournament.

The second semi final was a disappointment, with Canada missing far too many high percentage area shots. Only three Canadian players performed with distinction, Billy Robinson, Lars Hansen and Phil Tollestrup (27 points), as they had in previous games, and coach Jack Donohue, another American, resigned himself to battling for the bronze medal the next day. USA led 48–35 at the half time, and went on to cement their berth in the final 95–77.

The final was won and lost in the opening minutes. Dean Smith had clearly prepared his players well for the occasion, but had not really expected the Russians to be playing for third place. Yugoslavia looked a little apprehensive, and following a series of unsuccessful shots, unfortunate passes and American interceptions, found themselves trailing 8–0. Slavnic was in difficulty, with successive turnovers, and subsequently sustained a leg injury which was so bad that it prevented him receiving his medal on the rostrum. By contrast his opponent, Phil Ford, from the same university as the coach, that of North Carolina, was superb. Although this team's smallest player 1·86 (6ft 1in) and only 19 years of age, amazingly quick reflexes brought him several timely interceptions or "steals", and such was his play throughout the ten days of competition that he would get my vote as the Player of the Tournament.

Yugoslavia never recovered from their poor start, or rather, were never allowed to get back into the game. By half-time the Americans led 50–38 and seemed to have learnt from their experiences in the pool match against the European Champions, Kicarovic, Delipagic and Cosic tried desperately to keep their team in the game, but Kupchak the American's tallest player at 6ft 10in was playing well. Adrian Dantley, after a brief departure from the game following a nasty cut just above the eye, shot superbly well hitting successfully with 13 of his 19 attempts, and all of his free throws, and it was he who finished as the game's top scorer with 30 points. The final seconds were truly memorable as Phil Ford and then Quin Buckner completed their victory celebrations with the game in progress to a standing ovation from the Montreal Forum crowd. This time no doubt surrounded the victory, as USA took the title 95–74, and once again the Americans had been restored to their number one position in the world of basketball, a place which, of course, many, especially Americans, believed they have never lost, with a team although not the tallest, of exceptional speed, high quality players, excellently organised by coach Dean Smith. America's pride has been restored.

By contrast the result of the women's competition was never in any doubt. Given Olympic recognition for the first time, the Soviet Union confirmed their supremacy. Undefeated at international level since 1958 when they lost to Bulgaria, USSR continued their success in Montreal. Most onlookers would probably credit this to the mere presence of a woman, Iuliyaka Semenova from Riga, 7ft tall, some 6 inches taller than our own Geoffrey Capes, and weighing only a stone less. However, although the highest scorer for the Russian team, and equal second in the overall classification with 97 points (an average of 19·4 points per game), with 71% success from her shots, she only played for 97 of a possible 200 minutes in the tournament. Even without her the Russians would still have won with the oustanding skills of the athletic Tamara Daunene at 6ft 3in, the ball handling ability of Nadezhda Zakharova, their captain, the additional rebounding strength of Nelli Feryabnikova, and the outside shooting of both Nadezhda Shuvaeva and Tatjana Ovetchkina.

No team got close to the Russians who won all five games convincingly. However, the contest that went on for the other medal placings was remarkably close. The competition was organised on a league basis and surprisingly the results from last year's World Championship in Colombia were no guide to form. Both Japan and Czechoslovakia the respective medallists at Cali disappointed with essentially the same teams, and it was left to the United States of America (surprisingly) to take the silver medal. The Bulgarians far surpassed their expectations by taking the bronze medal, inspired by Penka Stoyanova who also scored 97pts in the tournament.

The men's and women's handball titles went, as expected to the Soviet Union in an East European dominated competition. And in the volleyball the Japanese women retained their domination by a wide margin with the men's gold medal going to Poland. In each case the Soviet Union were runners-up.

11

SOCCER AND HOCKEY

THE Olympic soccer tournament has become a farce. No one seems to want it, except a few FIFA officials and the communist countries who use it as practice for the World Cup. Football has its own world championship and what the Olympics has increasingly turned into is a pale imitation of the World Cup—but without the concentration of interest and attention which the major international team game deserves. In 1972, four Communist countries formed the semi-finalists with teams including players who were to perform in the World Cup two years later. In Montreal three of the four semi-finalists came from Eastern Europe—the remaining team, not unexpectedly for a country so imbued with football, was Brazil. The one argument for permitting soccer to be part of the Games is that it does allow a wider scattering of nations than can be accommodated at a World Cup when only the best countries are able to take part because of the difficult qualifying tournaments. As it is, one is confronted with some excellent players—Poland's goalkeeper Jan Tomaszewski as one example—taking part in a sub-standard tournament. It really is time that the International Olympic Committee did something about it.

Britain, with rare commonsense, have declared all footballers "players", thus removing the amateur status and effectively banning Britain from the Olympic competition. It is a pity that other countries are not honest enough to follow suit.

Nine of the 16 nations which qualified for Montreal came from outside the established soccer Continents of Europe and South America. Both Brazil and Uruguay qualified but niether could have been expected to challenge the Eastern Europeans because their most talented players turn professional at an early age. Two Western European nations who did sneak through were Spain (over Bulgaria) and France who pipped Rumania on goal average.

It was the Brazilians, joint winners with Mexico of last year's Pan-American soccer tournament, who were the sole representatives of the Western World in the semi-finals. In their quarter-final tie they were held 0–0 by Israel at half-time but attacked with flair and foresight after the interval. Jarbas scored twice, Junior once and Erivelto once to give them a safe 4–1 victory. Since they had already drawn with East Germany in a preliminary game they were clearly capable of reaching the final where in fact they would have met East Germany again. But in a taut semi-final they faced Poland, who had gently warmed up for the tie by defeating North Korea 4–0 in the quarter-final. Poland's worst performance was only to draw 0–0 with Cuba.

It was an interesting clash of styles with Poland doing more of the attacking, particularly in the second half when they had a number of worthwhile shots, netting two goals through Andrzej Szarmach. The Brazilians showed plenty of intricate moves in mid-field but were finally beaten by the more reliable approach of the Poles.

Poland thus were in the final for the second successive Olympics—they had shocked Hungary in Munich after the dazzling Wlodzimierz Lubanski had been their inspiration. This time they met a well-drilled East German side, who had defeated Russia 2–1 in the other semi-final. Both their semi-final goals had come in the second half. Jurgen Dorner converting a penalty and Lothar Kurbjuweit racing through from mid-field in the 66th minute to add a second. Viktor Kolotov's 84th minute goal was too late to alter the flow of the game. In the final East Germany had a 2–0 lead within 14 minutes. Hartmut Schade and Martin Hoffman netting the goals. Poland promptly substituted Tomaszewski.

Poland then played with more confidence and after some insistent pressure on the East German defence pulled one goal back in the 59th minute through Grzegorz Lato. But the East Germans went carefully on with Reinhard Hafner scoring a third goal six minutes before the end. It was a fine match to end an unsatisfactory tournment.

Hockey

The dominance of India and Pakistan over world hockey, which was cracked at the Munich Games, was flung off in Montreal. From 1928 until 1972 one of these two Asian nations took the gold medal at the Games. But the West German victory in Munich marked a crucial moment in the development of the game. It is true that between Munich and Montreal, West Germany themselves did not play with the zest and skill that they displayed in the Olympics—they had indifferent results in two World Cup tournaments and the European Cup. And in the Games, although favourites because of their experience of playing on artificial surfaces and their victory in the Pre-Olympic tournament, they went the same way as the countries they deposed. The final, unbelievably, was between Australia and New Zealand, who finished off what West Germany had started in Munich.

India, winners of the World Cup and seven times Olympic gold medallists, were crushed 6-1 by Australia, who tired the former masters of the game by using every inch of the pitch, stretching the defence and then riddling it with constant attacks. As Frank Van Rooij, one of Europe's top coaches, remarked: "The only thing India have left is their fantastic stick work." Both in this defeat and in their 3-1 defeat at the hands of Holland they looked spiritless. There was a lack of enterprise and they were criticised by many for not abandoning their pyramid formation. They also seemed to possess fewer outstanding players than they had in the past.

Their reliance on the traditional 5-3-2 formation with strong-running wingers was not flexible enough to match the tactics which other countries used against them. And their insistence on not appointing officials for long periods meant that they have not been able to build up any sort of regular understanding between players and management.

Pakistan eventually picked up third place but it was scant compensation for the amount of money and time that they had spent on the game. They had a major international tour of America and Europe and were clearly determined to regain the title they lost in Munich. They had plenty of experienced players, goalkeeper Saleem Sherwani and Abdul Rashid, but lacked the co-ordination to reach the final. Holland, without the injured Ties Kruize, did splendidly to reach the last four and only lost 3-2 to Pakistan after an even game.

West Germany, like India, often looked jaded. When their opponents scored the first goal in their pool matches they lacked the zest to recover. The injury to the brilliantly talented left winger Peter Trump, one of the heroes of the 1972 victory and at 25 expected to be at the peak of his career, was a grievous blow. Michael Krause, their ferocious-hitting full-back, was not the force that he had been in the past; it was Krause who scored the only goal of the game to defeat Pakistan in 1972. After losing to Spain 4-1 in the pool match they overwhelmed them 9-1 in the match for fifth place.

In the final New Zealand playing with tremendous stamina and determination just edged out Australia 1-0. Some stout defensive play—Australia forced eight penalty corners of which the New Zealanders managed to block seven and one shot missed—and some brisk breakaways brought them the title for the first time.

The decisive goal came after a penalty corner in the 42nd minute. Tony Ineson crashed home a short corner. They had had a chance to go ahead in the sixth minute but Ramesh Patel hit a penalty stroke wide. Australia's star striker Ronald Riley, who netted seven goals in the tournament, was carefully controlled by the New Zealanders, who went on to an unexpected but famous win.

12

BOXING

In an Olympics that saw the USA lose so many titles in events which they used to believe were their prerogative, the American boxers fought with powerful precision to take five gold medals—equalling the record set at Helsinki in 1952. It was a triumph for ceaseless aggression and ferocious hitting over the more disciplined approach of the communist countries. Since 1952 the Iron Curtain nations have been the principal winners in Olympics, European Championships and in the inaugural world championships of 1974. Apart from such famous fighters as Muhammad Ali, Joe Frazier and George Foreman—all of whom won Olympic gold medals—the majority of the leading boxers have come from countries like Russia and Poland.

But this performance by the Americans may force them to change their style—something they will be loth to do because they have always been critical of the vicious approach and violent punching which they see in American professional boxing. One of their arguments against professional boxing is that it tends to degenerate into street fighting instead of what they believe is a scientific sport of physical education value; another, incidentally, is the old chestnut about the exploitation of the young.

What the Americans, and to a certain extent, the Cubans, displayed in Montreal was that in boxing success can be earned (and suffered) through heavy punching and the ability to withstand similar punishment. As if the experience of professional boxing had not taught one that for every stylist like Ali and Gene Tunney there has been a Dempsey or Harry Greb. Amateur boxing has been handicapped in many countries by enthusiasts deploring the degeneracy of the professional ring and holding up the amateur sport as an example of manliness and good sportsmanship.

There will be some serious soul-searching in places like Russia and Poland over the next few years before a distinct policy is formulated. Perhaps the demands for medals in Moscow will overcome the ethical values so many people believe can be acquired through boxing.

For the USA, who had only one champion in 1972, this was the most splendid of comebacks. The boxers, who exemplified their resurgence in style and success, were the Spinks brothers who won both their finals in the last round. Leon met the Cuban Sixto Soria, who had knocked out three opponents on his way to the final in little over 10 minutes. Leon had come to Montreal with a satisfactory but not outstanding record—three AAU titles, a second place in the Pan American Games and only eight losses of his 127 contests. Spinks was not concerned with defence and attacked the Cuban with clusters of clubbing blows. He knocked him down once and was quickly in trouble again as Spinks crammed on the pace. In the second round Spinks was given a public warning for ignoring an instruction from the referee. But in the third round Spinks began to wear down his opponent and eventually the referee had to halt the bout.

His 20-year-old brother, Michael, two inches taller but only a middleweight, was equally formidable. In the final he fought Russia's Rufat Riskiev, the world amateur champion. Riskiev has been a member of the Russian team for seven years and was seemingly experienced enough not to be caught by the hard-hitting American. In the second round he was hitting the American and scoring valuable points. But in the last round Spinks landed a firm blow to the stomach which forced the Russian to double up in painful surprise. The referee stopped the contest.

There is always particular interest in the heavyweight class. The pedigree of the role of winners down the years is unquestioned and for many successful Americans the gold medal has been a lucrative stepping-stone to a fortune in the professional ring. Teofilo Stevenson, Cuba's 1972 Olympic champion, was different. Because professional boxing is unknown in Cuba, Stevenson, then 20, was obliged to remain an amateur. Between Munich and Montreal he was glimpsed occasionally and usually successfully by the outside world. He won the heavyweight crown at the first World Championships in 1974 and the Pan American Games title the following year. Despite beliefs that he had declined he was the clear favourite for the Montreal title.

His most important asset was his timing. This enabled him to land blows of extraordinary force which were graphically described by West Germany's Peter Hussing, whom he defeated inside the distance in Munich, in the words: "I have never been hit so hard in all my 212 bouts. You just don't see his right hand. All of a sudden it is there ... on your chin!" Timing is something that is not lost, just as it is not easily acquired. It is a physical quality which is largely inbred, the result of natural co-ordination.

Since Munich he had added a stone to his 13½-stone frame, was more experienced and had yet to lose a competition that mattered. When Angelo Dundee, the manager of Muhammad Ali, rated his valuation to turn professional in 1972 as two million dollars he was not exaggerating. Indeed he was probably being miserly. The prices of heavyweights in boxing have an inflation rate affected not only by the world's currency but also by the market in talented big boxers. By Montreal even Ali's amazing reign as the supreme professional boxer seemed to be coming to an end, and that raised Stevenson's value by even more.

That didn't concern Stevenson apparently. In Montreal he repeated what he had said in Munich and on subsequent occasions. "I don't like professional boxing. I want to be an athlete and if I turn professional I am not an athlete any more." He felt certain that Castro would not ask him to change his mind. "Castro knows what is going on in professional boxing. Pro boxers are pieces of merchandise. I don't want to be exploited."

In Munich Stevenson had hammered America's Duane Bobick to defeat. By 1974 the USA had produced a new heavyweight Marvin Stinson and Stevenson beat him for the world title. In 1976 they had John Tate, a truck driver in Tennessee, who had barely 18 months experience but looked the part at 6ft 4in and 16 stone, Tate had a traditional upbringing for a negro from the Southern States —cotton-picking at the age of eight. He had only begun boxing at a late age of 20 but he showed his potential by taking a points victory off Poland's European champion Andrezey Biegalski in the early rounds of the Olympics, But he was less impressive against West Germany's Peter Hussing, barely getting through their quarter-final bout on a split decision. What was equally significant was that Tate suffered damage to his left eye, which had been cut earlier in the tournament. Plainly he could be hit and hurt.

Just how hard Stevenson was punching was demonstrated in his bout with Finland's Pekka Ruokola. The Cuban knocked the Finn down three times with crisply-timed short right hand crosses. When Ruokola rose for the third count the referee counted him out. Everyone therefore expected Stevenson to win his semi-final bout with Tate, but were nevertheless fascinated to discover whether he could repeat his destructive punching on the larger American.

He did. After 1min 29sec of the opening round he hammered in his right fist. Tate's knees buckled and he went staggering across the ring to a neutral corner, where he sank on his haunches to be counted out. The performance prompted George Foreman to remark from the ring-side that Stevenson could win the world professional title any time he chose. The Cuban was less exciting in the final. He met Rumania's Mricea Simon, who had been knocked out in the second round of the 1975 European Championships by Biegalski. After his semi-final victory over a mediocre Bermudan, Clarence Hill, it was laughingly suggested that the loser should have been made to fight Stevenson instead of the winner. But Simon stifled the patronising smiles by disturbing the Cuban with his sensible tactics although not any heavy punching. He would not be drawn out by his opponent and neither fighter would function other than to attempt counter-punching. The referee ordered them to be more aggressive. In the final round Stevenson hurt his opponent twice with left jabs and after a maul glimpsed a gap in his opponent's defence and landed his right hand. The Rumanian went down quickly and got up more slowly. The referee stopped the bout with 25 seconds to go—and Stevenson had become the first man to retain his Olympic heavyweight title. The experts were not content to leave it at that. Rumours began again—that Stevenson would turn professional after all, managed by Norman Manley, the son of the Jamaican Prime Minister. He simply is too talented a boxer to be allowed to compete for his own pleasure. However, I would not be surprised if he is not in Moscow in four years time to try to complete his hat-trick of victories.

Stevenson also epitomised Cuba's adoption of the strategy of the USA—their neighbours physically if not politically. Unlike the European communist nations they relied on hefty punching which brought them three titles—the same number as in Munich.

Eastern Europe only took two gold medals: welterweight Jochen Bachfeld (East Germany) who was fortunate to take a points decision from Venezuela's Pedro Gamarra, an ambitious and accurate puncher, and Poland's light-middleweight Jerzy Rybicki who got the Judge's verdict from Yugoslavia's Tadijia Kucar, who was suffering from a heavily damaged right eye.

For Britain these were less successful Games than either Mexico or Munich. The boycott of so many of the African boxers disrupted the draw which resulted in the organisers redrawing the four categories. The British team had trained for a number of awkward bouts. As Kevin Hickey, the most able of successors to David James as team coach, admitted: "This has been an odd tournament. We came out here preparing for a man to fight four or five times to reach the final and all the team were fit for that. But the withdrawal of the Africans ruined that. Moreover, some of the boys, instead of feeling their way against moderate opponents as they would have done, have been thrown in with world class opponents after only one contest." Hickey agreed that in terms of medals it had been a disappointing Games—only bantamweight Pat Cowdell getting as far as the semi-finals where he got a bronze. There were other reasons, some of which were controversial and not completely untypical of the whole shape of the sport in Britain.

The naming of Cardiff Chris Davies as the British light-welterweight in the team which was managed by his father, John, aroused consernation in the sport. Davies had been preferred to Clinton McKenzie, the ABA champion from Croydon, and the decision infuriated Hickey who threatened to resign.

Hickey was explicit in his attitude. "I was flabbergasted when they told me the names of the team and my first impulse was to chuck the whole thing in. I'm glad I was able to give the matter a deal of thought after I drove home from the selection meeting. Before the match against America the British team were told by John Davies that they were facing their last hurdle to the Olympics. McKenzie won in fine style then but so far as he is concerned those encouraging words accounted for nought. What has happened leaves so much to be desired as far as integrity is concerned." Davies' record internationally had not been outstanding. He had been beaten against Spain, Hungary, Sweden and England and failed to progress beyond the first series in two European and one Commonwealth championships. He was not even the current Welsh ABA champion. But the selectors were not given the full facts and by a split vote Davies was given the place.

After massive protests and discussions with Denis Howell, the Minister for Sport, the selection was changed and McKenzie went to Canada. What was so disturbing about the incident was that the selectors could have been persuaded to make the choice in the first place and it emphasised once again how out of touch with the form and ability of the leading competitors so many people controlling the sport were. One person who must be exonerated from this criticism is Hickey, whose support of the individual fighters and understanding of the sport, is considerable. The sooner that he is given the task of picking the team by himself—or with a few trusted and experienced advisers—the better it will be for the sport. Once again it revealed that beneath the progress achieved by men like James and Hickey there still exists reactionary attitudes and sometimes ignorance.

The team, whose morale understandably suffered because of the controversy, boxed determinedly in Montreal. Cowdell, the Commonwealth champion and European bronze medallist, was thought by Hickey to have a strong chance before the team left for the Games. "He is a perfect competitor in terms of temperament," Hickey said. In his quarter-final contest he got the verdict from four judges but really managed only to take control of the bout in the final two minutes. His opponent, Reynaldo Fortaleza (The Philippines) was a southpaw who disturbed Cowdell in the first two rounds. The opening round produced little positive work from either boxer and Fortaleza was on top on the second. But in the final round the Briton was the dominating figure.

In the semi-final he lost a split decision to Yong Jo Ku (North Korea). Many experienced onlookers thought Cowdell was unlucky. He was ahead in the first round by moving nimbly in and out behind an accurate left jab but had to sustain some firm left hooks from his opponent. But in the second the Korean landed some strong blows and seemed to be ahead in the third when Cowdell dropped him with a left counter to the jaw. From then on Cowdell was in control. The judges were possibly influenced by a number of warnings—none of them public—which Cowdell received for the careless use of his head in clinches. Hickey, who tries to smother his subjectivity as much as possible, believed that Cowdell had won. The Briton was probably a victim of the alteration in the judges' scoring allocation. In Montreal they preferred the close-punching American method of hitting whereas in the past they have tended to be wooed by the long-range style adopted by the Russians and the other communist competitors.

Britain's other principal hope, Charlie Magri, the ABA flyweight champion and a European Championships bronze medallist, was surprisingly stopped in the final round of his opening bout. He seemed to be moving to a comfortable points victory when Canada's Ian Clyde struck him with a right hook (Clyde was a southpaw). Magri went down but was up at four. The referee after completing the mandatory eight count ended the contest.

13

GYMNASTICS, FENCING AND CYCLING

GYMNASTICS now generates vast aesthetic appreciation at the Olympics. Visually it is the most striking of the sports and a distinct contrast to the boisterous, rugged atmosphere of the field events in athletics, judo, weight-lifting, wrestling and boxing. Although such outstanding performers of the 1960's as Larissa Latynina and Vera Caslavska were admired by ordinary sports enthusiasts as well as gymnastic experts, it was not until the Munich Games that the sport became so popular because of television. The exploits of Russia's Olga Korbut initiated waves of enthusiasm for the sport that had Western Europe and the USA, in particular, in rhapsodies over a sport that for many people had previously consisted of memories of bruised knees, strained limbs and didactic schoolmistresses. In Britain there was simply a shortage of suitably qualified coaches to accommodate the demand for tuition from the many schoolchildren who were eager to emulate Olga.

The Montreal Olympics sustained this popularity partly because it occurred at the beginning of the Games when the major counter-attraction of athletics had not yet started. Television producers were delighted to interrupt their portrayal of mediocre boxing matches and swimming events, which have not the visual impact of athletics, with long periods of gymnastics. And they were not disappointed.

Once more a woman gymnast proved herself the outstanding figure of the first week of the Games. If Nadia Comaneci, the 14-year-old Rumanian girl, failed to arouse the same emotions as Olga Korbut did at Munich, it was because she was too skilled a competitor to fall off the apparatus as the Russian did in Munich. To many people she seemed an automaton—but this did not preclude fascination in seeing a difficult human skill being done supremely well.

Miss Comaneci's arrival on the international gymnastics scene has been astonishingly swift. In 1974 she had been regarded as not being talented enough for the Rumanian team at the World Championships when Russia's Ludmila Tourischeva, the 1972 Olympic Combined Exercises champion, confirmed her pre-eminence in the sport by winning the most important international event in the gymnastics calendar for the fifth successive year.

Miss Comaneci was first noticed when she competed in the Champions All event at Wembley in 1974. Her first place there was only a prelude to her victory in the European Championships. Not only did she take the Combined Exercises title but she also finished first on three of the four apparatus. The fourth gold medal (the floor) went to Miss Tourischeva, who claimed that she was suffering from a back injury.

Britain then had contrived to create a new international competition—the World Cup—originated primarily to get financial benefit and public exposure rather than because gymnastics needed such a competition. The Rumanians declined the invitation at the last moment, perhaps because they did not want Miss Comaneci to have the same intensive publicity that had attracted Miss Korbut. It might affect her concentration for the Olympics and interrupt her training when she was recasting her voluntary routines in preparation for Montreal.

In her absence Miss Tourischeva took the World Cup and plainly would be difficult to defeat in 1976. Pauline Prestidge, Britain's National Women's Coach, has been a great admirer of Miss Tourischeva but she had quickly recognised the concentrated skill of the Rumanian.

"I have a tremendous admiration for the way that Ludmila combines skill with an emotional style that makes me almost want to cry whenever she steps on to the mat. But Nadia is too precise technically. She is doing movements on the beam that 10 years ago would have been attempted only on the floor exercises. And her bar routine and vault are the best we have seen. She has more fluency on her back somersaults than even Olga Korbut, but with no pause either before or after her movements." Mrs Prestidge's words were worth recalling as the Women's Team Event began in the Forum, the splendidly constructed indoor arena that usually houses the famous Montreal Canadians Ice Hockey Team.

The pattern of the Women's competition was set from the opening exercise. The Russians were delightful on the asymetric bars and scored fine marks. They finished their routines before the Rumanians, who were working on the beam, had completed their exercises. Consequently they were obliged to sit and watch the exhibition of Nadia Comaneci. It was her first routine in the Olympics and she could have been excused if she had been flustered or inexact in her movements—particularly on the beam which requires such measured care and is the least favourite of the gymnasts to begin a competition with because it is the apparatus with the highest premium on meticulous skill. It was probably the critical moment of the whole women's competition. But Miss Comaneci did not hesitate. She went through her routine without apparent error. On one handstand she lifted her legs overhead so gradually that it appeared as if she could not have the momentum to reach the position. But she did—and then held it there as if to stress the smoothness of the action before proceeding with the exercise.

The applause was louder than anything the Russians had received—and deservedly so for she received 9·90pts for the exercise. The Russian squad turned away from the cheering which Miss Comaneci greeted by returning to the arena for a victory salute. The Russians suspected then they would lose the Individual Combined Exercises title. Miss Comaneci was clearly as proficient as she had been at the European Championships the previous year. It was not the crowd's applause that was so significant, nor the mark that she received, it was that she had been clapped by the other gymnasts. Only the great gymnasts receive this accolade in a sport where the competitors are more discriminating than the most pedantic of judges. As the Russians marched on to the beam, their next exercise, they were aware that they were attempting to beat someone whom the competitors themselves accepted as the premier gymnast in the world.

The contrast between Miss Comaneci's beam exhibition and that of the Russians was evident. Both Miss Tourischeva and Nelli Kim, winner of the USSR Cup in May, performed competently and Miss Korbut displayed her old dexterity and style. But although Miss Korbut received 9·80pts, the other two Russian girls only obtained 9·40. Both swayed during one movement on the apparatus and recovered their balance with difficulty. It was a defect—but Miss Comaneci doesn't have defects. Many gymnasts at international level can complete the compulsory exercises without mistakes in training but few can do it during the Olympics. Miss Comaneci clearly had the temperament which made her such a rational favourite for the Combined Exercises title. And unlike Russia's Olga Korbut the charm in her routines is not obvious. She does not appear to be trying to entice the judges or spectators and this restraint is all the more effective because of it.

As the first day proceeded this trend became manifest. Miss Comaneci was clearly in the lead even if the Russians were superior as a team. It is, of course, an advantage to be a member of a team such as the Soviet Union during a gymnastics event, apart from the more evident assistance which applies to other sports like the benefit from training with other top competitors. A shrewd gymnastic coach will arrange the order of competitors for an exercise so that the judges are confronted with a crescendo of talent. For instance, the Russians often put Elvira Saadi, or Svetlana Grozdova totally reliable but not brilliant gymnasts, first for many of the events. And on their high but not outstanding mark, they try to build up the scores. Thus, for instance if Olga Korbut gets 9·70pts for the floor exercises then Miss Tourischeva or Miss Kim, who are more gifted in this exercise, must get higher scores because the judges have Miss Korbut's routine fresh in their minds, and know that Miss Tourischeva and Miss Kim have done better. Consequently they receive more than 9·70pts. To be an outstanding gymnast in an indifferent team—as the USA's Cathy Rigby discovered in 1970 and 1972—is a disadvantage. Then, if the early team members have scored, say 9·00pts the judges, although recognising the superiority of the later performances may reward the gymnast with 9·70pts instead of the 9·85pts which she might well have got if she were a member of a great team.

All six Russian female competitors were in the first nine in the overall classification after compulsory and voluntary exercises which shows what an advantage Miss Tourischeva and Miss Kim had in their competition with Miss Comaneci. What Miss Comaneci did have however was the assistance of Theodora Ungureanu, her training partner and fellow combatant in the pillow fights they indulge in as relaxation.

Miss Ungureanu eventually finished fourth and her presence offset the comparative—and it is only marginal—weakness of the rest of the Rumanian team which took the silver medal. Even in the individual all-round competition, when the team event had been settled, one noticed Miss Comaneci interrupting her concentration on her own asymetric bars routine to leap up on to the apparatus to sandpaper down the bar before her friend was due to exercise.

Although one had expected Russia to finish the first day well ahead of the other countries in the team competition, and, although one believed that Miss Comaneci would probably have been in the lead in the individual classification, what one hadn't anticipated was that Miss Comaneci would be so dominant at that stage in the event. And what stressed her superiority was her 10pts out of 10 on the asymetric bars—the first perfect score in Olympic history but by the end of these Games certainly not the last. Miss Comaneci said she was not surprised when she became the first woman to achieve this, stating categorically: "I knew it was an immaculate routine. I've done it 16 times before in my career." This may have been true but she did not say that most of these had been achieved in domestic events when the judging has not been so discriminatingly even and when the pressures of competition not so intense. Miss Comaneci agreed that she was encouraged by the active response of the crowd who aided her confidence after that first testing performance on the beam.

The Rumanian was 1·50pts ahead of both Miss Tourischeva and Miss Ungureanu after the first day. It was a large enough margin to concern Larissa Latynina, now the Russian coach. She complained that Miss Comaneci did not deserve the maximum score because she took two steps on dismounting instead of one.

Although there was certainly some validity in her observation it was probably motivated by a wish to restore confidence in the girls whom she had been advising. The British coaches, who were able to make assessments without being influenced by such considerations, believed that Miss Comaneci deserved a perfect score because she had accomplished everything that the compulsory exercise had demanded without blemish. And on that basis she should have received 10pts. One can't ask more than that.

On the second day of the Team Event, when the voluntary exercises are exhibited, Miss Comaneci confirmed everything that she had indicated on the opening day. She received maximum points for both the beam and asymetric bars and her performance eclipsed Russia's victory in the team event. Her achievement on the opening day had taken the results computer unawares. It rejected the 10pts because it was unprecedented in the Games. But even a computer can be influenced to accept the progress of sport and there were no such difficulties in recording Miss Comaneci's perfection in the voluntary exercises. Although everyone was discussing her flawless scores what impressed me was that she dropped only 0·30pts over the four apparatus—consistency of excellence without parallel in the history of the sport.

The contrast with the Russians was evident to even an untrained observer. Miss Korbut lost 0·30pts—as many as Miss Comaneci did all evening—when her feet stuttered on landing on one attempt and on the other she indecorously fell to the mat. And neither Miss Kim nor Miss Tourischeva, who finished equal second 0·80pts behind the Rumanian showed the definition in skill of Miss Comaneci.

They were trying, striving to improve their marks however much they may have disguised their determination behind their smiles and charming demeanour. An indication was that for the first time Miss Tourischeva was eager to commit herself to a display of self-advertisement by acknowledging the crowd's applause during the actual competition. She was trying to recover the whole-hearted approval of the spectators who were being seduced by another. On the beam the Russians 9·85pts brought only perfunctory applause because they were watching Miss Comaneci elsewhere. And when Miss Comaneci collected her silver medal for the team event the applause made the team winners look shame-facedly aside and mutter among themselves. Still there was some gratifying compensation in the fact that Russia had again won the team event—something that they have never lost since they returned to the Games in 1952.

The margin of Miss Comaneci's superiority was not so considerable that some slipshod performances on the evening of the Combined Exercises would not let the Russians through. But since she had not faltered before in international competition the odds were that she wouldn't do so now. And this is what happened. She had the qualities of a rubber ruler—flexibility and exactness of measurement. Miss Tourischeva recognised Miss Comaneci's right to the title after the beam when the Russian woman walked over to the Rumanian girl and with a lack of ostentation patted her on the shoulder. And when the medals were decided she declined to mount the medal rostrum until she had kissed the winner—a more noticeable gesture but none the less sincere for that.

She received two perfect scores again for her exhibitions on the asymetric bars and beam, where meticulous movement is the most important facet of the exercise. But Miss Kim was also in unprecedented form. She received a maximum score for the vault where her athletic ability can be fulfilled. She curved her body over the horse with captivating agility and landed without any shift of her position.

The Rumanian was not finished yet. On the last day of the women's gymnastics she collected two further gold medals for both individual apparatus—the team scores counting half towards the individual events. But this time she was matched title for title, perfect score for perfect score and almost medal for medal by Nelli Kim. And the day's gymnastics stressed that if Miss Comaneci has no superior for precision of technique there are competitors who have a slightly greater ability at other aspects of the sport. There was an absence of sensuality in her routines so that only her youth prevented her from appearing clinically efficient. The Rumanian finished first (with perfect scores making a total of seven) on the asymetric bars and beam. Miss Kim received the gold medals for the vault and floor exercises, which need respectively acrobatic ability and a deep feeling for the rhythm of the sport. The contrast could not have been more manifest.

Miss Kim missed her grip on the asymetric bars in attempting a deft change of hand positions and fell to the mat. But on the other exercises she displayed a charming fluency of movements. She blended her technique to the music on the floor exercises with a deep appreciation for the emotions of the sport. The Russians, of course, have always excelled in this department of the sport partly because of their country's interest and prominence in ballet. And Miss Kim was in the tradition of Larissa Latynina and 'Natasha' Kuchinskaya.

Miss Kim conveyed her pleasure to the audience producing a joy that was evident in all her moves. Her spontaneity, too, was juxtaposed with the Rumanian whose enthusiasm for the sport is less apparent. Admiring as one was of the mobility and facility of Miss Comaneci occasionally one was chilled by her performance. One does not get bored with beauty so quickly.

Miss Korbut seemed overshadowed by all this. But she still emerged to take the silver medal in the beam. She hopes to enter the theatre now. But gymnastics will not easily forget the woman, who popularised the sport even if she never won the Olympic or European Combined Exercises title. Gymnastics, like every other sport, is about more than just winning.

It is interesting that of all the Olympic events gymnastics is the only one in which the men's competition is so overshadowed by the women's. Frequently it is the other way round—how many enthusiasts are there for women's shot putting?—partly because the men's performances are so demonstrably superior. But gymnastics is a sport apart. Despite the visual attraction of gymnastics it is not art and anyone who tries to equate it with ballet is doing gymnastics a grave disservice. It is simply unrealistic to pretend that gymnastics can enhance one's understanding of life. But equally it is different from most other Olympic sports, if only because results are assessed on people's judgements on other people; this is something which leads many people to believe that gymnastics should not be part of the Games. But because it is a sport apart other qualities are esteemed—like grace and skilled movement, talents which women are better equipped to express than men.

This is not to denigrate men's gymnastics. But it is a sport that in Munich and Mexico, received comparatively little recognition. It is true that the 18,000 seater stadium was full every day but nevertheless there was a lack of atmosphere which was so apparent because it was interwoven with the women's competition. When it comes to gymnastics women are better than men at the qualities which this sport has in profusion. There was no excessive demands on gymnastics instruction for men after the Munich Games as there had been for women.

This is not to derogate men's gymnastics. But it is a sport that in the public's eye has none of the coruscating quality of the female side of gymnastics. Despite all this one found plenty of drama and interest in the men's competition which saw the familiar contrast between the Japanese and the Russians which has been such a feature of the sport in recent years.

This year's competition was transformed by the injury in the week before the event to the Japanese Shigeru Kasamatsu, who in the World Championships two years earlier had not only taken the overall title, but also the gold medals on the floor and vault. He was taken to hospital for an emergency appendix operation and missed the Games completely. He was, of course, favourite for the event and the man who expected to lead Japan to the Team title—something that they have taken in every Olympics and world championships since 1960.

His absence placed a burden on Sawao Kato, who had emerged from semi-retirement to become a member of the team. Kato, the

Combined Exercises champion in Munich and Mexico, was the best of the group of proficient competitors who abound in Japan.

These included Eizo Kenmotsu, a silver medallist in Munich and third in the World Championships, and Mitsuo Tsukahara, whose technical contribution to the vault had been considerable. But both Tsukahara and Hiroshi Kajiiama had been beaten by Russia's leading competitor, Nikolai Andrianov, in the 1975 World Cup. Andrianov was clearly going to be a threat to the Japanese. At 22 he was at the age when male gymnasts are approaching their peak, still agile enough to move fluently but having acquired the strength through the years of training which is necessary for control in the exercises on the rings, pommel horse and parallel bars. He had split Kasamatsu and Kenmotsu in finishing runner-up in the World Championships and had been a consummate winner of the European title.

The men's gymnastics event was to resolve itself into a struggle between the Japanese, coaxed by the experience of Kato who was trying to compensate for the absence of Kasamatsu, and the vibrant skill of the young Russians for whom Andrianov was an example in his determination and talent.

The Japanese were comparatively careless in the early stages of the first day and almost imperceptibly slipped behind. Kenmotsu was lacking his customary polish—he received only 9·00pts on the parallel bars, and Shun Fujimoto got only 9·00pts for the vault and 9·10pts for pommel horse. The Russians, with one exception—Vladimir Marchenko's catastrophic 8·50pts on the parallel bars—were splendidly consistent. Andrianov was masterly everywhere. The one surprise in the Russian team was the prominence of Vladimir Markelov instead of Alexander Detiatin, who had been third in the European Championships in 1975 and was expected to be the outsider whom everyone feared—a person rapidly fulfilling his potential in the year of the Games.

Instead it was Markelov, who at 18-years-old had finished second in the USSR Cup in May, who had the distinction of preceeding Andrianov in the Russian line-up. He totally justified his fifth position. He finished the compulsory exercises in second place to Andrianov and his form—and Kasamatsu's absence—disturbed the predictions of the experts.

It was only the last two apparatuses that the Japanese performed on—the parallel bars and the high bar that they recovered their aplomb and the support of the crowd. The spectators jeered the judges' assessment of Kenmotsu's High Bar routine of 9·65pts because they believed that he should have received more. They recovered 0·45pts after the parallel bars and then 0·55pts on the High Bar—both exercises that by tradition they are skilled in—but still trailed the Russians by 0·50pts in total.

On the optional exercises Japan continued their recovery. It was a tortuous struggle which was frequently interrupted by disagreements between officials, sustained booing and yet some amazingly agile moves by both teams. Shun Fujimoto limped out of the arena with a damaged knee after the rings to reduce the Japanese team to five men. It later transpired that Fujimoto had broken his leg in the warm-up but struggled on to help his team—a typical example of Japanese stoicism in sport. The tense situation aroused the Japanese to their finest form after the comparatively mediocre exhibition of the compulsory exercises. They performed with skilled purpose—and finally took the title by 0·40pts.

The disputes over the marking began after a splendidly controlled ring routine by Kato, which was awarded 9·80pts. The crowd booed the marking for over a minute, insisting that it should have been higher. Arthur Gander, the Swiss President of the International Gymnastics Federation, walked over to the officials and spoke to the Russian judge Asaraian.

Then when Andrianov was given 9·50pts for a high bar routine the Russian coach raced across the arena to talk to Gander. And finally after a masterly High Bar exhibition by Hisato Igarashi, which received 9·85pts, the Russian Head Judge Boris Shakhlin, the former Olympic champion and an esteemed figure in the sport, had a conference of officials. But the score remained unaltered.

But Adrianov had remained solidly in the lead although Kato had equalled Andrianov on the voluntary exercises both receiving 58·40pts; Tsukahara was only 0·50 behind. The Russian was to cling on to his advantage in the Combined Exercises Final. It was his consistency which ultimately determined the title, moving with neat style on the floor exercises and rugged firmness on the rings. Sadly Andrianov received only scanty applause. The enthralling competition earlier in the evening of the Women seemed to exhaust the audience. He may not be adventurous in selecting his routines—he admitted afterwards that he had deliberately tried exercises in which there were few opportunities for error—but his ability is uniform if undemonstrative.

He finished a clear point ahead of Kato and never received less than a mark of 9·65pts for any apparatus. Kato was slightly less good. Tsukahara took the bronze medal. Markelov damaged a foot on a double back-flip with twist on warming up for the Floor Exercises and was forced to withdraw. But there is plenty of time for him to win medals in the future.

Andianov's combination of power and mobility brought even more prominent success in the individual apparatus finals. He took three gold medals bringing his total to four gold, two silver and a bronze—equalling the previous post-war record set by Shakhlin in 1960. The two exercises which the Japanese won were the parallel bars and the high bar; this was predictable for a country whose gymnasts excel at the swinging movements. Kato had an immaculate routine on the parallel bars and was steadier in the static positions and neater in his hand movements than Andrianov. The Russian attempted one reverse turn, returned to his starting position and then had to restart the movement. This cost him valuable points. The Russian did not qualify for the final of the high bar which was magnificently won by Tsukahara, who whirled spectacularly round the bar and deserved his 9·85pts. Hungary's Zoltan Magyar, the reigning world champion, took the pommel horse but otherwise Andrianov was supreme. Despite his prominence one wondered how many people have even heard of him, people for whom Nadia Comaneci is as familiar as the daughter of their next door neighbour.

As far as the British team were concerned one can only say that Averil Lennox reached the final, a commendable effort and a justifiable reward for all the hard work that she had put in. She finished 35th in the Combined Exercises.

The support of Bill McLaughlin, who scrutinises her training, resulted in her placing higher than anyone has done for a long time. The men did not finish in the first 70. Despite all the money that has been ploughed into the sport in recent years Britain still lag behind the rest of the world.

Fencing

As had been expected no one country dominated the fencing events. If Russia were supreme at the sabre and the women's team foil competition, then West Germany and Sweden took the honours in the men's epée, an Italian won the foil and a Hungarian the women's foil. It remains however, a sport which is deeply entrenched in Europe with few competitors from other Continents placing in the leading positions.

France had expected to take the individual men's foil—traditionally the first event to be staged at the Games—but their distinguished representative, Christian Noel, world champion in 1973 and 1975 finished seventh. He had seemed in top form earlier in the year when in an eight nation team event he won 24 out of 27 events. But the 1972 Olympic bronze medallist was never able to capture his finest form and was decisively beaten. The highest-placed Frenchman was indeed Bernard Talvard who finished third. The event was narrowly won by Italy's Fabio dal Zotto who took the gold medal from Russia's Alexander Ramankov, the 1974 world champion. France also hoped to take the team event but finished third in an event won by West Germany, whose highest-placed team member in the individual competition was Harald Hein in ninth place; it was triumph for team strength over individual excellence. Both Matthias Behr and Klaus Reichert had finished in the top 13.

Italy took the silver medal with a formidable team led by Dal Zotto and also including Carlo Montano, whose cousin Mario was fifth in the individual sabre. Much interest in the sabre centred on whether the hefty and overweight Montano and Maffei could beat the slim-line Russians, Victor Sidiak, the 1972 gold medallist, Vladimir Nazlymov, last year's world champion, and Victor Krovopouskov. The latter was the man in form. He took the Russian title earlier in the year and won the sabre with a dexterous display which combined both force and finesse. The other heavy men, Michael Maffei (Italy), the 1971 world champion, who had had to shed nearly two stone to get fit for the Games, Peter Marot (Hungary) and Rumania's Dan Irimicuic were convincingly beaten by the slender Russians. The result was no advertisement for eating. Russia finished clear of Italy in the team competition.

In the epée, Russia's weakest weapon, West Germany's Alexander Pusch, last year's world champion, finished in front of his compatriot Dr. Jurgen Hehn. But Sweden, who had showed their depth of talent in the individual competition, came through to take the title. They had gifted fighters in Rolf Edling, whose enormous reach and gangling frame brought him two world titles, and Hans Jacobsen, who had won two 1976 major tournaments.

Among the women Hungary's Ildiko Schwarczenberger took the gold medal in the individual competition and they also were third in the team event, won, as expected by Russia.

Britain, who used to be so successful in this sport, only briefly raised hopes of breaking their long run without an Olympic medal. In the men's epée Ralph Johnson had a 5–2 victory against Alex Pusch, the eventual winner. But he faded after finishing first in his poll to end in 13th position. In the epée event Bill Hoskyns, the last Briton to win a medal in Olympic fencing, led a team that promised to do well but were beaten 8–5 by Norway, Hoskyns, the 1958 world champion and competing uniqely in his sixth Olympics, won two bouts against Norwegians but was defeated 5–2 by Ole Moerch.

Cycling

There was one particular disappointment in the cycling events—that France's Daniel Morelon failed to take his third successive gold medal in the sprint. A smooth rider of impeccable fairness he was competing in his fourth Olympics (he was a bronze medallist in 1964). He had lost the world title in Montreal in 1974 but regained it the following year in Liège and there were justifiable hopes that he would have the acceleration to win the gold medal. But it was not to be. For the second time in Montreal he lost to Anton Tkac (Czechoslovakia), who took the 1974 world title from the Frenchman, in a deciding match after the final. Tkac just swooped home ahead of the Frenchman to take the gold medal.

Another sentimental gold medallist would have been Britain in the 4000 metres team pursuit. This would not have been so much in recognition of their considerable ability but rather as a tribute to their sportsmanship. In 1973 they met West Germany in the World Championships final and were losing by more than a second as the Germans wheeled round the last curve.

The front man moved up slightly to avoid an official who was replacing the markers by the edge of the track. The rider behind touched his wheel, affecting his balance. His fall on to the concrete track caused the whole team to collide with him. The Britons rode on to an unsatisfactory victory. Britain were awarded the gold medal but refused to take it. The organisers consequently presented the West Germans with the gold medal for "sporting reasons" and allowed Britain the opportunity to protest at the decision. They didn't.

The admiration for the British riders was deserved. Their action was regarded as that of true British sportsmen on the Continent and the quartet were voted "Sportsmen of the Year" in West Germany. They were presented with gold watches and fêted in a number of major cities.

In the 1974 World Championships Britain were the third fastest qualifiers for the quarter-finals but, in their race against Czechoslovakia, Ian Hallam's back wheel shed a spoke and he tumbled to the track. Britain's chances were ruined. Consequently there were plenty of international observers who wanted Britain to take the title in Montreal. With Ian Hallam, the Commonwealth champion, on the verge of retirement but still anxious to add another Olympic medal to the bronze that he took in Munich there was also Michael Bennett, another member of the 1972 team. The quartet was completed by Ian Banbury and Robin Croker.

Against West Germany in the semi-final they led for the first 2000 metres but, after being passed, eased off, knowing that they wouldn't defeat their fitter opponents. This gave them the resources necessary for the third-place with East Germany, who had been the fastest qualifiers but who had lost to Russia in the other semi-final.

The crowd, remembering Britain's sportsmanship and bad luck in the past, supported them eagerly. With just two laps left of the 4,000 metres race Britain had secured almost a three-second lead. Bennett after a tremendous full lap, eased and left it for the remaining trio. Hallam did not realise that he had gone and also went up the banking from the front position. Banbury then took up the pace so keenly that Hallam was left struggling. Hallam's time was crucial since he was the third man and as he accelerated to catch up his team-mates the East Germans continued their final burst. On the last lap Hallam, who had been one of the most persistent in the pace-setting, urged himself for a late sprint and steered the British home by three-tenths of a second. It was a suitable end to a superb career. West Germany eventually took the gold medal.

Britain also did commendably well in the 100 kilometre time trial when they finished sixth. But this race was dominated by the Russians who were always in the lead. They opened up a 45 second gap on East Germany after 35 kilometres and a 50 second gap on Poland, the world champions. This lead stretched to 69 seconds over Poland at the half-way stage but the world champions mounted a determined attack in the final stages and got within 20 seconds of Russia at the finish. A strong wind blowing straight down the road made the race harder than it might have been and, in particular, the last haul up to the line into the wind was the place where the race was decided. The Russians, the 1972 Olympic champions, were experienced and well trained enough to maintain their lead at the end of the race. Britain, too, showed their stamina by surging through from 11th over the last 25 kilometres to finish sixth.

In the kilometre time trial, Klaus-Jurgen Grunke (East Germany) had an epic victory to add the gold medal to the world title he took in 1975. With 12 competitors still to ride, Michel Vaarten, the Belgian champion, swept home in 1min 7·51sec and then had to watch from the track centre to see if anyone could beat his performance. Man after man tried and failed. Poland's Janusz Kierskowski, third in the 1975 World Championships, failed and then Eduard Rapp (Russia), who has twice taken the world title, was eliminated. He began before the gun and decided of his own free-will that he should restart. But the officials had never indicated that he ought to begin again and promptly eliminated him. But as a climax to the drama Grunke started briskly and sustained his momentum to take the gold medal.

Perhaps the most startling result of all the cycling events was the triumph of Gregor Braun, the young West German, in the 4000 metres individual pursuit. Although only 20 Braun defeated Vladimir Osokin (Russia), the 1975 World Championship's silver medallist, in the semi-final Osokin had been enormously impressive earlier in the Games by recording 4min 45·10sec in the preliminaries—the fastest time ever recorded other than at high altitude. The fine Velodrome track, roofed in and with an excellent surface, helped the competitors. But Osokin still looked the favourite. But in the semi-final Braun won a desperately close match—only 0·17sec separating the pair after the 14 laps. Both men recorded their best-ever times for the distance. Braun clocked 4min 45·50sec—a time which he did not need to reproduce to take the final from Holland's Herman Ponsteen.

14

ARCHERY AND SHOOTING

Archery

Luann Ryon, a 23-year-old Californian student who took a year off to prepare for the Olympics and Darell Pace, a computer expert, took both archery titles back to the United States, emulating the achievement, four years earlier of Doreen Wilbur and John Williams. By contrast Britain, in 21st and 23rd positions (women) and 21st and 30th (men) could not even emulate their predecessors of four years earlier.

Exceptionally high standards were set by the women. The silver medallist Valentina Kovpan, runner up at the 1973 and 1975 world and 1974 European championships, broke two world and three Olympic records. Her world standards of 327 for a single distance 60 metres and 346 at 30 metres and her double Olympic record totals of 589 at 70 metres, 626 at 60 metres moved her up from fifth to second at the end. She lost the title, however, as the result of her second 50 metres FITA round with a 254 for 22nd place, compared with Miss Ryon's 307 at the same postion.

Miss Ryon's total of 2499 was an Olympic record by some 75 pts. A remarkable competitor was the Polish woman Irena Szydlowska, a silver medallist in Munich and yet at 48 she still held her own for much of the competition before slipping back over the second half.

This was only the second time since 1920 that archery had been included and proved yet another sport where Britain has yet to make any impact. David Pink did equal Ted Gamble's 90 metres record with a 286 but other than that there was little to report.

Shooting

Alas, no Bob Braithwaite to emulate Britain's gold medal of 1968 when he won the clay pigeon shooting nor even as good results as in Munich when John Kynoch came close in the "moving target" for a bronze medal. In fact the best Britain produced was a 12th by Laslo Antal in the free pistol and a 15th by Brian Girling in the rapid fire pistol.

The results were noteworthy in that a woman, Margaret Murdock, took a silver medal in this the one of two Olympic spots where women and men compete on equal footing, the other being the riding events.

Poor weather conditions were responsible for the low scoring in the Olympic trap shooting, the title going to the American Donald Haldeman. It took a shoot off to decide the destination of the silver medal. Haldeman's total would have put him no higher than 11th in Munich.

The rest of the results reached the expected standards: an East German, Uwe Potteck, led another, Harold Vollmar to a gold and silver in an Olympic record in the free pistol. To redress the balance, two West Germans took the major honours in the small bore rifle (prone position) with the winner Karl Heinz Smieszek shooting 99, 100, 100, 100, 100, 100. Yet another double came in the three bore rifle (three positions) with Lanny Bassham taking the gold medal from Margaret Murdock on the basis of three perfect 100s as opposed to two by his female rival. East Germany's second 1–2 came in the rapid fire pistol with another Olympic record, this time by Norbert Klaar while the remaining gold and silver double to go to one country was in the running games target where the Soviet Union collected an Olympic record through Alexandr Gazov.

15

"NO COMMENT"

To the hundreds of millions for whom the Olympic Games are marked by extra long sessions in front of the television, the Montreal Games, like all others, started and ended with harmonious and colourful ceremonies conjuring up all that is best in the human spirit.

But for the international Press—as indeed for so many of those actually taking part in the Games—they began, ended and were dogged throughout by politics, to an extent possibly equalled only by the Berlin Olympiad of 1936 when Hitler attempted to impose his will on the completing nations.

Great individual team performances, tales of triumph and failure, of cheating and sportsmanship there unquestionably were, but they were overshadowed, to the detriment of the competitors in the Games, by a series of international disputes which had little if anything to do with what was going on in the Olympic arenas.

The political controversies were threefold, and all by their timing critical. They began with the refusal of Canada, some days before the Games were to open, to admit members of the team of the Republic of China (Taiwan). The argument of the Canadian Government was that the Taiwan regime was staking a bogus claim to be the government of China, a claim it did not accept and which the majority of the world rejected.

Intensive lobbying for a change of heart began, with the United States making a hastily-withdrawn threat to pull out of the Games and the International Olympic Committee working for compromise. Finally, with most of the Taiwan team waiting in Boston and Detroit for their visas (a handful with dual American nationality were already in Canada) it was accepted by Canada and the IOC that the team could take part in the Games, bear its national flag and have its national anthem played, provided that it competed under the name Taiwan and did not claim to be the team of the Republic of China. The Taiwanese rejected the compromise and returned home to a heroes' welcome.

Then, with the opening ceremony rapidly approaching, a second and more dangerous dispute erupted around the Games. This time it was centred on the team from New Zealand, innocent in its own right but from a country whose Rugby authorities had persisted in sending teams to South Africa and had indeed despatched one there as the Games approached.

Black African nations, motivated partly by anger at the mass shooting of black rioters in Soweto not long before, began to make threatening noises designed to persuade the IOC to tell the New Zealand team to stay at home. When no such decision came, the more militant among them began, raggedly, to pull out.

The first withdrawals, by Tanzania and Mauritius, began before athletes had even begun arriving in Montreal. Others announced before the opening ceremony that they would not compete—Nigeria was one. But as the Queen took the salute for the parade of national teams that traditionally marks the start of the Games, neither she, nor Lord Killanin next to her, could have had any idea how many teams they would see or which team would come out of the tunnel next. In the event 19 failed to show up, but the authorities were left with no idea how many of these would in fact pull out.

On the Sunday, the morning after the opening, the first events got under way. By this time several other nations had said definitely that they would not be taking part, Congo-Brazzaville, Ethiopia, Ghana, Chad and Zambia. But the first clues the organisers had in their cases were when teams or individuals failed to show up for their events. Even this was not a thorough guide as the Egyptians, for example, took part in the Games for three days before deciding to withdraw.

By the time the position stabilised, 24 nations had called their teams home and 33 who had originally planned to take part in the Olympics were absent for a variety of reasons. What made the mass boycott so poignant was that many of the athletes and Olympic officials from these countries fought to the bitter end to stay. The Kenyans fought hardest but gave in after only a day, the Moroccans and Tunisians lasted until the Wednesday, five days after the opening ceremony.

For once in African sport, the politicians were pushing the participants and not the other way round. Whereas sportsmen had long been campaigning for action against South Africa, it had not in the past suited their political leaders to take it. Now, backed up by active lobbyists in Montreal from SANROC (The South African Non-Racial Committee for Olympic Sports) and the Supreme Council for Sport in Africa, the Organisation of African Unity took such a tough line that only two states, Senegal and the Ivory Coast, defied it. This was made up for by symbolic support from Guyana and Iraq, though a number of Caribbean and Arab states who flirted with the idea of withdrawal decided against it.

The mass walkout deprived the Games of a number of star competitors, but they continued nonetheless. As they closed, however, a third political storm blew up, and one which proved doubly embarrassing to Canada as host nation. One of Canada's most notable features is the large communities within it descended from refugees and emigres from lands now under Communist control, notably the Ukraine and the Baltic States. The more militant Ukranians had determined that as the Russians were going to be at the Games in force with a team containing many of their countrymen, they would seize on the occasion to demonstrate powerfully their dislike of the Soviet system and the case for Ukrainian independence. This they did in a fashion that rapidly got under the Russians' skins, with protestors running on to pitches, the burning of the Soviet flag, and a campaign of rumours that Valeriy Borzov, the Ukrainian who lost his 100 metres title by finishing third, and failed to turn up to defend his 200 metres title, had defected to the West.

Thus the Russians were already in an angry mood when one of their divers, 17-year-old Sergei Nemtsamov, did just that. Their anger was doubled by reports in the Canadian papers that when a Rumanian oarsman had sought asylum a couple of days before, he had been assisted by a hostess assigned to the Rumanian team. The effect of this was that they came out fighting, accusing COJO, the committee organising the Games, of planting hostesses on the Soviet team trained in persuading them to defect, and alleging that Nemtsamov had been "kidnapped".

When the Canadians refused to return the diver to the Soviet team despite Soviet claims that, as a minor, he could not legally be granted asylum, the Russians announced bluntly that unless their request was complied with they would withdraw from the final two days' events (it was by now the last Friday of the Games) and pull out of the closing ceremony. As this last included a live television hook-up with Moscow where the 1980 Games are to be held, such an action would have had a serious effect on the front of international good humour which the organisers were still endeavouring to cultivate.

Frenzied negotiations began, in which the IOC took a leading part. The Russians were told firmly that any withdrawal now would jeopardise the 1980 Games, and the Canadians agreed to let Nemtsamov see a Soviet official, though under conditions which were not at first accepted. The meeting duly took place, and a few minutes before the closing ceremony began it was announced that the diver still wanted to stay in Canada and had been given six months in which to reach a final decision. Although a Soviet spokesman alleged Nemtsamov had been "brainwashed", the closing ceremony went ahead unblemished. Nemtsamov later changed his mind and decided to return to the Soviet Union.

Politics apart, the theme of the Games was of the dilemma of COJO, the Montreal committee which had ensured that the Games took place and whose arrangements were, for the most part, excellent. COJO's problem was that it needed to ensure that the Games took place in something like the spirit of openness and friendship envisaged by Baron de Coubertin, and yet at the same time make them so secure that a repetition of the Munich massacre, in which 11 Israelis had died four years previously, was unthinkable.

They succeeded in the latter, but at a price. While humour and craziness burst through from time to time, COJO took itself so seriously that only personal kindness and warmth broke through the barrier of permafrost which Mme Monique Berlioux, executive director of the IOC, described as an "iron collar".

COJO's reaction to her comments was typical. Instead of saying they realised security was suffocating but that it had to be, M. Louis Chantigny, COJO's head of public relations and a man who, in the words of an American reporter, "gave the word 'information' a whole new meaning", launched into Mme Berlioux, a Swiss, for defaming the French–Canadian people. While one ought to have applauded M. Chantigny, who after a few days had earned the active dislike of all but the domestic Press, for saying anything at all, the reluctance of both COJO and himself to accept that she had a valid point did them little credit.

Just how tight the security needed to be was shown by a series of scares about the arrival of Palestinian guerrillas, some based on fact and others apparently "planted" by the Israeli intelligence service in an effort to keep the Canadians up to scratch. These were highlighted by an incident in the Olympic village which led to the expulsion of the Canadian sprinter Robert Martin on his 26th birthday. Martin had smuggled an American male friend—a fellow athlete not competing in the Games—into the Village and kept him there, despite the stringent security, with the acquiescence of his colleagues. Newspaper reports that someone had done just this were denied in the most crushing terms by the Canadian team management after an abortive police investigation, only for grudging apologies to be given once it became clear the entire security apparatus had broken down.

Martin was by no means the only competitor to end the Games prematurely in disgrace. The Russian pentathlete Boris Onishenko, almost certain to win at least a silver, was sent home after it was found that he had been fencing with a "bugged" epée designed to register hits that had not been made. Several boxing judges were suspended for bias and incompetence, a Canadian yachtsman was the first of several competitors to fail dope tests and five Canadian swimmers were expelled from the Olympic Village for breaking the rules about drinking and staying out late.

Amid all this the arguments about security rumbled on. The Canadian armed forces and the local police, faced with the task of protecting the Queen against threats of assassination by Quebec separatists as well as making sure the Games were not disrupted, appeared stretched to the limit. And yet it was not so, as a squad of Montreal police found when they raided the boxing arena at the end of the first week after repeated complaints by journalists and ticket-holders that their seats had been taken. In those seats they found 692 colleagues who had got in free by waving their security passes. They were told not to do so again, but when M. Chantigny was asked about the occurrence he replied that the police had an interest in learning about self-defence.

There was also a chorus of protest about the handling of reporters and photographers by the security forces. For some reason no-one was ever quite able to fathom, all but one of the incidents involved representatives of the West German media. Some of them had clearly been trying to get into restricted areas and had provoked the police; others appeared to have been assaulted without cause. All, plus a Swede, had a hard time in the cells, but in almost every case they either did not reach the courts or were given an absolute dis-

Ludmila Tourisheva makes a most difficult position look matter-of-fact on the beam (above) while a composed Nadia Comaneci (below) looks unusually serious. Right (above) with graceful ease Nadia Comaneci flies off the asymmetrical bars and (below) an impudent pose by the tiny Maria Filatova.

Dave Starbrook holds down the Korean Jeaki Cho to guarantee himself a second successive Olympic judo medal and (below) Pat Cowdell, Britain's only boxing medallist of the Games lands a most effective jab on the chin of Reynaldo Fortaleza during their quarter final match.

The strongest man in the world, Vassili Alexeev, hoists the bar over his head during his successful defence of the super-heavyweight weightlifting title and (below) Kornelia Ender, one of East Germany's wonder-children, powers her way to yet another gold medal.

Britain's only Olympic swimming champion for very many years takes his bow: David Wilkie, after winning the 200 metres breaststroke title. (Below) John Naber, of the United States, during one of his gold medal swims, the 200 metres backstroke.

charge when they got there. Much of the difficulty appeared to have been caused by lack of liaison between COJO and the various security forces; in one classic incident photographers arriving for the canoeing events were placed in an enclosure by COJO, only to be forcibly evicted by the police as the first race got under way.

Two incidents best sum up the heavy-handedness of the organisers compared with the sheer joie de vivre which was never far below the surface as far as the competitors were concerned, and which visitors to Montreal experienced among the crowds dancing to a brass band in the Crescent area, noted for its frantic night life. When a resident complained about the band, it was marched, still playing and accompanied by hundreds of dancers, to the police station, where the desk sergeant sent the revellers, still dancing, on their way.

The first of these occurred early in the second week of the Games—the Tuesday, to be precise—when the Olympic flame in the main arena went out during a cloudburst. Showing great presence of mind, M. Pierre Bouchard, a plumber working in the empty stadium, rushed up the steps of the plinth, kindled a flame with his cigarette lighter and pieces of paper, and relit the contraption. Instead of laughing the whole incident off, COJO officials were horrified. The gas was hurriedly turned off, the Keeper of the Flame summoned to the stadium under police escort and the Flame re-lit with a torch which had in its turn been lit from the authentic Olympic flame. That the flame had gone out at least twice en route to Montreal was conveniently overlooked.

By complete contrast, two British yachtsmen injected just the right note of zany humour into the proceedings after their boat Gift 'Orse had finished well down the field in the Tempest class. Possibly spurred on by the fact that the craft had been donated to them by a cigarette company, they put a match to it and watched it burn until a coastguard cutter rammed it and sent it to the bottom of Lake Ontario. As the craft drifted into the yachtsmen's Valhalla, its crew (David Hunt) remarked wistfully: 'My skipper has style, but not that much. I tried to persuade him to burn with the ship, but he wouldn't agree."

Against this background, and despite everything which might bring the Games into disrepute around the world, Canadians took to the entire Olympic programme with enthusiasm. Montrealers forgot the crippling cost of staging them, turned out to events in force and cheered Mayor Jean Drapeau to the echo at the opening and closing ceremonies. Canadians as a whole suddenly realised that as a nation they had neglected international sport, and that it could be fun.

By some accident of history possibly connected with their erratic climate, Canadians have involved themselves with sports which they share either with the Americans (baseball, American football and basketball), with the Russians (ice hockey) or with nobody (Canadian football). But as the Games wore on there were signs that they might produce a lasting interest in such sports as soccer (73,000 watched the Olympic final between Poland and East Germany), swimming and athletics.

Throughout the Games the Canadian media were searching for a superstar of track and field on whom they could build this interest. They thought they had found one in Diane Jones, a blonde schoolteacher from Saskatoon whom Mick Jagger asked out on the eve of her final. She gave a disappointing performance in the Pentathlon, finishing sixth. But they finally came up with one where they least expected, in the high jump where on the penultimate evening of the Games the third-string Canadian, Greg Joy, won a silver medal in atrocious conditions to become the toast of his countrymen.

Yet whatever the lasting impact of the Games on Canadians (and after the political storms the Canadian Government must have been relieved to see them end) the questions that remain are the same as after previous Olympics, only bigger. Can the Games survive in this or any other form? How can a balance be struck between true amateurs and crypto-professionals? Who determines the criteria for taking part? How can the standard of refereeing be improved? How can a free country restrain spectators from insulting a visiting team, and how, above all, can security be balanced against the neutral zest of competitors? Montreal answered none of these questions, and that it did not do so was amplified by a letter sent at the close from the Greek Prime Minister, Mr. Karamanlis, to Lord Killanin. In it the politician called for the Games to return to their spiritual home of Greece in an effort to end the national jealousies which have dogged them, and to rekindle the true Olympic flame. It was a solution few could see being accepted, but after Moscow in 1980 and probably Teheran in 1984 one wonders how many cities and nations will readily shoulder the burden.

16

WINTER GAMES

THE METAMORPHOSIS of John Curry from being a good figure skater to one of uniquely outstanding ability was not an overnight happening. There was no flash of inspiration which made this quiet Birmingham-born sportsman into the supreme champion of all: European champion, followed by the Olympic gold medal and finally the world title. After that there was nothing further to offer. John had reached the zenith every sportsman, whether amateur or, later in his career, professional, hopes to attain.

The life of John Curry started on September 9th, 1949. He recalls attending his first ice show at the age of six and then naturally gravitated towards the ballet. His father, however, felt it was not sufficiently masculine for his son and suggested ice skating instead. In 1957 he started to skate at the Springhill Ice Rink, near his home in Streetly, before moving first to Silver Blades, Birmingham, and then to the Solihull rink where he learned the basic techniques from coach Ken Vickers.

Curry always gave Vickers his due credit. "At first I was not really devoted to the sport but I must admit that my first coach instilled in me a basic technique which from the earliest age prevented me from incorporating instinctive errors in my programme. I didn't exactly burn the house down with my progress at first. I recall working on the axel for weeks and months in an effort to perfect the movement while my young colleagues were already attempting double axels, before they had learned an adequate single axel."

Soon John was making progress, though. At 16 he came to London to take a part-time job as a bank clerk, earning £50 a month, which enabled him to train at Richmond under such famous coaches as the Swiss, Arnold Gerschwiler, and later Alison Smith. In 1967 he was the British junior champion, but already there were those predicting that his career would never be properly fulfilled as his arm and hand movements would only serve to antagonise the judges, especially the Eastern bloc, who would construe his style as insufficiently masculine. This was not a particularly happy time for John. "I do not have happy memories of this period of my life. I had a small, insignificant job, barely enough money to keep me alive. Yet most important of all I had the facilities to train six to seven hours a day, but with the bank job as well it was a back-breaking task."

1970 saw the start of the breakthrough. He won the British title for the first time, and finished twelfth in the European championships. He lost his crown to Haig Oundjian the following year but started to make an impact in the outside world; seventh in the European, fourteenth in the world. In 1972, Olympic year, he was again champion of Britain, fifth in Europe, ninth in the world and eleventh in the Olympics.

But 1973 was the watershed year. For before fourth placings in Europe and the world, an American industrialist (a devotee of skating) saw him compete, realised his potential and offered him sponsorship. Initially John did not know who his benefactor was, although he learned eventually that his money was responsible for the preparation of not a few famous skaters, including the girl who would take the golden crown at Innsbruck at the same time as John, Dorothy Hammill.

However, the plans almost went awry. With such an offer at stake John had to do materially better than he did in 1972. Alas, he could only finish fourth and, disappointed, he went to his new-found friend and sponsor, Ed Moser, and offered either to release him from his sponsorship or to come to the United States and prepare at Lake Placid with Gus Luss, the coach to Don McKellen, and at Denver with Carlo Fassi, coach to former Olympic champion, Peggy Fleming, and to Dorothy Hammill. In America he could be assured of practice alone on ice. In Britain he had to take his chance while members of the public wobbled their way around the ice.

In 1975 he was second in the European Championships in Copenhagen, after which he declared what everyone had been saying under their breath; that the East European judges were always ganging up on western opposition to ensure their own competitors' success. In his case he was to finish behind Vladimir Kovalev and was to hear and read that certain judges would never give him the points he deserved as they felt his type of skating was not right for the ice. Others were more cruel; encouraging their countries' skaters to make rude remarks about John's programme, that it was "fit for a woman", and so on.

After his attack on the judges the Soviet Federation attempted to have him disqualified, a sure sign that they realised his potential greatness. The request was inevitably rejected and the Russians themselves were given certain discreet warnings about biased markings. After the world championships, in which he was third behind two Russians, Sergei Volkov and Kovalev, John did not attempt to blame the judges as he had skated badly on his own admission.

Then came 1976 and the peak. John explains his final flourish thus; "I learned a lot from Carlo Fassi, who is without doubt the most competent trainer in the world. He knows all the techniques necessary for competition and has practical experience of all the top championships. Moreover he is able to exert a strong psychological influence over his pupils." Fassi also advised John to enrol with the Erhard Seminar Training School. This enabled him to conquer his nerves before competition and go out on to the ice feeling strong, without butterflies in the stomach, and with a cool head. All this from two concentrated weekends in New York.

This was the seal that John Curry needed. Before, both Fassi and Gerschwiler say that when they saw John he had the necessary attributes to become world and Olympic champion. It was merely a question of approach and belief in himself, which EST finally brought home.

And so to Innsbruck and the supreme test for the young man who throughout his career had always attempted to make figure skating into an art instead of the sport it had always been considered. Whereas in previous years he had concentrated on skating a beautiful programme with the jumps an adjunct to the competition (losing favour as a result with the judges) he realised that it was vital to conform to the rules and changed his choreography so that the jumps became the vital part of the programme. And what Jumps, Axels, Lutzs, Spins. They were all there in a performance of such dexterity and sheer perfection never before seen in an Olympics. To say that he was first and the others nowhere does seem a trifle unfair to the Russians, Sergei Volkov, Vladimir Kovalev, the Canadian Toller Cranston (perhaps his nearest rival in style) and even the American Terry Kubicka, who produced a rare backward somersault that nearly didn't come off.

But is was true. There was no other skater and even the overcritical judges could not rob him of his superb glory. Had he skated last in the programme there is little doubt that he would have rated 6·0 (maximum points) nearly all the way. As it was he reaped so many 5·9s that when the other contenders came after him even the Eastern bloc judges did not dare over-mark their men for risk of being lynched by the crowd, or worse, being expelled from the jury for making the entire skating world look completely idiotic. It was Britain's first Winter Games medal since Tony Nash and Robin Dixon won the two-man bob, also in Innsbruck, twelve years earlier and the third figure skating gold medal for Britain, following Madge Syers (1908) and Jeannette Altwegg (1952).

Inevitably, in these Winter Games the Eastern Bloc dominated the medals table—although the biggest surprise was perhaps the two bronze of tiny Lichtenstein, who entered the lists for the first time ever, in both Summer or Winter Games. The Soviet Union and East Germany collected between them 46 medals out of 111 available, with the remainder of the awards split among 14 countries, including France, who despite their massive infusion of money, extensive winter sports programme and thriving tourist season, had to be content with a mere bronze. Canada, as usual, was the only other Commonwealth country in the medal lists with three, one of each colour, from Kathy Kreiner in the women's giant slalom (gold), 500 metres speed skating, Cathy Priestner (silver) and Toller Cranston, bronze in the figure skating.

There was, as is now normal, controversy over the doping tests. Galina Koulakova, perhaps the Soviet Union's most prestigious cross country skiier with eight Olympic medals of various hues to her credit, was tested after placing third in the 5km and found to have minute traces of a prohibited substance inside her. As she was streaming from a cold it did not seem unreasonable to expect that she used a nasal spray and, although it was accepted that the quantity was so minute that it could not possibly have helped her, she was, a trifle harshly, disqualified. However, the IOC Medical Commission was gracious enough to permit her to start in the 10km and 4 × 5kms relay from which she collected a bronze and gold respectively. And as the fourth woman in the 5kms had also been a Russian, Nina Baldicheva, at least that country could not complain that it had lost a medal.

The ice hockey, although it produced a surprisingly classic, sporting, final between those two old rivals the Soviet Union and Czechoslovakia, almost did not take place. The Czechs had had several competitors ruled out because the team doctor had given them certain antibiotics to counteract the epidemic of 'flu which raged through the Olympic Village, but forgot to inform the IOC. Both the International Ice Hockey Federation and the Czech Ice Hockey Federation complained to the IOC about the ban, which affected their captain, Frantisek Pospisil, using as fuel the arguments of Ludwig Prokop, Austrian doctor member of the IOC who declared that the medicine absorbed by the Czech was a tranquilliser, not a stimulant. The Czech trainer, Karel Gut, pointed out that in future any competitor who might have 'flu and wished to cure himself runs the risk of disqualification. The result was that Czechoslovakia lost the two points they had gained against Poland (the match in question) but still made the final easily. There is no doubt that their medical team did try to pull a fast one for they did not report their use of codeine until it was apparent that two of those who had been given the pills would be tested. It had been a gamble which did not pay off. However, they threatened not to play the final if certain of their players were ruled out and in face of this threat the IOC gave way. It would have been a tragic loss had the match not taken place and certainly the victors merited their 4-3 margin.

With the entire winter sports industry and the ski manufacturers, not to mention clothing and other equipment makers, praying for an Austrian ski success, they were not disappointed with Erich Klammer rising above the problems of being favourite on his home course to sweep away with the downhill after as thrilling a run as has ever been seen in an Olympics. He threw away the textbook, seemed to spend as much time in the air as on the ground, took his corners wide, yet overcame a first half deficit on Switzerland's Bernard Russi (1min 13·05sec) and Herbert Plank (Italy) (1 min 13·21sec). Klammer had gone down in 1min 13·24sec and although less than one fifth of a second may seem nothing to mere mortals used to standing in a bus queue for half an hour, to a skiier it is an eternity. Little wonder that Austria mourned after the first section, simply hoping against the odds. Yet that second stretch which is replayed time and again in Austria proved decisive. In that final stretch he made up so much that he actually crossed the winning line in 1min 45·73sec, compared with Russi's 1min 46·06sec, and Plank's 1min 46·59sec. From nineteen one hundredths down he finished thirty-three one hundredths ahead. Also half a second. Victory for Austria, but spare a thought for poor Russi who had been so close to winning his second successive gold medal.

The zenith of all skiing achievements is to win the grand slam in an Olympics. Only Toni Sailer (Austria) and Jean Claude Killy (France) in 1956 and 1968 respectively have achieved this among men but little Rosi Mittermaier came close, so close for West Germany. First the downhill, and a sweeping victory over her rivals, then the slalom and yet another first place. Then with the giant slalom to come Kathy Kreiner, almost apologetically, pushed her into second place, a position 98 per cent of Olympic competitors would have been satisfied to achieve but the margin of defeat, 0·12sec was so small that little wonder Rosi was bitterly upset. Yet she did not complain, nor offer any excuse. Admittedly she was a little surprised by the girl who beat her but not that much. A gate taken too close here, a bad line there, all combined to bring her just that minute fraction off the grand slam.

Despite the fact that the International Olympic Committee is committed to decreasing rather than increasing the Winter and Summer Games programmes, there was one extra event at Innsbruck—Ice dancing, in which the Russian supremacy was again apparent in the flawless form of Ludmilla Pakjomova and Aleksandr Gorshkov, Irina Moiseeva and Andrei Minenkov and Natalia Linichuk and Gennadiy Karponosov, who finished first, second and fourth with only the brave American couple, Colleen O'Connor and James Mills preventing the clean sweep with the bronze medal. However, the story for the gossip writers was the follow up to the famous "affaire" of 1972 in the pairs. In that Games Irina Rodnina and Alexei Oulanov won the gold, Ludmilla Smirnova and Andrei Souraikin, the silver. Scarcely before the Games had finished Oulanov had married Smirnova, leaving Rodnina, the champion and mentor, partnerless. It was thought that she might team up with Souraikin but after trails before their own Russian judges, it was obvious that the spark lacked. Eventually Rodnina picked up Zaitsev, her new partner, off a skating rink and moulded him into her form. As one headline described her, "Amazing Irina—but no Grace". A complete description of a competitor who seemed to be more akin to an automaton than a human being; no errors, no joy, apparently her competition was as much of a duty to her as to a soldier drilling on the barracks square.

The East Germans dominated the bob and luge, using new techniques to produce top competitors, and copied, with a complete lack of success, by Britain. The GDR took sportsmen of the right build, strength and explosive energy, javelin throwers or hurdlers, for instance, at the end of their career, showed them what to do and sat back and waited for the gold medals. Though rare, it is not unique for sportsmen to compete in both Winter and Summer Games; that is, until these Games. In the bob, as an example, the new champions Meinhard Nehmer and Bernhard Germeshausen were top class track and field men; the first had a javelin performance of 81·50m (267ft 4in) and the second was a solid decathlon man with a total of 7,534pts behind him. Among the West Germans, Manfred Schumann, in the silver medal bob, was a former high hurdles Olympic semi finalist.

Altogether a most exciting Winter Games, which also proved that a small country can host at reasonably low cost.

17

RESULTS

Abbreviations

AFG	Afghanistan
AHO	Netherlands Antilles
ALB	Albania
ALG	Algeria
ARG	Argentina
ARS	Saudi Arabia
AUS	Australia
AUT	Austria
BAH	Bahamas
BAR	Barbados
BEL	Belgium
BER	Bermuda
BIR	Burma
BOL	Bolivia
BRA	Brazil
BUL	Bulgaria
CAF	Central African Republic
CAN	Canada
CEY	Ceylon
CGO	Congo
CHA	Chad
CHI	Chile
CIV	Ivory Coast
CMR	Cameroon
COL	Colombia
CRC	Costa Rica
CUB	Cuba
DAH	Dahomey
DEN	Denmark
DOM	Dominican Republic
ECU	Ecuador
ETH	Ethiopia
EGY	Egypt
FIJ	Fiji Islands
FIN	Finland
FRA	France
GAB	Gabon
GBR	United Kingdom
GDR	German Democratic Republic
GER	Germany (West)
GHA	Ghana
GRE	Greece
GUA	Guatemala
GUI	Guinea
GUY	Guyana
HAI	Haiti
HBR	British Honduras
HKB	Hong Kong
HON	Honduras
HUN	Hungary
INA	Indonesia
IND	India
IRL	Ireland
IRN	Iran
IRQ	Iraq
ISL	Iceland
ISR	Israel
ISV	Virgin Islands
ITA	Italy
JAM	Jamaica
JOR	Jordan
JPN	Japan
KEN	Kenya
KHM	Cambodia
KOR	Korea
KUW	Kuwait
LBA	Libya
LBR	Liberia
LES	Lesotho
LIB	Lebanon
LIE	Lichtenstein
LUX	Luxembourg
MAD	Madagascar
MAL	Malaysia
MAR	Morocco
MAW	Malawi
MEX	Mexico
MGL	Mongolia
MLI	Mali
MLT	Malta
MON	Monaco
MRI	Mauritius

NCA	Nicaragua
NEP	Nepal
NETH	Netherlands
NGR	Nigeria
NIG	Niger
NOR	Norway
NZL	New Zealand
PAK	Pakistan
PAN	Panama
PAR	Paraguay
PER	Peru
PHI	Philippines
POL	Poland
POR	Portugal
PRK	Democratic People's Republic of Korea
PUR	Puerto Rico
RHO	Rhodesia
ROC	Republic of China
ROM	Rumania
SAL	El Salvador
SEN	Senegal
SIN	Singapore
SLE	Sierra Leone
SMR	San Marino
SOM	Somali Republic
SPA	Spain
SUD	Sudan
SWIT	Switzerland
SUR	Surinam
SWE	Sweden
SWZ	Swaziland
SYR	Syria
TAN	Tanzania
TCH	Czechoslovakia
THA	Thailand
TOG	Togo
TRI	Trinidad and
TOB	Tobago
TUN	Tunisia
TUR	Turkey
UGA	Uganda
URS	USSR (Soviet Union)
URU	Uruguay
USA	United States of America
VEN	Venezuela
VNM	Vietnam
VOL	Upper Volta
YUG	Yugoslavia
ZAM	Zambia
ZAI	Zaire

SUMMER GAMES

Archery

(*Men*)

			total
1.	Darrell Pace (USA)	(Olympic record)	2571
2.	Hiroshi Michinga (JPN)		2502
3.	Carlo Ferrari (ITA)		2495
4.	Richard McKinney (USA)		2471
5.	Vladimir Chendarov (URS)		2467
6.	Willi Gabriel (GER)		2435
7.	Dave Mann (CAN)		2431
8.	Takanobu Nishi (JPN)		2422
13.	David Anear (AUS)		2407
16.	Edward Gamble (CAN)		2362
21.	David Pink (GBR)		2347
30.	Stewart Littlefair (GBR)		2238

(*Women*)

			total
1.	Luann Ryon (USA)	(Olympic record)	2499
2.	Valentina Kovpan (URS)		2460
3.	Zebiniso Rustamova (URS)		2407
4.	Sun Yong Jang (PRK)		2405
5.	Lucille Lemay (CAN)		2401
6.	Jadwiga Wilejto (POL)		2395
16.	Wanda Allen (CAN)		2303
21.	Patricia Conway (GBR)		2257
23.	Rachael Fenwick (GBR)		2199

Men's Athletics

100 Metres

		sec
1.	Haseley Crawford (TRI)	10·06
2.	Don Quarrie (JAM)	10·08
3.	Valeriy Borzov (URS)	10·14
4.	Harvey Glance (USA)	10·19
5.	Gay Abrahams (PAN)	10·25
6.	John Jones (USA)	10·27
7.	Dieter Kurrat (GDR)	10·31
8.	Petar Petrov (BUL)	10·35

200 Metres

		sec
1.	Don Quarrie (JAM)	20·23
2.	Millard Hampton (USA)	20·29
3.	Dwayne Evans (USA)	20·43
4.	Pietro Mennea (ITA)	20·54
5.	Ruy da Silva (BRA)	20·84
6.	Bogdan Grzejszczak (POL)	20·91
7.	Colin Bradford (JAM)	21·17

abandoned: Haseley Crawford (TRI)

400 Metres

		sec
1.	Alberto Juantorena (CUB)	44·26
2.	Fred Newhouse (USA)	44·40
3.	Herman Frazier (USA)	44·95
4.	Alfons Brijdenbach (BEL)	45·04
5.	Maxie Parks (USA)	45·24
6.	Richard Mitchell (AUS)	45·40
7.	David Jenkins (GBR)	45·57
8.	Jan Werner (POL)	45·63

800 Metres

		min	sec
1.	Alberto Juantorena (CUB) (World record)	1	43·50
2.	Ivo van Damme (BEL)	1	43·86
3.	Richard Wohlhuter (USA)	1	44·12
4.	Willi Wuelbeck (GER)	1	45·26
5.	Steve Ovett (GBR)	1	45·44
6.	Luciano Susanj (YUG)	1	45·75
7.	Sriram Singh (IND)	1	45·77
8.	Carlo Grippo (ITA)	1	48·49

1500 Metres

		min	sec
1.	John Walker (NZL)	3	39·17
2.	Ivo Vandamme (BEL)	3	39·27
3.	Paul Wellmann (GER)	3	39·33
4.	Eamonn Coghlan (IRL)	3	39·51
5.	Frank Clement (GBR)	3	39·65
6.	Richard Wohlhuter (USA)	3	40·64
7.	David Moorcroft (GBR)	3	40·94
8.	Graeme Grouch (AUS)	3	41·80
9.	Janos Zemen (HUN)	3	43·02

5000 Metres

		min	sec
1.	Lasse Viren (FIN)	13	24·76
2.	Dick Quax (NZL)	13	25·16
3.	Klaus Peter Hildenbrand (GER)	13	25·38
4.	Rod Dixon (NZL)	13	25·50
5.	Brendan Foster (GBR)	13	26·19*
6.	Willy Polleunis (BEL)	13	26·99
7.	Ian Stewart (GBR)	13	27·65
8.	Aniceto Silva (POR)	13	29·38
9.	Knut Kvalheim (NOR)	13	30·33
10.	Detlef Uhlemann (GER)	13	31·07

* Olympic record of 13 min 20·34 sec in heat.

10,000 Metres

		min	sec
1.	Lasse Viren (FIN)	27	40·38
2.	Carlos Lopes (POR)	27	45·17
3.	Brendan Foster (GBR)	27	54·92
4.	Tony Simmons (GBR)	27	56·26
5.	Ilie Floroiu (ROM)	27	59·93
6.	Mariano Haro (SPA)	28	00·28
7.	Mark Smet (BEL)	28	02·80
8.	Bernard Ford (GBR)	28	17·28
12.	Chris Wardlaw (AUS)	28	29·91
14.	David Fitzsimons (AUS)	29	17·74

110 Metres Hurdles

		sec
1.	Guy Drut (FRA)	13·30
2.	Alejandro Casanas (CUB)	13·33
3.	Willie Davenport (USA)	13·38
4.	Charles Foster (USA)	13·41
5.	Thomas Munkelt (GDR)	13·44
6.	James Owens (USA)	13·73
7.	Vyacheslav Kulebyakin (URS)	13·93
8.	Victor Myasnikov (URS)	13·94

400 Metres Hurdles

			sec
1.	Edwin Moses (USA)	(World record)	47·64
2.	Michael Shine (USA)		48·69
3.	Evgeniy Gavrilenko (URS)		49·45
4.	Quentin Wheeler (USA)		49·86
5.	Jose Carvalho (POR)		49·94
6.	Yanko Bratanov (EUL)		50·03
7.	Damaso Alfonso (CUB)		50·19
8.	Alan Pascoe (GBR)		51·29

3000 Metres Steeplechase

			min	sec
1.	Anders Garderud (SWE)	(World record)	8	08·02
2.	Bronislaw Malinowski (POL)		8	09·11
3.	Frank Baumgartl (GDR)		8	10·36
4.	Tapio Kantanen (FIN)		8	12·60
5.	Michael Karst (GER)		8	20·14
6.	Evan Robertson (NZL)		8	21·08
7.	Dan Glans (SWE)		8	21·53
8.	Antonio Campos (SPA)		8	22·65
9.	Dennis Coates (GBR)		8	22·99
11.	Tony Staynings (GBR)		8	33·66

Marathon

			hr	min	sec
1.	Waldemar Cierpinski (GDR)	(Olympic record)	2	09	55·0
2.	Frank Shorter (USA)		2	10	45·8
3.	Karel Lismont (BEL)		2	11	12·6
4.	Don Kardong (USA)		2	11	15·8
5.	Lasse Viren (FIN)		2	13	10·8
6.	Jerome Drayton (CAN)		2	13	30·0
7.	Leonid Mosseev (URS)		2	13	33·4
8.	Franco Fara (ITA)		2	14	24·6
17.	Jack Foster (NZL)		2	17	53·4
26.	Jeff Norman (GBR)		2	20	04·8
31.	Keith Angus (GBR)		2	22	18·6
45.	Barry Watson (GBR)		2	28	32·2

20 Kilometres Walk

		hr	min	sec
1.	Daniel Bautista (MEX)	1	24	40·6
2.	Hans Reimann (GDR)	1	25	13·8
3.	Peter Frenkel (GDR)	1	25	29·4
4.	Karl-Heinz Stadtmuller (GDR)	1	26	50·6
5.	Raul Gonzalez (MEX)	1	28	18·2
6.	Armando Zanbaldo (ITA)	1	28	25·2
11.	Brian Adams (GBR)	1	30	46·2
12.	Ross Haywood (AUS)	1	30	59·2
14.	Oliver Flynn (GBR)	1	31	42·4
23.	Marcel Jobin (CAN)	1	34	33·4
30.	Paul Nihill (GBR)	1	36	40·4

High Jump

		ft	in
1.	Jacek Wszola (POL)	7	4¾
2.	Greg Joy (CAN)	7	3¾
3.	Dwight Stones (USA)	7	3
4.	Sergey Budalov (URS)	7	3
5.	Sergey Seniukov (URS)	7	1¾
6.	Rodolfo Bergamo (ITA)	7	1¾
7.	Rolf Beilschmidt (GDR)	7	1¾
8.	Jesper Torring (DEN)	7	1¾
12.	Claude Ferragne (CAN)	7	0¼

Long Jump

		ft	in
1.	Arnie Robinson (USA)	27	4¾
2.	Randy Williams (USA)	26	7¾
3.	Frank Wartenburg (GDR)	26	3¾
4.	Jacques Rousseau (FRA)	26	3¾
4.	Joao de Oliviera (BRA)	26	3¾
6.	Nenad Stekic (YUG)	25	10¾
7.	Valeriy Podlujnyi (URS)	25	10¼
8.	Hans Baumgartner (GER)	25	8¾

Triple Jump

		ft	in
1.	Viktor Saneyev (URS)	56	8¾
2.	James Butts (USA)	56	4½
3.	Joao de Oliviera (BRA)	55	5½
4.	Pedro Perez (CUB)	55	1¾
5.	Tommy Haynes (USA)	55	0¾
6.	Wolfgang Komsee (GER)	54	8¾
7.	Eugenius Biskipski (POL)	54	1¼
8.	Carol Corbu (ROM)	53	11

Pole Vault

		ft	in
1.	Tadeusz Slusarski (POL) (Equals Olypmpic rcd)	18	0½
2.	Antti Kalliomaki (FIN)	18	0½
3.	Dave Roberts (USA)	18	0½
4.	Patrick Abada (FRA)	17	10½
5.	Wojciech Buciarski (POL)	17	10½
6.	Earl Bell (USA)	17	10½
7.	Michel Bellot (FRA)	17	8½
8.	Itsuo Takanezawa (JPN)	17	8½
12.	Don Baird (AUS)	17	2¾
16.	Brian Hooper (GBR)	16	5

Shot Putt

		ft	in
1.	Udo Beyer (GDR)	69	0¾
2.	Evgeni Mironov (URS)	69	0
3.	Alexander Barisnikov (URS)	68	10¾*
4.	Al Feuerbach (USA)	67	5
5.	Hans Peter Gies (GDR)	67	2
6.	Geoff Capes (GBR)	66	9½

* Olympic record of 69ft 11½ in qualifying round.

Discus

		ft	in
1.	Mac Wilkins (USA)	221	5*
2.	Wolfgang Schmidt (GDR)	217	3
3.	John Powell (USA)	215	6
4.	Norbert Thiede (GDR)	210	11
5.	Siegfried Pachale (GDR)	210	9
6.	Pentti Kahma (FIN)	207	1
7.	Knut Hjeltnes (NOR)	206	10
8.	Jay Silvester (USA)	203	4

* Olympic record of 224ft in qualifying round.

Hammer

		ft	in
1.	Yuriy Sedyh (URS) (Olympic record)	254	4
2.	Alexey Spiridinov (URS)	249	7
3.	Anatoliy Bondarchuk (URS)	247	7½
4.	Karl Heinz Riehm (GER)	247	7
5.	Walter Schmidt (GER)	245	2
6.	Jochen Sachse (GDR)	243	9
7.	Chris Black (GBR)	240	1
12.	Peter Farmer (AUS)	223	1

Javelin

			ft	in
1.	Miklos Nemeth (HUN)	(World record)	310	4
2.	Hannu Siitonen (FIN)		288	5
3.	Gheorghe Megelea (ROM)		285	11
4.	Piotr Bielczyk (POL)		283	9
5.	Sam Colson (USA)		282	8
6.	Vasiliy Ershov (URS)		279	8
7.	Seppo Hovinen (FIN)		276	5
8.	Janis Lusis (URS)		263	4
11.	Philip Olsen (CAN)		254	11

Decathlon

			pts
1.	Bruce Jenner (USA)	(World record)	8618
2.	Guido Kratschmer (GER)		8411
3.	Nikolay Avilov (URS)		8369
4.	Raimo Pihl (SWE)		8218
5.	Ryszard Skowronek (POL)		8113
6.	Siegfried Stark (SDR)		8048
7.	Leonid Litvinenko (URS)		8025
8.	Lennart Hedmark (SWE)		7974
18.	Daley Thompson (GBR)		7434

4 × 100 Metres

		sec
1.	United States	38·33
2.	East Germany	38·66
3.	Soviet Union	38·78
4.	Poland	38·83
5.	Cuba	39·01
6.	Italy	39·08
7.	France	39·16
8.	Canada	39·47

4 × 400 Metres

		min	sec
1.	United States	2	58·56
2.	Poland	3	01·83
3.	West Germany	3	01·98
4.	Canada	3	02·64
5.	Jamaica	3	02·84
6.	Trinidad & Tobago	3	03·46
7.	Cuba	3	03·81
8.	Finland	3	06·51

Women's Atheletics

100 Metres

			sec
1.	Annagret Richter (GER)		11·08 *
2.	Renate Stecher (GDR)		11·13
3.	Inge Helten (GER)		11·17
4.	Raelene Boyle (AUS)		11·23
5.	Evelyn Ashford (USA)		11·24
6.	Chandra Cheeseborough (USA)		11·31
7.	Andrea Lynch (GBR)		11·32
8.	Marlis Oelsner (GDR)		11·34

* Set world record of 11·01 sec in semi-finals.

200 Metres

			sec
1.	Barbel Eckert (GDR)	(Olympic record)	22·37
2.	Annegret Richter (GER)		22·39
3.	Renate Stecher (GDR)		22·47
4.	Carla Bodendorf (GDR)		22·64
5.	Inge Helten (GER)		22·68
6.	Tatyana Prorochenko (URS)		23·03
7.	Denise Robertson (AUS)		23·05
8.	Chantal Rega (FRA)		23·09

400 Metres

			sec
1.	Irena Szewinska (POL)	(World record)	49·29
2.	Christina Brehmer (GDR)		50·51
3.	Ellen Streidt (GDR)		50·55
4.	Pirjo Haggman (FIN)		50·56
5.	Rosalyn Bryant (USA)		50·65
6.	Sheila Ingram (USA)		50·90
7.	Riita Salin (FIN)		50·98
8.	Debra Sapenter (USA)		51·66

800 Metres

		min	sec
1.	Tatiana Kazankina (URS) (World record)	1	54·94
2.	Nikolina Chtereva (BUL)	1	55·42
3.	Elfi Zinn (GDR)	1	55·60
4.	Anita Weiss (GDR)	1	55·74
5.	Svetlana Strykina (URS)	1	56·44
6.	Svetlana Zlateva (BUL)	1	57·21
7.	Doris Gluth (GDR)	1	58·99
8.	Miriana Wuman (ROM)	2	02·21

1500 Metres

		min	sec
1.	Tatiana Kazankina (URS)	4	05·48
2.	Gunhild Hoffmeister (GDR)	4	06·02
3.	Ulrike Klapezynski (GDR)	4	06·09
4.	Nikolina Chtereva (BUL)	4	06·57
5.	Ludmilla Bragina (URS)	4	07·20
6.	Gabriella Dorio (ITA)	4	07·27
7.	Ellen Wellman (GER)	4	07·91
8.	Janice Merrill (USA)	4	08·54
9.	Nina Holmen (FIN)	4	09·55

100 Metres Hurdles

		sec
1.	Johanna Schaller (GDR)	12·77
2.	Tatiana Anasimova (RUS)	12·78
3.	Natalia Lebedeva (URS)	12·80
4.	Gudrun Berend (GDR)	12·82
5.	Grazyna Rabsztyn (POL	12·96
6.	Esther Rot (ISR)	13·04
7.	Valeria Stefanescu (ROM)	13·35
8.	Ilieana Ongar (ITA)	13·51

High Jump

		ft	in
1.	Rosemarie Ackermann (GDR) (Olympic rcd)	6	4
2.	Sara Simeoni (ITA)	6	3¼
3.	Yorkanka Blagoeva (BUL)	6	3¼
4.	Maria Mcranova (TCH)	6	2½
5.	Joni Huntley (USA)	6	2½
6.	Tatyana Shlyahto (URS)	6	1¾
7.	Annette Tannander (SWE)	6	1¾
8.	Cornelia Popa (ROM)	6	1¾
10.	Julie White (CAN)	6	1¾
20.	Louise Graeme (CAN)	5	10

Long Jump

		ft	in
1.	Angela Voigt (GDR)	22	0½
2.	Kathy McMillan (USA)	21	10¾
3.	Lidiya Alfeeva (URS)	21	7¾
4.	Siegrun Siegl (GDR)	21	7½
5.	Ildiko Szabo (HUN)	21	6¾
6.	Jarmila Nygrynova (TCH)	21	5½
9.	Sue Reeve (GBR)	20	7

Shot Putt

			ft	in
1.	Ivanka Christova (BUL)	(Olympic record)	69	5
2.	Nadejda Chijova (URS)		68	9¼
3.	Helena Fibingerova (TCH)		67	9¾
4.	Marianne Adam (GDR)		67	5
5.	Ilona Schoknecht (GDR)		67	4¾
6.	Margitta Droese (GDR)		64	11¼
7.	Eva Wilms (GER)		63	3½
8.	Elena Stoyanova (BUL)		61	11¾
13.	Lucette Moreau (CAN)		50	9½

Discus

			ft	in
1.	Evelin Schlaak (GDR)	(Olympic record)	226	4
2.	Maria Vergova (BUL)		220	9
3.	Gabriele Hinzmann (GDR)		219	3
4.	Faina Melnik (URS)		217	10
5.	Sabine Engel (GDR)		216	1
6.	Argentina Menis (ROM)		214	6
7.	Maria Betancourt (CUB)		209	6
8.	Natalia Gorbacheva (URS)		208	2

Javelin

			ft	in
1.	Ruth Fuchs (GDR)	(Olympic record)	216	4
2.	Marion Becker (GER)		212	3
3.	Kathy Schmidt (USA)		209	10
4.	Jacqueline Hein (GDR)		209	5
5.	Sabine Sebrowski (GDR)		206	11
6.	Svetlana Babich (URS)		194	11
10.	Tessa Sanderson (GBR)		187	0

Pentathlon

		pts
1.	Siegrun Siegl (GDR)	4745
2.	Christine Laser (GDR)	4745
3.	Burglinda Pollak (GDR)	4740
4.	Liudmila Popovskaya (URS)	4700
5.	Nadejda Tkachenko (URS)	4669
6.	Diane Jones (CAN)	4582
12.	Sue Longdon (GBR)	4276
15.	Andrea Bruce (JAM)	4198
18.	Miriama Tuisorisori (FIJ)	3827

4 × 100 Metres

			sec
1.	East Germany	(Olympic record	42·55
2.	West Germany		42·59
3.	Soviet Union		43·09
4.	Canada		43·17
5.	Australia		43·18
6.	Jamaica		43·24
7.	United States		43·35
8.	Great Britain (Wendy Clarke, Denise Ramsden, Sharon Colyear, Andrea Lynch)		43·79

4 × 400 Metres

			min	sec
1.	East Germany	(World record)	3	19·23
2.	United States		3	22·81
3.	Soviet Union		3	24·24
4.	Australia		3	25·56
5.	West Germany		3	25·71
6.	Finland		3	25·87
7.	Great Britain (Liz Barnes, Gladys Taylor, Verona Elder, Donna Murray)		3	28·01
8.	Canada		3	28·91

Basketball

Finals (*Men*)

Yugoslavia 74, United States 95; Soviet Union 100, Canada 72; Italy 98, Czechoslovakia 75; Australia 81, Cuba 92; Puerto Rico 89, Mexico 84.

Standings

1. United States
2. Yugoslavia
3. Soviet Union
4. Canada
5. Italy
6. Czechoslovakia
7. Australia

Leading Scorers

	baskets
Edward Palubinskas (AUS)	219
Arturo Guerrero (MEX)	167
Philip Tollestrup (CAN)	149
Alejandro Urgelles (CUB)	126
Ruperto Herrera (CUB)	122
Adrian Dantley (USA)	116

Women

			baskets		
	won	lost	for	against	pts
1. Soviet Union	5	0	504	346	10
2. United States	3	2	415	417	8
3. Bulgaria	3	2	365	377	8
4. Czechoslovakia	2	3	351	359	7
5. Japan	2	3	405	400	7
6. Canada	0	5	336	477	5

Boxing

48 Kilogrammes
1. Jorge Hernandez (CUB)
2. Uk Byong Li (PRK)
3. Payao Pooltarat (THA)
3. Orlando Maldonado (PUR).

51 Kilogrammes
1. Leo Randolph (USA)
2. Ramon Duvalon (CUB)
3. David Torosyan (URS)
3. Leszek Blazynski (POL)

54 Kilogrammes
1. Yong Jo Gu (PRK)
2. Charles Mooney (USA)
3. Patrick Cowdell (GBR)
3. Victor Rybakov (URS)

57 Kilogrammes
1. Angel Herrera (CUB)
2. Richard Nowakowski (GDR)
3. Leszek Kosedowski (POL)
3. Davey Armstrong (USA)

60 Kilogrammes
1. Howard Davis (USA)
2. Simion Cutov (ROM)
3. Vasiliy Solomin (URS)
3. Tzvetan Tzvetkov (BUL)

63·5 Kilogrammes
1. Ray Leonard (USA)
2. Andres Aldama (CUB)
3. Vladimir Kolev (BUL)
3. Kazimierz Szczerba (POL)

67 Kilogrammes
1. Jochen Bachfeld (GDR)
2. Pedro Gamarro (VEN)
3. Reinhard Skricek (GER)
3. Victor Zilberman (ROM)

71 Kilogrammes
1. Jerzy Rybicki (POL)
2. Tadija Kacar (YUG)
3. Victor Savchenko (URS)
3. Rolando Garbey (CUB)

75 Kilogrammes
1. Michael Spinks (USA)
2. Rufat Riskiev (URS)
3. Luis Martinez (CUB)
3. Alec Nastac (ROM)

81 Kilogrammes
1. Leon Spinks (USA)
2. Sixto Soria (CUB)
3. Costica Dafinoiu (ROM)
3. Janusz Gortat (POL)

Over 81 Kilogrammes
1. Teofilo Stevenson (CUB)
2. Mircea Simon (ROM)
3. Clarence Hill (BER)
3. Johnny Tate (USA)

Canoeing

K1 500 Metres (Men)

		min	sec
1.	Vasile Diba (ROM)	1	46·41
2.	Zoltan Sztanity (HUN)	1	46·95
3.	Rudiger Helm (GDR)	1	48·30
4.	Herminio Menendez (ESP)	1	48·40
5.	Grzegorz Sledziewski (POL)	1	48·49
6.	Sergey Lizunov (URS)	1	49·21
7.	Oreste Perri (ITA)	1	50·27
8.	Douglar Parnham (GBR)	1	50·33

K2 500 Metres (Men)

		min	sec
1.	East Germany	1	35·87
2.	Soviet Union	1	36·81
3.	Rumania	1	37·43
4.	Spain	1	38·50
5.	Hungary	1	38·81
6.	Finland	1	39·59
7.	Sweden	1	39·63
8.	Australia	1	39·77

K1 1000 Metres (Men)

		min	sec
1.	Rudiger Helm (GDR)	3	48·20
2.	Geza Csapo (HUN)	3	48·84
3.	Vasile Deba (ROM)	3	49·65
4.	Oreste Perri (ITA)	3	51·13
5.	Aleksandr Shaparenko (URS)	3	51·45
6.	Berndt Andersson (SWE)	3	52·64
7.	Douglas Parnham (GBR)	3	52·64
8.	Grzegorz Sledziewski (POL)	3	54·29

K2 1000 Metres (Men)

		min	sec
1.	Soviet Union	3	29·01
2.	East Germany	3	29·33
3.	Hungary	3	30·36
4.	France	3	35·05
5.	Spain	3	33·16
6.	Belgium	3	33·86
7.	Rumania	3	34·27
8.	Canada	3	34·46

K4 1000 Metres (Men)

		min	sec
1.	Soviet Union	3	08·69
2.	Spain	3	08·95
3.	East Germany	3	10·76
4.	Rumania	3	11·35
5.	Poland	3	12·17
6.	Norway	3	12·28
7.	Bulgaria	3	12·94
8.	Hungary	3	14·67

C1 1000 Metres (Men)

		min	sec
1.	Ljubek Matija (YUG)	4	09·51
2.	Vasiliy Urchenko (URS)	4	12·57
3.	Ramas Wichmann (HUN)	4	14·11
4.	Borislav Ananiev (BUL)	4	14·41
5.	Ivan Patzaichin (ROM)	4	15·08
6.	Iche Roland (FRA)	4	18·23
7.	Stephan Wildrief (GDR)	4	22·43
8.	Ulrich Eicke (GER)	4	22·77

C2 1000 Metres (Men)

		min	sec
1.	Soviet Union	3	52·76
2.	Rumania	3	54·28
3.	Hungary	3	55·66
4.	Poland	3	59·56
5.	East Germany	4	00·37
6.	Czechoslovakia	4	01·48
7.	Bulgaria	4	02·44
8.	West Germany	4	03·86

K1 500 Metres (Women)

		min	sec
1.	Carola Zirzow (GDR)	2	01·05
2.	Tatiana Korshunova (URS)	2	03·07
3.	Klara Rajnai (HUN)	2	05·01
4.	Ewa Kaminska (POL)	2	05·16
5.	Maria Mihoreanu (ROM)	2	05·40
6.	Anastazie Hajna (TCH)	2	06·72
7.	Julie Leach (USA)	2	06·92
8.	Irene Peppinhage (GER)	2	07·80

K2 500 Metres (Women)

		min	sec
1.	Soviet Union	1	51·15
2.	Hungary	1	51·69
3.	East Germany	1	51·81
4.	Rumania	1	53·77
5.	West Germany	1	53·86
6.	Poland	1	55·05
7.	Bulgaria	1	55·95
8.	Canada	1	56·75

Cycling

1000 Metres Time Trial

		min	sec
1.	Klaus Jurgen Grunke (GDR)	1	05·927
2.	Michel Vaarten (BEL)	1	07·516
3.	Niels Fredborg (DEN)	1	07·617
4.	Janusz Kierzkowski (POL)	1	07·660
5.	Eric Vermeulen (FRA)	1	07·846
6.	Hans Michalsky (GER)	1	07·878
11.	David Weller (JAM)	1	08·534
12.	Stephen Goodall (AUS)	1	08·610
13.	Jocelyn Lovell (CAN)	1	08·852
19.	Paul Medhurst (GBR)	1	10·167
20.	Anthony Sellier (ANT)	1	11·103

4000 Metres Team Pursuit

1. West Germany bt
2. Soviet Union
3. Great Britain (Ian Banbury, Michael Bennett, Robin Croker, Ian Hallam bt
4. East Germany

4000 Metres Individual Pursuit

		min	sec
1.	Gregor Braun (GER)	4	47·61
2.	Herman Ponsteen (HOL)	4	49·72
3.	Thomas Huschke (GDR)	4	52·71
4.	Vladimir Osokin (URS)	4	57·34

100 Kilometres Team Time Trial

		hr	min	sec
1.	USSR	2	08	53
2.	Poland	2	09	13
3.	Denmark	2	12	20
4.	West Germany	2	12	35
5.	Czechoslovakia	2	12	56
6.	Great Britain (Paul Carbutt, Phil Griffiths, Dudley Hayton, Bill Nickson)	2	13	10
9.	Australia	2	13	43
16.	Canada	2	17	15
26.	Hong Kong	2	39	43

27 teams started, 26 finished

Scratch Sprint

1. Anton Tkac (TCH) bt
2. Daniel Morelin (FRA)
3. Hans Jurgen Geschke (GDR) bt
4. Dieter Berkmann (GER)
5. Sergei Kravtsov (URS)
6. Yoshika Cho (JPN)
7. Niels Freborg (DEN)
8. Giorgio Rossi (ITA)

Individual Road Race

		hr	min	sec
1.	Bernt Johansson (SWE)	4	46	52·0
2.	Giuseppe Martinelli (ITA)		+31 sec	
3.	Mieczysl Nowicki (POL)		group	
4.	Alfons de Wolf (BEL)		,,	
5.	Nikolai Gorelev (URS)		,,	
6.	George Mount (USA)		,,	
7.	Jean Rene Bernardeau (FRA)		,,	
8.	Vitterio Algeri (ITA)		,,	
15.	Garry Bell (NZL)	+2	min 9	sec
24.	Pierre Harvey (CAN)		group	
28.	Clyde Sefton (AUS)		,,	
34.	Remo Sansonetti (AUS)		,,	
35.	Joseph Waugh (GBR)		,,	
42.	Dudley Hayton (GBR)	+7	min 34 sec	

Equestrian Sports

Three Day Event
Team

		pts
1.	United States	441·00
2.	West Germany	584·60
3.	Australia	599·54
4.	Italy	682·24
5.	Soviet Union	721·55
6.	Canada	808·81
7.	Ireland	822·05

Eliminated

Great Britain—	Lucinda Prior-Palmer on Be Fair	ret.
	Richard Meade on Jacob Jones	141·35
	Hugh Thomas on Playamar	ret.
	Princess Anne on Goodwill	299·30

Individual

		dressage	cross country	show jumping	pts
1.	Edmund Coffin (USA)	63·59	50·4	00	114·99
2.	John Plumb (USA)	66·25	49·6	10·00	125·85
3.	Karl Schulz (Ger)	46·25	63·2	20·00	129·45
4.	Richard Meade (GBR)	73·75	57·6	10·00	141·35
5.	Wayne Roycroft (AUS)	80·84	97·2	00	178·04
6.	Gerard Sinnott (IRL)	101·25	77·6	00	178·85
11.	Juliet Graham (CAN)	110·84	81·6	10·25	202·69
12.	Mervyn Bennett (AUS)	120·84	85·2	00	206·04
24.	Princess Anne (GBR)	91·25	204·8	3·25	299·30

Grand Prix (Team) Show Jumping

		pt
1.	France	40·00
2.	West Germany	44·00
3.	Belgium	63·00
4.	United States	64·00
5.	Canada	64·50
6.	Spain	71·00
7.	Great Britain (Roland Fernyhough, Peter Robeson, Debbie Johnsey, Graham Fletcher)	76·00

Jumping Grand Prix

		pt
1.	Alwin Schockemoehle (GER)	0·00
2.	(after jump off) Michel Vaillancourt (CAN)	12·00
3.	(after jump off) Francois Mathy (BEL)	12·00
4.	(after jump off) Debbie Johnsey (GBR)	12·00
5.	Guy Creighton (AUS)	16·00
5.	Marcel Rozier (FRA)	16·00
5.	Frank Chapot (USA)	16·00
5.	Hugo Simon (AUT)	16·00
14.	Peter Robeson (GBR)	27·75

Individual Dressage

		pt
1.	Christine Stueckelberger (SUI)	1486·0
2.	Harry Boldt (GER)	1435·0
3.	Reiner Klimke (GER)	1395·0
4.	Gabriela Grillo (GER)	1257·0
5.	Dorothy Morkis (USA)	1249·0
6.	Viktor Ugriomov (URS)	1247·0
7.	Chris Boylen (CAN)	1217·0
11.	Lorraine Stubbs (CAN)	1153·0

Team Dressage

		total
1.	West Germany	5155·0
2.	Switzerland	4684·0
3.	United States	4647·0
4.	Soviet Union	4542·0
5.	Canada	4538·0
6.	Denmark	4448·0
7.	Holland	4380·0
8.	Great Britain (Sarah Whitmore, Jennie Loriston Clarke, Diana Mason)	4076·0

Fencing

Individual Foil (*Men*)

		wins	hits given	hits rcd
1.	Fabio dal Zotto (ITA)	4	24	15 (b)
2.	Alexandr Romankov (URS)	4	21	13 (b)
3.	Bernard Talvet (FRA)	3	19	21
4.	Vassili Stankovich (URS)	2	19	18
5.	Frederic Pietruska (FRA)	2	13	19
6.	Gregory Benko (AUS)	0	15	25

(b) After fight off.

Team Foil (*Men*)

		wins	hits given	hits recd
1.	West Germany	9	64	57
2.	Italy	6	57	64
3.	France	9	55	36
4.	Soviet Union	4	36	55
5.	Poland	9	48	24
6.	Great Britain (Nicholas Bell, Barry Paul, Robert Bruniges, Graham Paul)	1	24	48

Individual Epée (*Men*)

		wins	hits given	hits rcd
1.	Alexander Pusch (GER)	3	22	18 (b)
2.	Jurgen Hehn (GER)	3	19	20 (b)
3.	Gyozo Kulcsar (HUN)	3	22	19 (b)
4.	Istvan Osztrics (HUN)	2	18	20
5.	Jerzy Janikowski (POL)	2	20	21
6.	Rolf Edling (SWE)	2	18	21
13.	William Johnson (GBR)			
28.	Edward Bourne (GBR)			
39.	Timothy Belsen (GBR)			

(b) After fight off.

Teofilo Stevenson deals savagely with one of his early opponents, the Finn Pekka Ruokola, on the way towards his second gold medal. (Below) An excited British pursuit bronze medal team hold their mascot aloft on the medal stand.

John Curry during his immaculate display of figure skating which brought Britain a rare Winter Games gold medal and put Curry on the path to a grand slam of Olympic, World and European titles.

"A Study in Perfection" by the Ice Dance champions Ludmila Pakhomova and Alexsander Gorshkov, and (below) the West German skier Rosi Mittermaier takes the air during the downhill run en route for her second gold medal of the games.

A ski-jumper's view of the City of Innsbruck as he soars high above the heads of the spectators.

Epée Team (Men)

		wins	hits given	hits rcd
1.	Sweden	8	64	59
2.	West Germany	5	59	64
3.	Switzerland	9	57	43
4.	Hungary	3	43	57
5.	Soviet Union	9	54	31
6.	Rumania	2	31	54
9.	Great Britain			
11.	Canada			

Individual Sabre

		wins	hits given	hits rcd
1.	Viktor Krovonouskov (URS)	5	25	14
2.	Vladimir Nazylmov (URS)	4	23	18
3.	Viktor Sidiak (URS)	3	22	20
4.	Ioan Pop (ROM)	2	19	20
5.	Mario Montano (ITA)	1	16	21
6.	Michele Maffei (ITA)	0	13	25
27.	Richard Cohen (GBR)			
30.	Marc Lavoie (CAN)			
31.	John Deanfield (GBR)			
32.	Eli Sukunda (CAN)			
34.	Peter Mather (GBR)			

Team Sabre (Men)

		wins	hits given	hits rcd
1.	Soviet Union	9	44	59
2.	Italy	4	59	44
3.	Rumania	9	55	36
4.	Hungary	4	36	55
5.	Cuba	9	66	56
6.	Poland	6	55	66

9. Great Britain (Bill Hoskyns, Peter Mather, John Deanfield, Richard Cohen).

Foil (Women)

		wins	hits given	hits rcd
1.	Ildiko Schwarczenbereer (HUN)	8	6	15
2.	Maria Collino (ITAL)	8	12	12
3.	Elena Belova (URS)	6	2	19
4.	Brigitte Dumont (FRA)	4	0	17
5.	Cornelia Hamisch (GER)	2	−9	22
6.	Ildiko Bobis (HUN)	2	−11	24
13.	Susan Wrigglesworth (GBR)			
19.	Clare Halsted (GBR)			
22.	Wendy Agar (GBR)			

Women's team foil

		wins	hits given	hits rcd
1.	Soviet Union	9	52	26
2.	France	2	26	52
3.	Hungary	9	53	39
4.	West Germany	4	39	53
5.	Italy	9	63	64
6.	Poland	7	64	63
7.	Great Britain (Wendy Ager, Susan Wrigglesworth, Hilary Cawthorne, Clare Halsted)			
9.	Canada			

Gymnastics

Team Competition (Men)

		pt
1.	Japan (Hasato Igarashi, Shun Fujimoto, Sawao Kato, Hiroshi Kajiyama, Eizo Kemmotsu, Mitsuo Tsukahara)	576·85
2.	Soviet Union	576·45
3.	East Germany	564·65
4.	Hungary	564·45
5.	West Germany	557·40
6.	Rumania	557·30

Individual All Round Competition (Men)

1.	Nikolai Andrianov (URS)	116·650
2.	Sawao Kato (JPN)	115·650
3.	Mitsuo Tsukahara (JPN)	115·575
4.	Alexandr Ditiatin (URS)	115·525
5.	Hiroshi Kajiyama (JPN)	115·425
6.	Andrzej Szajina (POL)	114·625
22.	Philip Delesalle (CAN)	110·750
35.	Pierre Leclerc (CAN)	73·750

Floor Exercises (Men)

1.	Nikolai Andrianov (URS)	19·450
2.	Vladimir Marchenko (URS)	19·425
3.	Peter Kormann (USA)	19·300
4.	Roland Bruckner (GDR)	19·275
5.	Sawao Kato (JPN)	19·250
6.	Eizo Kemmotsu (JPN)	19·100

Side Horse (Men)

1.	Zoltan Magyar (HUN)	19·700
2.	Eizo Kemmotsu (JPN)	19·575
3.	Nikolai Andrianov (URS)	19·525
3.	Michael Nikolay (URS)	19·525
5.	Sawao Kato (JPN)	19·400
6.	Alexandr Ditiatin (URS)	19·350

Rings (Men)

		pt
1.	Nikolai Andrianov (URS)	19·650
2.	Alexandr Ditiatin (URS)	19·550
3.	Danut Grecu (ROM)	19·500
4.	Ferenc Donath (HUN)	19·200
5.	Eizo Kemmotsu (JPN)	19·175
6.	Sawao Kato (JPN)	19·125

Vault (Men)

1.	Nikolai Andrianov (URS)	19·450
2.	Mitsuo Tsukahara (JPN)	19·375
3.	Hiroshi Kajiyama (JPN)	19·275
4.	Danut Grecu (ROM)	19·200
5.	Zoltan Magyar (HUN)	19·150
5.	Imre Molnar (HUN)	19·150

Parallel Bars (Men)

1.	Sawao Kato (JPN)	19·675
2.	Nikolai Andrianov (URS)	19·500
3.	Mitsuo Tsukahara (JPN)	19·475
4.	Bernd Jeger (GDR)	19·200
5.	Miloslav Netusil (TCH)	19·125
6.	Andrzej Szajna (POL)	18·850

Horizontal Bar (Men)

1.	Mitsuo Tsukahara (JPN)	19·675
2.	Eizo Kemmotsu (JPN)	19·500
3.	Eberhard Gienger (GER)	19·475
3.	Henri Boerio (FRA)	19·475
5.	Gennadi Kryssin (URS)	19·250
6.	Ferenc Donath (HUN)	19·200

Team Competition (Women)

1.	Soviet Union (Svetlana Grozdova, Elvira Saadi, Maria Filatova, Ludmila Tourisheva, Nelli Kim)	390.35
2.	Rumania	387·15
3.	East Germany	385·10
4.	Hungary	380·15
5.	Czechoslovakia	378·25
6.	United States	375·05

Individual All Round Competition (Women)

		pt
1.	Nadia Comaneci (RUM)	79·275
2.	Nelli Kim (URS)	78·675
3.	Ludmila Tourisheva (URS)	78·625
4.	Teodora Ungureanu (RUM)	78·375
5.	Olga Korbut (URS)	78·025
6.	Gitta Escher (GDR)	77·750
27.	Karen Kelsall (CAN)	74·625
29.	Patti Rope (CAN)	74·500
33.	Nancy McDonnell (CAN)	70·050
35.	Avril Lennox (GBR)	73·875

Horse (Women)

1.	Nelli Kim (URS)	19·800
2.	Ludmila Tourisheva (URS)	19·650
3.	Carola Domback (GDR)	19·650
4.	Nadia Comaneci (ROM)	19·625
5.	Gitta Escher (GDR)	19·550
6.	Marta Egervari (HUN)	19·450

Asymetrical Bars (Women)

1.	Nadia Comaneci (ROM)	20·000
2.	Teodora Ungureanu (ROM)	19.800
3.	Marta Egervari (HUN)	19·775
4.	Marion Kische (GDR)	19·750
5.	Olga Korbut (URS)	19·300
6.	Nelli Kim (URS)	19·225

Beam (Women)

1.	Nadia Comaneci (ROM)	19·950
2.	Olga Korbut (URS)	19·725
3.	Teodora Ungureanu (ROM)	19·700
4.	Ludmila Tourisheva (URS)	19·475
5.	Angelika Hellmann (GDR)	19·450
6.	Gitta Escher (GDR)	19·275

Floor Exercises (Women)

1.	Nelli Kim (URS)	19·850
2.	Ludmila Tourisheva (URS)	19·825
3.	Nadia Comaneci (ROM)	19·750
4.	Anna Pohludkova (TCH)	19·575
5.	Marion Kische (GDR)	19·475
6.	Gitta Escher (GDR)	19·450

Handball

Finals (Men)

Soviet Union 19, Rumania 15
West Germany 16, Poland 21
Yugoslavia 21, Hungary 19
Denmark 21, Czechoslovakia 25
Japan 27, United States 20

Standings

1. Soviet Union
2. Rumania
3. Poland
4. West Germany
5. Yugoslavia
6. Hungary
11. Canada

Women

		w	l	d	for	agst	pts
1.	Soviet Union	5	0	0	92	40	10
2.	East Germany	3	3	1	89	47	7
3.	Hungary	3	1	1	85	55	7
4.	Rumania	2	3	0	73	83	4
5.	Japan	1	4	0	72	115	2
6.	Canada	0	5	0	35	106	0

Hockey

Finals

New Zealand 1, Australia 0
Holland 2, Pakistan 3
West Germany 9, Spain 1
India 2, Malaysia 0

Standings

1. New Zealand
2. Australia
3. Holland
4. Pakistan
5. West Germany
6. Spain
7. India
8. Malaysia

Leading scorers:

	goals
Paul Litjens (HOL)	11
Juan Amat (ESP)	7
Ronald Riley (AUS)	7
Wolfgang Stroedter (GER)	7
Munawar Khan (PAK)	6
Serge Dubois (BEL)	4
Manzoor Hussain (PAK)	4
Tony Inseon (NAL)	4
Surjit Singh (IND)	4

Judo

63 Kilogrammes

1. Hector Rodriguez (CUB)
2. Eunkyung Chang (KOR)
3. Felice Mariani (ITA)
3. Jozsef Tuncsik (HUN)

70 Kilogrammes

1. Vladimir Nevzorov (URS)
2. Koji Kuramoto (JPN)
3. Patrick Vial (FRA)
3. Marian Talaj (POL)

80 Kilogrammes

1. Isamu Sonoda (JPN)
2. Valeriy Dvoinikov (URS)
3. Slavko Obadov (YUG)
3. Youngchul Park (KOR)

93 Kilogrammes

1. Kazuhiro Ninomiya (JPN)
2. Ramaz Harshiladze (URS)
3. Dave Starbrook (GBR)
4. Juergun Roethlisberger (SUI)

Over 93 Kilogrammes

1. Sergei Novikov (URS)
2. Gunther Neureuther (GDR)
3. Sumio Endo (JPN)
3. Allen Coage (USA)

Open

1. Haruki Uemura (JPN)
2. Keith Remfrey (GBR)
3. Chota Chochishvila (URS)
3. Jeaki Cho (KOR)

Modern Pentathlon

Team

		pt
1.	Great Britain (Adrian Parker, Danny Nightingale, Jim Fox)	15,559
2.	Czechoslovakia	15,451
3.	Hungary	15,395
4.	Poland	15,343
5.	United States	15,285
6.	Italy	15,031

		total	riding	fencing	shooting	swimming	running
1.	Janusz Pyciak-Peciak (Pol)	5520	1066	928	1044	1164	1318
2.	Pavel Lednev (URS)	5485	1032	1096	1022	1092	1243
3.	Jan Bartu (TCH)	5466	1100	976	1044	1184	1162
4.	Daniele Masala (ITA)	5433	1090	832	1066	1244	1201
5.	Adrian Parker (GBR)	5298	1100	712	868	1240	1378
6.	John Fitzgerald (USA)	5286	1036	952	1000	1232	1066
10.	Danny Nightingale (GBR)	5187	1012	760	934	1172	1309
15.	Jim Fox (GBR)	5074	1100	784	846	1080	1264

Rowing

Single Sculls (Men)

		min	sec
1.	Pertti Karppinen (FIN)	7	29·03
2.	Peter Kolbe (GER)	7	31·67
3.	Joachim Dreifke (GDR)	7	38·03
4.	Sean Drea (IRL)	7	42·53
5.	Nikolai Dougan (URS)	7	57·39
6.	Ricardo Ibarra (ARG)	8	03·05
8.	Edward Hale (AUS)		

Double Sculls (Men)

		min	sec
1.	Norway	7	13·20
2.	Great Britain (Chris Baillieu, Michael Hart)	7	15·26
3.	East Germany	7	17·45
4.	Soviet Union	7	18·87
5.	West Germany	7	22·15
6.	France	7	50·18

Coxless Pairs (Men)

		min	sec
1.	East Germany	7	23·31
2.	United States	7	26·73
3.	West Germany	7	30·03
4.	Yugoslavia	7	34·17
5.	Bulgaria	7	37·42
6.	Czechoslovakia	7	51·06
9.	Canada		
12.	Great Britain (David Sturge, Henry Clay)		

Coxed Pairs (Men)

		min	sec
1.	East Germany	7	58.99
2.	Soviet Union	8	01·82
3.	Czechoslovakia	8	03·28
4.	Bulgaria	8	11·27
5.	Italy	8	15·97
6.	Poland	8	23·02
7.	Great Britain (Neil Christie, James Macleod, David Webb)		

Quadruple Sculls (Men)

		min	sec
1.	East Germany	6	18·25
2.	Soviet Union	6	19·89
3.	Czechoslovakia	6	21·77
4.	West Germany	6	24·81
5.	Bulgaria	6	32·04
6.	United States	6	34·33
9.	Great Britain (Andrew Justice, Mark Hayter, Allan Whitwell, Charles Imbert)		
11.	Canada		

Coxless Fours (Men)

		min	sec
1.	East Germany	6	37·42
2.	Norway	6	41·22
3.	Soviet Union	6	42·52
4.	New Zealand	6	42·23
5.	Canada	6	46·11
6.	West Germany	6	47·44
12.	Great Britain (Neil Keron, David Townsend, Richard Avling, William Mason)		

Coxed Fours (Men)

		min	sec
1.	Soviet Union	6	40·22
2.	East Germany	6	42·70
3.	West Germany	6	46·96
4.	Czechoslovakia	6	50·15
5.	Bulgaria	6	52·86
6.	New Zealand	7	00·17
7.	Ireland		

Eights (Men)

		min	sec
1.	East Germany	5	58·29
2.	Great Britain (Richard Lester, John Yallop, Tim Crooks, Hugh Matheson, David Maxwell, James Clark, Fred Smallbone, Leonard Robertson, Patrick Sweeney)	6	00·82
3.	New Zealand	6	03·51
4.	West Germany	6	06·15
5.	Australia	6	09·75
6.	Czechoslovakia	6	14·29
8.	Canada		

Single Sculls (Women)

		min	sec
1.	Christine Scheiblich (GDR)	4	05·56
2.	Joan Lind (USA)	4	06·21
3.	Elena Antonova (URS)	4	10·24
4.	Rossitza Spassova (URS)	4	10·85
5.	Ingrid Munneke (HOL)	4	18·71
6.	Mariann Ambrus (HUN)	4	22·59
11.	Colette Peppin (CAN)	4	34·76

Double Sculls (Women)

		min	sec
1.	Bulgaria	3	44·36
2.	East Germany	3	47·86
3.	Soviet Union	3	49·93
4.	Norway	3	52·18
5.	United States	3	58·25
6.	Canada	4	06·23

Coxless Pairs (Women)

		min	sec
1.	Bulgaria	4	01·22
2.	East Germany	4	01·64
3.	West Germany	4	02·35
4.	Soviet Union	4	03·27
5.	Canada	4	08·09
6.	Rumania	4	15·44
10.	Great Britain (Linda Clark, Beryl Mitchell)		

Coxed Fours (Women)

		min	sec
1.	East Germany	3	29·99
2.	Soviet Union	3	32·49
3.	Rumania	3	32·76
4.	Bulgaria	3	34·13
5.	Czechoslovakia	3	42·53
6.	Denmark	3	46·99
9.	Canada	3	57·72

Coxed Fours Sculls (Women)

		min	sec
1.	East Germany	3	29·99
2.	Soviet Union	3	32·49
3.	Rumania	3	32·76
4.	Bulgaria	3	34·13
5.	Czechoslovakia	3	42·53
6.	Denmark	3	46·99
9.	Canada	3	57·72

Coxed Fours (Women)

		min	sec
1.	East Germany	3	45·08
2.	Bulgaria	3	48·24
3.	Soviet Union	3	49·38
4.	Rumania	3	51·17
5.	Holland	3	54·36
6.	United States	3	56·50

Eights (Women)

		min	sec
1.	East Germany	3	33·32
2.	Soviet Union	3	36·17
3.	United States	3	38·68
4.	Canada	3	39·52
5.	West Germany	3	41·06
6.	Rumania	3	44·79

Shooting

Small Bore Rifle, 3 Positions

		pt
1.	Lanny Bassham (USA)	1162
2.	Margaret Murdock (USA)	1162
3.	Werner Seibold (GER)	1160
4.	Srecko Pejovic (YUG)	1156
5.	Sven Johansson (SWE)	1152
6.	Ho Jun Li (PRK)	1152
14.	Hans Adloch (CAK)	1144
18.	Malcolm Cooper (GBR)	1143
24.	Barry Dagger (GBR)	1137

Small Bore Rifle Prone Position

		pt
1.	Karl Heinz Smieszek (GER) (equals Wld record)	599
2.	Ulrich Lind (GER)	597
3.	Gennady Luschikov (URS)	595
4.	Anton Mueller (SUI)	595
5.	Walter Frescura (ITA)	594
6.	Arne Sorenson (CAN)	593
20.	Ian Ballinger (NZL)	590
20.	Anthony Greenfield (GBR)	590
28.	Hans Adloch (CAN)	589
41.	Donald Brook (AUS)	586
51.	Alister Allen (GBR)	584

Trap

		pt
1.	Donald Haldeman (USA)	190
2.	Armando Silva Marques (POR)	189
3.	Ubaldesc Baldi (ITA)	189
4.	Burckhardt Hoppe (GDR)	186
5.	Alexandr Androshkin (URS)	185
6.	Adam Smelcynski (POL)	183
18.	Malcolm Jenkins (GBR)	177
28.	Peter Boden (GBR)	169

Running Target Game

			pt
1.	Alexandr Gazov (URS)	(Olympic record)	579
2.	Alexandr Keydarov (URS)		576
3.	Jerzy Greszkiewicz (POL)		571
4.	Thomas Pfeffer (GDR)		571
5.	Wolfgang Hamberger (GER)		567
6.	Helmut Bellingradt (COL)		567
19.	Graeme McIntyre (NZL)		547
21.	John Gough (GBR)		543
23.	John Anthony (GBR)		537
24.	Grant Taylor (NZL)		536
25.	Daniel Nadeau (CAN)		526

Rapid Fire Pistol

			pt
1.	Norbert Glaar (GDR)	(Olympic record)	597
2.	Jurgen Wiefel (GDR)		596
3.	Roberto Ferraris (ITA)		595
4.	Afansy Kuzmin (URS)		595
5.	Corneliu Ion (ROM)		595
6.	Erwin Glock (GER)		594
15.	Brian Girling (GBR)		587
31.	John Cooke (GBR)		583
31.	Jules Sobrian (CAN)		583
34.	Alexander Taransky (CAN)		380
38.	Steven Kelly (CAN)		570

Skeet

		pt
1.	Josef Panacek (TCH)	198
2.	Eric Swinkels (HOL)	198
3.	Wieslaw Gawlikowski (POL)	196
4.	Klaus Reschke (GDR)	196
5.	Franz Schitzhofer (AUT)	195
6.	Edgardo Zachrisson (GUA)	194
22.	Joseph Neville (GBR)	191
26.	John Woolley (NZL)	190
35.	Harry Willsie (CAN)	188
47.	Brian Hebditch (GBR)	184

Free Pistol

			pt
1.	Uwe Potteck (GDR)	(Olympic record)	573
2.	Harald Vollmer (GDR)		567
3.	Rudolf Dollinger (AUT)		562
4.	Heinz Mertel (GER)		560
5.	Ragnar Skanaker (SWE)		559
6.	Vincenzo Tondo (ITA)		559
12.	Antal Laslo (GBR)		553
23.	Thomas Guinn (CAN)		548
24.	Jules Sobrian (CAN)		547
32.	Norman Harrison (AUS)		540
42.	John Gillman (AUS)		525
46.	Camilo Pedro (HKG)		490

Soccer

Brazil 4, Israel 1 Poland 5, North Korea 0	Brazil 0, Poland 2
France 0, East Germany 4 Soviet Union 2, Iran 1	East Germany 2, Soviet Union 1

Third Place

Brazil 0, Soviet Union 2

Final

Poland 1, East Germany 3

Standings

1. East Germany
2. Poland
3. Soviet Union
4. Brazil

		goals
Leading Scorers:	Andrzev Szarmach (POL)	6
	Jurgen Dorner (GDR)	4
	Victor Rangel (MEX)	3
	Michel Platini (FRA)	3
	Grzegorz Lato (POL)	3
	Vladimir Onischenko (URS)	3

Swimming

100 Metres Freestyle (Men)

			sec
1.	Jim Montgomery (USA)	(World record)	49·99
2.	Jack Babashoff (USA)		50·81
3.	Peter Nocke (GER)		51·31
4.	Klaus Steinbach (GER)		51·68
5.	Marcello Guarducci (ITA)		51·70
6.	Joe Bottom (USA)		51·79
7.	Vladimir Bure (URS)		52·03
8.	Andrey Krylov (URS)		52·15

200 Metres Freestyle (Men)

			min	sec
1.	Bruce Furniss (USA)	(World record)	1	50·29
2.	John Naber (USA)		1	50·50
3.	Jim Montgomery (USA)		1	50·58
4.	Andrei Kyylov (URS)		1	50·73
5.	Klaus Steinbach (GER)		1	51·09
6.	Peter Nocke (GER)		1	51·71
7.	Gordon Downie (GBR)		1	52·78
8.	Andrei Bogdanov (URS)		1	53·33

400 Metres Freestyle (Men)

			min	sec
1.	Brian Goodell (USA)	(World record)	3	51·93
2.	Tim Shaw (USA)		3	52·54
3.	Vladimir Raskatov (URS)		3	55·76
4.	Djan Magruda (BRA)		3	57·18
5.	Stephen Holland (AUS)		3	57·59
6.	Sandor Nagy (HUN)		3	57·81
7.	Vladimir Mikheev (URS)		4	00·79
8.	Stephen Badger (CAN)		4	02·83

1500 Metres Freestyle (Men)

			min	sec
1.	Brian Goodell (USA)	(World record)	15	02·40
2.	Bobby Hackett (USA)		15	03·91
3.	Stephen Holland (AUS)		15	04·66
4.	Djan Madruga (BRA)		15	19·84
5.	Vladimir Salnikov (URS)		15	29·45
6.	Max Metzker (AUS)		15	31·53
7.	Paul Hartloff (USA)		15	32·08
8.	Zoltan Waldar (HUN)		15	46·97

100 Metres Backstroke (Men)

			sec
1.	John Naber (USA)	(World record)	55·49
2.	Peter Rocca (USA)		56·34
3.	Roland Matthes (GDR)		57·22
4.	Carlos Berrocal (PUR)		57·28
5.	Lutz Wanja (GDR)		57·49
6.	Bob Jackson (USA)		57·69
7.	Mark Kerry (AUS)		57·94
8.	Mark Tonelli (AUS)		58·42

200 Metres Backstroke (Men)

			min	sec
1.	John Naber (USA)	(World record)	1	59·19
2.	Peter Rocca (USA)		2	00·55
3.	Dan Harrigan (USA)		2	01·35
4.	Mark Tonelli (AUS)		2	03·17
5.	Mark Kerry (AUS)		2	04·07
6.	Miloslav Rolko (TCH)		2	05·81
7.	Robert Rudolf (HUN)		2	07·30
8.	Zoltan Verraszto (HUN)		2	08·23

100 Metres Breaststroke (Men)

			min	sec
1.	John Hencken (USA)	(World record)	1	03·11
2.	David Wilkie (GBR)		1	03·43
3.	Arvidas Iouzaytis (URS)		1	04·23
4.	Graham Smith (CAN)		1	04·26
5.	Giorgio Lalle (ITA)		1	04·37
6.	Walter Kusch (GER)		1	04·38
7.	Duncan Goodhew (GBR)		1	04·66
8.	Chris Woo (USA)		1	05·13

200 Metres Breaststroke (Men)

			min	sec
1.	David Wilkie (GBR)	(World Record)	2	15·11
2.	John Hencken (USA)		2	17·26
3.	Rick Colella (USA)		2	19·20
4.	Graham Smith (CAN)		2	19·42
5.	Charles Keating (USA)		2	20·79
6.	Arvidas Iuozaytis (URS)		2	21·87
7.	Nikolay Pankin (URS)		2	22·21
8.	Walter Kusch (GER)		2	22·36

100 Metres Butterfly (Men)

		sec
1.	Matt Vogel (USA)	54·35
2.	Joe Bottom (USA)	54·50
3.	Gary Hall (USA)	54·65
4.	Roger Pyttel (GDR)	55·09
5.	Roland Matthes (GDR)	55·11
6.	Clay Evans (CAN)	55·81
7.	Hideaki Hara (JPN)	56·34
8.	Neil Rogers (AUS)	56·57

200 Metres Butterfly (Men)

			min	sec
1.	Mike Bruner (USA)	(World record)	1	59·23
2.	Steve Gregg (USA)		1	59·54
3.	Bill Forrester (USA)		1	59·96
4.	Roger Pyttel (GDR)		2	00·02
5.	Michael Kraus (GER)		2	00·46
6.	Brian Brinkley (GBR)		2	01·49
7.	Jorge Delgado (ECU)		2	01·95
8.	Aleksandr Manachinskiy (URS)		2	04·61

400 Metres Medley (Men)

			min	sec
1.	Rod Strachan (USA)	(World record)	4	23·68
2.	Tim McKee (USA)		4	24·62
3.	Andrey Smirnov (URS)		4	26·90
4.	Andras Hargity (HUN)		4	27·13
5.	Graham Smith (CAN)		4	28·64
6.	Steve Furniss (USA)		4	29·23
7.	Andy Ritchie (CAN)		4	29·87
8.	Ha-Jo Geisler (GER)		4	34·95

4 × 100 Metres Medley (Men)

			min	sec
1.	USA (John Naber, John Hencken, Matt Vogel, Jim Montgomery)	(World record)	3	42·22
2.	Canada		3	45·94
3.	West Germany		3	47·29
4.	Great Britain (James Carter, David Wilkie, John Mills, Brian Brinkley)		3	49·56
5.	Soviet Union		3	49·90
6.	Australia		3	51·54
7.	Italy		3	52·92
8.	Japan		3	54·74

4 × 200 Metres Freestyle (Men)

		min	sec
1.	USA (Mike Bruner, Bruce Furniss, John Naber, Jim Montgomery) (World record)	7	23·22
2.	Soviet Union	7	27·97
3.	Great Britain (Alan McLatchey, David Dunne, Gordon Downie, Brian Brinkley)	7	32·11
4.	West Germany	7	32·27
5.	East Germany	7	38·92
6.	Holland	7	42·56
7.	Sweden	7	42·84
8.	Italy	7	43·39

High Diving (Men)

		pt
1.	Klaus Dibiasi (ITA)	600·51
2.	Gregory Lousanis (USA)	576·99
3.	Vladimir Aleynik (URS)	548·61
4.	Kent Vosler (USA)	544·14
5.	Patrick Moore (USA)	538·17
6.	Falk Hoffmann (GDR)	531·60
7.	David Ambartsumian (URS)	516·21
8.	Carlos Giron (MEX)	513·93

Springboard Diving (Men)

		pts
1.	Philip Boggs (USA)	619·05
2.	Franco Cagnotto (ITA)	570·48
3.	Aleksandr Kosenkov (URS)	567·24
4.	Falk Hoffmann (GDR)	553·53
5.	Robert Cragg (USA)	548·19
6.	Gregory Louganis (USA)	528·96
7.	Carlos Giron (MEX)	523·59
8.	Klaus Dibiasi (ITA)	516·18

Water Polo

country	played	won	lost	goals for	goals against	pts
1. Hungary	04	00	01	30	24	09
2. Italy	02	01	02	21	20	06
3. Holland	02	01	02	18	17	06
4. Romania	01	01	03	26	25	05
5. Yugoslavia	00	02	03	21	24	03
6. Germany	00	04	01	15	21	01

round progress

	Hol.	Ita.	Ger.	Hun.	Rom.	Yug
Holland	x	3– 3	3– 2	3– 5	4– 4	5– 3
Italy	3– 3	x	4– 3	5– 6	4– 4	5– 4
Germany	2– 3	3– 4	x	3– 5	3– 5	4– 4
Hungary	5– 3	6– 5	5– 3	x	9– 8	5– 5
Romania	4– 4	4– 4	5– 3	8– 9	x	5– 5
Yugoslavia	3– 5	4– 5	4– 4	5– 5	5– 5	x

100 Metres Freestyle (Women)

			sec
1.	Kornelia Ender (GDR)	(World record)	55·65
2.	Petra Priemer (GDR)		56·49
3.	Brigitha Enith (HOL)		56·65
4.	Kim Peyton (USA)		56·81
5.	Shirley Babashoff (USA)		56·95
6.	Claudia Hempel (GDR)		56·99
7.	Jill Sterkel (USA)		57·06
8.	Jutta Weber (GER)		57·26

200 Metres Freestyle (Women)

			min	sec
1.	Kornelia Ender (GDR)	(World record)	1	59·26
2.	Shirley Babashoff (USA)		2	01·22
3.	Brigitha Enith (HOL)		2	01·40
4.	Annelies Maas (HOL)		2	02·56
5.	Gail Amumdrud (CAN)		2	03·32
6.	Jennifer Hooker (USA)		2	04·20
7.	Claudia Hempel (GDR)		2	04·61
8.	Irina Vlasova (URS)		2	05·63

400 Metres Freestyle (Women)

			min	sec
1.	Petra Thumer (GDR)	(World record)	4	08·89
2.	Shirely Babashoff (USA)		4	10·46
3.	Shannon Smith (CAN)		4	14·60
4.	Rebecca Perrott (NZL)		4	14·76
5.	Kathy Heddy (USA)		4	15·50
6.	Brenda Borgh (USA)		4	17·43
7.	Annelies Maas (HOL)		4	17·44
8.	Sabine Kahl (GDR)		4	20·42

800 Metres Freestyle (Women)

			min	sec
1.	Petra Thumer (GDR)	(World record)	8	20·59
2.	Shirley Babashoff (USA)		8	37·59
3.	Wendy Weinberg (USA)		8	42·60
4.	Rosemary Milgate (AUS)		8	47·21
5.	Nicole Kramer (USA)		8	47·33
6.	Shannon Smith (CAN)		8	48·15
7.	Regina Jager (GDR)		8	50·40
8.	Jenny Turrall (AUS)		8	52·88

100 Metres Breaststroke (Women)

		min	sec
1.	Hannelore Anke (GDR)	1	11·16*
2.	Liubov Rusanova (URS)	1	13·40
3.	Marina Koshevaia (URS)	1	13·30
4.	Carola Nitschke (GDR)	1	13·33
5.	Gabriele Askamp (GER)	1	14·15
6.	Marina Iurchenia (URS)	1	14·17
7.	Margaret Kelly (GBR)	1	14·20
8.	Karla Linke (GDR)	1	14·21

* World record of 1min 10·86sec in semi-finals

200 Metres Breaststroke (Women)

			min	sec
1.	Marina Koshevaia (URS)	(Olympic record)	2	33·35
2.	Marina Iurchenia (URS)		2	36·08
3.	Liubov Rusanova (URS)		2	36·22
4.	Anke Hannelore (GDR)		2	36·49
5.	Karla Linke (GDR)		2	36·97
6.	Carola Nitschke (GDR)		2	38·27
7.	Margaret Kelly (GBR)		2	38·37
8.	Deborah Rudd (GBR)		2	39·01

100 Metres Butterfly (Women)

			min	sec
1.	Kornelia Ender (GDR)	(Equals Wld record)	1	00·13
2.	Andrea Pollack (GDR)		1	00·98
3.	Wendy Boglioli (USA)		1	01·17
4.	Camille Wright (USA)		1	01·41
5.	Rosemarie Gabriel (GDR)		1	01·56
6.	Wendy Quirk (CAN)		1	01·75
7.	Lelei Fonoimoana (URS)		1	01·95
8.	Tamara Shelofastova (URS)		1	02·74

200 Metres Butterfly (Women)

			min	sec
1.	Andrea Pollack (GDR)	(Olympic record)	2	11·41
2.	Ulrike Tauber (GDR)		2	12·50
3.	Rosemarie Gabriel (GDR)		2	12·86
4.	Karen Thornton (USA)		2	12·90
5.	Wendy Quirk (CAN)		2	13·68
6.	Cheryl Gibson (CAN)		2	13·91
7.	Tamara Shelofastova (URS)		2	14·26
8.	Natalia Popov (URS)		2	14·50

100 Metres Backstroke (Women)

			min	sec
1.	Ulrike Richter (GDR)	(Olympic record)	1	01·83
2.	Birgit Treiber (GDR)		1	03·41
3.	Nancy Garapick (CAN)		1	03·71
4.	Wendy Hogg (CAN)		1	03·93
5.	Cheryl Gibson (CAN)		1	05·16
6.	Nadejda Stavko (URS)		1	05·19
7.	Antje Stille (GDR)		1	05·30
8.	Diane Edelijn (HOL)		1	05·53

200 Metres Backstroke (Women)

			min	sec
1.	Ulrike Richter (GDR)	(Olympic record)	2	13·43
2.	Birgit Treiber (GDR)		2	14·97
3.	Nancy Garapick (CAN)		2	15·60
4.	Nadejda Stavko (URS)		2	16·28
5.	Melissa Belote (USA)		2	17·27
6.	Antje Stille (GDR)		2	17·55
7.	Klavdia Studennikova (URS)		2	17·74
8.	Wendy Hogg (CAN)		2	17·95

400 Metres Individual Medley (Women)

			min	sec
1.	Ulrike Tauber (GDR)	(World record)	4	42·77
2.	Cheryl Gibson (CAN)		4	48·10
3.	Becky Smith (CAN)		4	50·48
4.	Birgit Treiber (GDR)		4	52·40
5.	Sabine Kahle (GDR)		4	53·50
6.	Donnalee Wennerstrom (USA)		4	55·34
7.	Joanne Baker (CAN)		5	00·19
8.	Monique Rodahl (NZL)		5	00·21

4 × 100 Metres Medley Relay (Women)

			min	sec
1.	East Germany (Ulrike Richter, Hannelore Anke, Andrea Pollack Kornelia Ender)	(World record)	4	07·95
2.	United States		4	14·55
3.	Canada		4	15·22
4.	Soviet Union		4	16·05
5.	Holland		4	19·93
6.	Great Britain (Joy Beasley, Margaret Kelly, Susan Jenner, Debby Hill)		4	23·25
7.	Japan		4	23·47
8.	Australia		4	25·91

4 × 100 metres Freestyle (Women)

			min	sec
1.	United States	(World record)	3	44·82
2.	East Germany		3	45·50
3.	Canada		3	48·81
4.	Holland		3	51·67
5.	Soviet Union		3	52·69
6.	France		3	56·73
7.	Sweden		3	57·25
8.	West Germany		3	58·33

Springboard (Women)

		pt
1.	Jennifer Chandler (USA)	506·19
2.	Christa Kohler (GDR)	469·41
3.	Cynthia McIngvale (USA)	466·83
4.	Heidi Ramlow (GDR)	462·15
5.	Karin Guthke (GDR)	459·81
6.	Olga Dmitrieva (URS)	432·24
7.	Irina Kalinina (URS)	417·99
8.	Barbara Nejman (USA)	365·07

High Diving (Women)

		pt
1.	Elena Vaytsekhovskaia (URS)	406·59
2.	Ulrika Knape (SWE)	402·60
3.	Debby Wilson (CAN)	401·07
4.	Irina Kalinina (URS)	398·67
5.	Cindy Shatto (CAN)	378·39
6.	Teri York (CAN)	378·39
7.	Melissa Briley (USA)	376·86
8.	Heidi Ramlow (GDR)	365·64

Volleyball

Finals (*Men*)

Soviet Union 2, Poland 3
Cuba 3, Japan 0
Czechoslovakia 3, Korea 1
Brazil 3, Italy 0

Standings

1. Poland
2. Soviet Union
3. Cuba
4. Japan
5. Czechoslovakia
6. Korea
7. Brazil
8. Italy

Finals (*Women*)

Japan 3, Soviet Union 0
Korea 3, Hungary 1
East Germany 0, Cuba 3
Canada 1, Peru 3

Standings

1. Japan
2. Soviet Union
3. Korea
4. Hungary
5. Cuba
6. East Germany
7. Peru
8. Canada

Weight-lifting

Flyweight (*52 Kilogrammes*)

			kg
1.	Alexandr Voronin (USSR)	(Olympic record)	242·5
2.	Gyorgy Koszegi (HUN)		237·5
3.	Mohammed Nassiri (IRN)		235·0
4.	Masatomo Takeuchi (JAP)		232·5
5.	Francisco Casamayor (CUB)		227·5
6.	Stefan Leletko (POL)		220·0
13.	Precious Mckenzie (GBR)		200·0

Bantam (*56 Kilogrammes*)

			kg
1.	Norair Nurikyan (BUL)	(Olympic record)	262·5
2.	Grzegorz Cziura (POL)		252·5
3.	Kenkichi Ando (JAP)		250·0
4.	Leszek Skorupa (POL)		250·0
5.	Imre Foldi (HUN)		245·0
6.	Bernhard Bachfisch (GER)		242·5

Featherweight (*60 Kilogrammes*)

			kg
1.	Nikolai Koleshikov (URS)	(Olympic record)	285·0
2.	Georgi Todorov (BUL)		280·0
3.	Kazamusa Hirai (JPN)		275·0
4.	Takashi Saito (JPN)		262·5
5.	Edward Weitz (ISR)		262·5
6.	Davoud Maleki (IRN)		260·0
13.	Victor Daniels (GBR)		227·5

Lightweight (67·5 Kilogrammes)

			kg
1.	Zbigniew Kaczmarek (POL)	(Olympic record)	307·5
2.	Piotr Korol (URS)		305·0
3.	Daniel Senet (FRA)		300·0
4.	Kazimierz Czarnecki (POL)		295·0
5.	Gunter Ambrass (GDR)		295·0
6.	Yatsuo Shimaya (JPN)		292·5
10.	Kevin Welch (GBR)		282·5
16.	Alan Winterbourne (GBR)		267·5

Middleweight (75 Kilogrammes)

			kg
1.	Yordan Mitkov (BUL)	(Olympic record)	335·0
2.	Vartan Militsyan (URS)		330·0
3.	Peter Wenzel (GDR)		327·5
4.	Wolfgang Hubner (GDR)		320·0
5.	Dragomir Cioroslan (ROM)		320·0
6.	Arvo Ala-Pontio (FIN)		315·0
13.	Robert Kabbas		297·5

Light Heavyweight (82·5 Kilogrammes)

			kg
1.	Valeri Shary (URS)	(Olympic record)	365·0
2.	Blagoi Blagoev (BUL)		362·5
3.	Trendafil Stoichev (BUL)		360·0
4.	Peter Baczako (HUN)		345·0
5.	Nicolaos Iliadis (GRE)		340·0
6.	Juhani Avellan (FIN)		330·0

Middle Heavyweight (90 Kilogrammes)

			kg
1.	David Rigert (URS)	(Olympic record)	382·5
2.	Lee James (USA)		362·5
3.	Atanas Shopov (URS)		360·0
4.	Philip Grippaldi (USA)		355·0
5.	Gheorghy Rehus (HUN)		350·0
6.	Peter Petzold (GDR)		345·0
10.	Gary Langford (GBR)		327·5
14.	Kenneth Price (GBR)		307·5

Heavyweight (110 Kilogrammes)

			kg
1.	Valentin Khristov (BUL)	(Olympic record)	400·0
2.	Yuri Zaitsev (URS)		385·0
3.	Krastio Semerdjiev (BUL)		385·0
4.	Tadeusz Rutkowski (POL)		377·5
5.	Pierre Gourrier (FRA)		372·5
6.	Jurgen Ciezki (GDR)		372·5
11.	Russ Prior (CAN)		362·5
16.	John Burns (GBR)		347·5
17.	John Barrett (NZL)		342·5
18.	Bob Santavy (CAN)		337·5

Superheavyweight (Over 110 Kilogrammes)

			kg
1.	Vasili Alexeev (URS)	(Olympic record)	440·0
2.	Gerd Bonk (GDR)		405·0
3.	Helmut Losch (GDR)		387·5
4.	Jan Nagy (TCH)		387·5
5.	Bruce Wilhelm (USA)		387·5
6.	Gerardo Fernandez (CUB)		365·0
7.	Robert Edmond (AUS)		347·5

Wrestling

Free Style

48 Kilogrammes

1. Khassan Issaev (BUL)
2. Roman Dnietrev (URS)
3. Akira Kudo (JPN)

52 Kilogrammes

1. Yuji Takada (JPN)
2. Alexandr Ivanov (URS)
3. Haex Sup Jeon (KOR)

57 Kilogrammes

1. Vladimir Umin (URS)
2. Hans Diester Bruchert (GDR)
3. Masao Arai (JPN)

62 Kilogrammes

1. Jung-Mo Yang (KOR)
2. Zeveg Oidov (MGL)
3. Gene Davis (USA)

68 Kilogrammes

1. Pavel Pinigin (URS)
2. Lloyd Keaser (USA)
3. Yasaburp Sugawara (JPN)

74 Kilogrammes

1. Jiichiro Date (JPN)
2. Mansour Barzegar (IRN)
3. Stanley Dziedzic (USA)

82 Kilogrammes

1. John Peterson (USA)
2. Viktor Novojilov (URS)
3. Adolf Seger (GER)

90 Kilogrammes

1. Levan Tediashvili (URS)
2. Ben Peterson (USA)
3. Stelica Morcov (ROM)

100 Kilogrammes

1. Ivan Yarygin (URS)
2. Russell Hellickson (USA)
3. Dimo Kostov (BUL)

Over 100 Kilogrammes

1. Soslan Andiev (URS)
2. Joszef Balla (HUN)
3. Ladislau Simon (ROM)

Greco-Roman Style

48 Kilogrammes

1. Alexey Shumakov (URS)
2. Gheorghe Berceanu (ROM)
3. Stefan Anghelov (BUL)
4. Yoshite Moriwake (JPN)
5. Dietmar Hinz (GDR)
6. Mitchell Kawasaki (CAN)

52 Kilogrammes

1. Vitaly Konstantinov (URS)
2. Nicu Ginga (ROM)
3. Koichiro Hirayama (JPN)
4. Rolf Krauss (GER)
5. Lajos Racz (HUN)
6. Morad-Ali Shirani (IRN)

57 Kilogrammes

1. Pettti Ukkola (FIN)
2. Ivan Grgic (YUG)
3. Farhat Mustafin (URS)
4. Yoshima Suga (JPN)
5. Mihai Botila (ROM)
6. Krasimir Stefanov (BUL)

62 Kilogrammes

1. Kazikierz Lipien (POL)
2. Nelson Davidian (URS)
3. Laszlo Reczi (HUN)
4. Teruhiko Miyahara (JPN)
5. Ion Paun (ROM)
6. Pekka Hjelt (FIN)

68 Kilogrammes

1. Suren Nalbandyan (URS)
2. Stefan Rusu (ROM)
3. Heinz Helmut Wehling (GDR)
4. Lars Skiold (SWE)
5. Andrzej Supron (POL)
6. Manfred Schondorfer (GER)

74 Kilogrammes

1. Anatolyi Bykov (URS)
2. Viteszlav Macha (TCH)
3. Karl Heinz Helbing (GER)
4. Mikko Huhtala (FIN)
5. Klaus Dieter Gopfert (GDR)
6. Gheorghe Ciobotaru (ROM)

82 Kilogrammes

1. Momir Petkovic (YUG)
2. Vladimir Cheboksarov (URS)
3. Ivan Kolev (BUL)
4. Leif Andersson (SWE)
5. Miroslav Janota (TCH)
6. Kazuhiro Takanishi (JPN)

90 Kilogrammes

1. Valery Rezantsev (URS)
2. Stoyan Ivanon (BUL)
3. Czeslaw Kwiecinski (POL)
4. Darko Nisavic (YUG)
5. Frank Andersson (SWE)
6. Istvan Sellyei (HUN)

100 Kilogrammes

1. Nikolai Bolboshin (URS)
2. Kamen Goranov (BUL)
3. Andrzej Skrylewski (POL)
4. Brad Rheingans (USA)
5. Tore Hem (NOR)
6. Heinz Schafer (GER)

Over 100 Kilogrammes

1. Alexandr Kolchinski (URS)
2. Alexandr Tomov (BUL)
3. Roman Codreanu (ROM)
4. Henryk Tomanek (POL)
5. William Lee (USA)
6. Janos Rovnyai (HUN)

Yachting

Finn

		total
1.	East Germany	35·40
2.	Soviet Union	39·70
3.	Australia	46·40
4.	Brazil	54·70
5.	Sweden	66·40
6.	Greece	77·00
7.	Great Britain (David Howlett)	77·70
8.	Canada	83·00
15.	New Zealand	109·00

470

		total
1.	West Germany	42·40
2.	Spain	49·70
3.	Australia	57·00
4.	Soviet Union	57·00
5.	New Zealand	59·70
6.	Great Britain (Philip Crebbin, Derek Clark)	69·40
16.	Canada	109·70

Flying Dutchman

		total
1.	West Germany	34·70
2.	Great Britain (Rodney Pattisson, Julian Brooke Houghton)	51·70
3.	Brazil	52·10
4.	Canada	57·10
5.	Soviet Union	59·40
6.	United States	65·70
9.	Australia	74·70
12.	New Zealand	85·00
19.	Ireland	142·00

Tempest

		total
1.	Sweden	14·00
2.	Soviet Union	30·40
3.	United States	32·70
4.	Germany	42·10
5.	Italy	55·40
6.	Denmark	62·70
7.	Canada	65·10
14.	Great Britain (Alan Warren, David Hunt)	119·00

Tornados

		total
1.	Great Britain (Reg White, John Osborn)	18·00
2.	United States	36·00
3.	West Germany	37·70
4.	Australia	44·40
5.	Sweden	57·40
6.	Switzerland	64·40
8.	Canada	69·70

Soling

		total
1.	Denmark	46·70
2.	United States	47·40
3.	East Germany	47·40
4.	Soviet Union	48·70
5.	Holland	58·00
6.	West Germany	60·70
8.	Canada	68·70
11.	Australia	92·70
13.	Great Britain (Iain Macdonald-Smith, Michael Baker-Harber, Barry Dunning)	102·00
19.	New Zealand	135·00

XIIth WINTER GAMES

Cross Country

15 Kilometres (Men)

		min	sec
1.	Nikolay Bajukov (USSR)	43	58·47
2.	Eugeniy Beliaev (USSR)	44	01·10
3.	Arto Koivisto (FIN)	44	19·25
4.	Ivan Garanin (USSR)	44	41·98
5.	Ivar Formo (NOR)	45	29·11
6.	William Koch (USA)	45	32·22
33.	Bert Bullock (CAN)	47	23·38
56.	Hans Skinstad (CAN)	49	30·36
59.	Edward Day (CAN)	49	59·43
63.	Paul Gibbins (GB)	51	48·02
65.	Douglas Elliott (GB)	52	14·27
67.	Ernie Lenie (CAN)	52	27·04
68.	Keith Oliver (GB)	52	31·00

(80 started, 78 finished)

30 Kilometres (Men)

		hr	min	sec
1.	Sergei Saveliev (USSR)	1	30	29·38
2.	William Koch (USA)	1	30	57·84
3.	Ivan Garanin (USSR)	1	31	09·29
4.	Juha Mieto (FIN)	1	31	20·39
5.	Nikolay Bajukov (USSR)	1	31	33·14
6.	Gert Dietmar Klause (GDR)	1	32	00·91
30.	Hans Skinstad (CAN)	1	36	16·95
31.	Bert Bullock (CAN)	1	36	24·55
42.	Edward Day (CAN)	1	38	09·10
56.	Reijo Puiras (CAN)	1	41	34·43

(69 started, 67 finished)

50 Kilometres (Men)

		hr	min	sec
1.	Ivar Formo (NOR)	2	37	30·05
2.	Gert Dietmar Klause (GDR)	2	38	13·21
3.	Benny Soedergren (SWE)	2	39	39·21
4.	Ivan Garanin (USSR)	2	40	38·94
5.	Gerhard Grimmer (GDR)	2	41	15·46
6.	Per Knut Aaland (NOR)	2	41	18·06
22.	Hans Skinstad (CAN)	2	46	11·83
37.	Edward Day (CAN)	2	51	58·75
41.	Ernie Lenie (CAN)	3	01	01·57

(44 started and finished)

4 × 10 Kilometres (Men)

		hr	min	sec
1.	Finland	2	07	59·72
2.	Norway	2	09	58·36
3.	USSR	2	10	51·46
4.	Sweden	2	11	16·88
5.	Switzerland	2	11	28·53
6.	USA	2	11	41·35
12.	Canada	2	15	31·85

(16 started, 14 teams finished)

5 Kilometres (Women)

		min	sec
1.	Helena Takalo (FIN)	15	48·69
2.	Raisa Smetanina (USSR)	15	49·73
3.	Nina Baldicheva (USSR)	16	12·82
4.	Hilkka Kuntola (FIN)	16	17·74
5.	Eva Olsson (SWE)	16	27·15
6.	Zinaida Amosova (USSR)	16	33·78
27.	Shirley Firth (CAN)	17	31·36
29.	Sharon Firth (CAN)	17	35·06
30.	Joan Groothuysen (CAN)	17	51·08
34.	Esther Miller (CAN)	18	05·05

(44 started, 43 finished)

10 Kilometres (Women)

		min	sec
1.	Raisa Smetanina (USSR)	30	13·41
2.	Helena Takalo (FIN)	30	14·48
3.	Galina Kulakova (USSR)	30	38·61
4.	Nina Baldicheva (USSR)	30	52·58
5.	Eva Olsson (SWE)	31	08·72
6.	Zinaida Amosova (USSR)	31	11·33
28.	Sharon Firth (CAN)	33	15·20
29.	Shirley Firth (CAN)	33	16·50
32.	Susan Holloway (CAN)	34	03·49
34.	Joan Groothuysen (CAN)	34	16·45

(44 started and finished)

4 × 5 Kilometre (Women)

		hr	min	sec
1.	USSR	1	07	49·75
2.	Finland	1	08	36·57
3.	E. Germany	1	09	57·95
4.	Sweden	1	10	14·68
5.	Norway	1	11	09·08
6.	Czechoslovakia	1	11	27·83
7.	Canada	1	14	02·72

Jumping

70 Metres (Men)

		pts
1.	Hans Georg Aschenbach (GDR)	252·0
2.	Jochen Danneberg (GDR)	246·2
3.	Karl Schnabl (AUT)	242·0
4.	Jaroslav Balcar (TCH)	239·6
5.	Ernst von Gruenigen (SWITZ)	238·7
6.	Reinhold Bachler (AUT)	237·2
36.	Peter Wilson (CAN)	207·6
48.	Richard Grady (CAN)	192·6
54.	Kim Fripp (CAN)	175·9
55.	Donald Grady (CAN)	164·9

90 Metres (Men)

		pts
1.	Karl Schnabl (AUT)	234·8
2.	Anton Innauer (AUT)	232·9
3.	Henry Glass (GDR)	221·7
4.	Jochen Danneberg (GDR)	221·6
5.	Reinhold Bachler (AUT)	217·4
6.	Hans Wallner (AUT)	216·9
45.	Peter Wilson (CAN)	154·7
46.	Richard Grady (CAN)	153·3
53.	Kim Fripp (CAN)	125·9

ALPINE EVENTS

Downhill

Men

		min	sec
1.	Franz Klammer (AUT)	1	45·73
2.	Bernhard Russi (SWITZ)	1	46·06
3.	Herbert Plank (ITA)	1	46·59
4.	Phillipe Roux (SWITZ)	1	46·69
5.	Ken Read (CAN)	1	46·83
6.	Andy Mill (USA)	1	47·06
8.	David Irwin (CAN)	1	47·41
10.	Jim Hunter (CAN)	1	47·52
18.	David Murray (CAN)	1	48·43
22.	David Griff (AUS)	1	49·02
30.	Alan Stewart (GB)	1	50·56
32.	Stuart Fitzsimmons (GB)	1	50·89
34.	Andrew Clifford (AUS)	1	51·64
37.	Peter Fuchs (GB)	1	52·75
53.	Stuart Blakely (NZ)	1	57·91
60.	Brett Kendall (NZ)	2	00·57

(74 started, 66 finished)

Women

		min	sec
1.	Rosi Mittermaier (W. GER)	1	46·16
2.	Brigitte Totschnig (AUT)	1	46·68
3.	Cynthia Nelson (USA)	1	47·50
4.	Andrea Spiess (AUT)	1	47·71
5.	Daniele Debernard (FRA)	1	48·48
6.	Jacqueline Rouvier (FRA)	1	48·58
16.	Laurie Kreiner (CAN)	1	49·97
19.	Kathy Kreiner (CAN)	1	50·48
22.	Betsy Clifford (CAN)	1	51·40
29.	Valentina Iliffe (GB)	1	53·31
31.	Sally Rodd (AUS)	1	54·82
34.	Fiona Easdale (GB)	1	57·66
35.	Hazel Hutcheon (GB)	1	58·33
36.	Patricia Henke (AUS)	1	59·59
37.	Theresa Wallis (GB)	1	59·77
38.	Sue Gibson (NZ)	2	03·49

(38 started and finished)

Slalom

Men

		min	sec
1.	Piero Gros (ITA)	2	03·29
2.	Gustavo Thoeni (ITA)	2	03·73
3.	Willy Frommelt (LIE)	2	04·28
4.	Walter Tresch (SWITZ)	2	05·26
5.	Christian Neureuther (W. GER)	2	06·56
6.	Wolfgang Junginer (W. GER)	2	07·08
23.	Jim Hunter (CAN)	2	17·06
27.	Robert Safrata (CAN)	2	17·98
35.	Stuart Blakely (NZ)	2	28·77
36.	Brett Kendall (NZ)	2	38·38

(62 started, 38 finished)

Women

		min	sec
1.	Rosi Mittermaier (W. GER)	1	30·54
2.	Claudia Giordani (ITA)	1	30·87
3.	Hanni Wenzel (LIE)	1	32·20
4.	Daniele Debernard (FRA)	1	32·24
5.	Pamela Behr (W. GER)	1	32·31
6.	Linda Cochran (USA)	1	33·24
14.	Laurie Kreiner (CAN)	1	39·38
15.	Valentina Iliffe (GB)	1	40·14
18.	Fiona Easdale (GB)	1	47·00
19.	Sue Gibson (NZ)	2	03·53

(30 started, 19 finished)

Giant Slalom

Men

		min	sec
1.	Heini Hemmi (SWITZ)	3	26·97
2.	Ernst Good (SWITZ)	3	27·17
3.	Ingemar Stenmark (SWE)	3	27·41
4.	Gustavo Thoeni (ITA)	3	27·67
5.	Phillip Mahre (USA)	3	28·20
6.	Engelhard Pargaetzi (SWITZ)	3	28·76
22.	Jim Hunter (CAN)	3	37·36
33.	Alan Stewart (GB)	3	49·64
44.	Brett Kendall (NZ)	4	04·05

(71 started, 52 finished)

Women

		min	sec
1.	Kathy Kreiner (CAN)	1	21·13
2.	Rosi Mittermaier (W. GER)	1	29·25
3.	Daniele Debernard (FRA)	1	29·95
4.	Lise Marie Morerod (SWITZ)	1	30·40
5.	Marie Terese Nadig (SWITZ)	1	30·44
6.	Monika Kaserer (AUT)	1	30·49
22.	Betsy Cliffors (CAN)	1	32·61
27.	Laurie Kreiner (CAN)	1	34·53
30.	Valentina Iliffe (GB)	1	35·48
33.	Sally Rodd (AUS)	1	37·52
37.	Fiona Easdale (GB)	1	41·09
38.	Theresa Wallis (GB)	1	41·66
39.	Serena Iliffe (GB)	1	45·09
40.	Patricia Henke (AUS)	1	45·40
41.	Janet Wells (NZ)	1	48·42
42.	Sue Gibson (NZ)	1	49·30

(45 started, 43 finished)

Combined (Cross country & jumping)

Men

		pts
1.	Ulrich Wehling (GDR)	423·39
2.	Urban Hettich (W. GER)	418·90
3.	Konrad Winkler (GDR)	417·47
4.	Rauno Miettinen (FIN)	411·30
5.	Claus Tuchscherer (GDR)	409·51
6.	Nikolay Nagovitzin (USSR)	406·44
33.	Kurt Sjolund (CAN)	252·22

(33 started and finished)

Speed Skating

500 Metres (Men)

			sec
1.	Eugeniy Kulikov (USSR)	(Olympic record)	39·17
2.	Valeriy Muratov (USSAR)		39·25
3.	Daniel Immerfall (USA)		39·54
4.	Mats Wallberg (SWE)		39·56
5.	Peter Mueller (USA)		39·57
6.=	Arnulf Sunde (NOR)		39·78
=	Jan Bazen (NETH)		39·78
11.	Tom Overend (CAN)		40·22
14.	Gaeten Boucher (CAN)		40·53
16.	Archie Marshall (GB)		40·85
25.	Victor Coates (AUS)		41·77

(29 started, 28 finished)

1000 Metres (Men)

		min	sec
1.	Peter Mueller (USA)	1	19·32
2.	Jorn Didriksen (NOR)	1	20·45
3.	Valeriy Muratov (USSR)	1	20·57
4.	Aleksandr Safronov (USSR)	1	20·84
5.	Hans van Helden (NETH)	1	20·85
6.	Gaeten Bucher (CAN)	1	21·23
11.	Victor Coates (AUS)	1	21·72
21.	Archie Marshall (GB)	1	24·00
23.	Tom Overend (CAN)	1	25·06

(31 started and finished)

1500 Metres (Men)

			min	sec
1.	Jan Egil Storholt (NOR)	(Olympic record)	1	59·38
2.	Yuri Kondakov (USSR)		1	59·97
3.	Hans van Helden (NETH)		2	00·87
4.	Sergei Riabev (USSR)		2	02·15
5.	Daniel Carroll (USA)		2	02·26
6.	Piet Kleine (NETH)		2	02·28
8.	Victor Coates (AUS)		2	03·34
14.	Gaeten Boucher (CAN)		2	04·45
24.	Geoffrey Sandys (GB)		2	09·17

(30 started and finished)

5000 Metres (Men)

			min	sec
1.	Sten Stensen (NOR)		7	24·48
2.	Piet Kleine (NETH)		7	26·47
3.	Hans van Helden (NETH)		7	26·54
4.	Victor Varlamov (USSR)		7	30·97
5.	Klaus Wunderlich (GDR)		7	33.82
6.	Daniel Carroll (USA)		7	36·46
10.	Victor Coates (AUS)		7	41·96
23.	Andrew Barron (CAN)		8	10·00
26.	Geoffrey Sandys (GB)		8	13·03

(31 started and finished)

10,000 Metres (Men)

			min	sec
1.	Piet Kleine (NETH)	(Olympic record)	14	50·59
2.	Sten Stensen (NOR)		14	53·30
3.	Hans van Helden (NETH)		15	02·02
4.	Victor Varlamov (USSR)		15	06·06
5.	Oerjen Sandler (SWE)		15	16·21
6.	Victor Coates (AUS)		15	16·80
18.	Geoffrey Sandys (GB)		16	26·27

(20 started & finished)

500 Metres (Women)

			sec
1.	Sheila Young (USA)	(Olympic record)	42·76
2.	Cathy Priestner (CAN)		43·12
3.	Tatiana Averina (USSR)		43·17
4.	Leah Poulos (USA)		43·21
5.	Vera Krasnova (USSR)		43·23
6.	Ljubov Sadchikova (USSR)		43·80
11.	Sylvia Burka (CAN)		44·35
21.	Kathleen Vogt (CAN)		45·62

(27 started and finished)

1000 Metres (Women)

			min	sec
1.	Tatiana Averina (USSR)	(Olympic record)	1	28·43
2.	Leah Poulos (USA)		1	28·57
3.	Sheila Young (USA)		1	29·14
4.	Sylvia Burka (CAN)		1	29·47
5.	Monika Holzner (W. GER)		1	29·54
6.	Cathy Priestner (CAN)		1	29·66
22.	Elizabeth Appleby (CAN)		1	34·27

(27 started, 26 finished)

3000 Metres (Women)

			min	sec
1.	Tatiana Averina (USSR)	(Olympic record)	4	45·19
2.	Andrea Mitscherlich (GDR)		4	45·23
3.	Lisbeth Korsmo (NOR)		4	45·24
4.	Karin Kessow (GDR)		4	45·60
5.	Ines Bautzmann (GDR)		4	46·67
6.	Sylvia Filipsson (SWE)		4	48·15
8.	Sylvia Burka (CAN)		4	49·04
18.	Elizabeth Appleby (CAN)		4	58·64
23.	Gayle Gordon (CAN)		5	07·09

(26 started and finished)

Figure Skating

Men

		placements	pts
1.	John Curry (GB)	11·0	192·74
2.	Vladimir Kovalev (USSR)	28·0	187·64
3.	Toller Cranston (CAN)	30·0	187·38
4.	Jan Hoffman (GDR)	34·0	187·34
5.	Sergei Vokov (USSR)	53·0	184·08
6.	David Santee (USA)	49·0	184·28
10.	Robin Cousins (GB)	83·0	178·14
14.	Stan Bohonek (CAN)	124·0	165·88
16.	Glyn Jones (GB)	141·0	157·24

(20 started, 16 finished)

Women

		placements	pts
1.	Dorothy Hammill (USA)	9·0	193·80
2.	Dianne de Leeuw (NETH)	20·0	190·24
3.	Christine Errath (GDR)	28·0	188·16
4.	Anett Poetzsch (GDR)	33·0	187·42
5.	Isabel de Navarre (W. GER)	59·0	182·42
6.	Wendy Burge (USA)	63·0	182·14
9.	Lynn Nightingale (CAN)	67·0	181·72
14.	Kim Alletson (CAN)	122·5	171·64
15.	Karena Richardson (GB)	137·0	166·52

(21 started, 20 finished)

Pairs

		placements	pts
1.	Irina Rodnina & Aleksandr Zaitsev (USSR)	9·0	140·54
2.	Romy Kermer & Rolf Oesterreich (GDR)	21·0	136·35
3.	Manuela Gross & Uwe Kagelmann (GDR)	34·0	134·57
4.	Irina Voroieva & Aleksandr Vlasov (USSR)	35·0	134·52
5.	Tai Babilonia & Randy Gardner (USA)	36·0	134·24
6.	Kerstin Stolfig & Veit Kempe (SWITZ)	59·0	129·57
11.	Erika & Colin Taylforth (GB)	108·0	124·40
14.	Candice Jones & Donald Fraser (CAN)	117·0	116·54

Dancing

		placements	pts
1.	Ludmilla Pakhomova & Aleksandr Gorshkov (USSR)	9·0	209·92
2.	Irina Moiseeva & Andrei Minenkov (USSR)	20·0	204·88
3.	Colleen O'Connor & James Mills (USA)	27·0	202·64
4.	Natalia Linichuk & Gennadiy Karponosov (USSR)	35·0	199·10
5.	Krisztina Regoczy & Andras Sallay (HUN)	48·5	195·92
6.	Matilde Ciccia & Lamberto Ceserani (ITA)	58·5	191·46
7.	Hilary Green & Glyn Watts (GB)	57·0	191·40
8.	Janet Thompson & Warren Maxwell (GB)	78·0	186·60
10.	Barbara Berezowski & David Porter (CAN)	86·0	182·90
12.	Kay Barsdell & Kenneth Foster (GB)	111·0	175·16
13.	Susan Carscallen & Eric Gillies (CAN)	107·0	175·96

Ice Hockey

		P	W	D	L	gls	pts
1.	USSR	5	5	0	0	40:11	10
* 2.	Czech	5	2	0	2	17:10	6
3.	W. Ger	5	2	0	3	21:24	4
4.	Finland	5	2	0	3	19:18	4
5.	USA	5	2	0	3	15:21	4
* 6.	Poland	5	0	0	4	9:37	0

* no point awarded for one game

Biathlon

(Men)

		hr	min	sec
1.	Nikolay Kruglov (USSR)	1	14	12·26
2.	Heikki Ikola (FIN)	1	15	54·10
3.	Aleksandr Elizarov (USSR)	1	16	05·57
4.	Willy Bertin (ITA)	1	16	50·36
5.	Aleksandr Tihonov (USSR)	1	17	18·33
6.	Esko Saira (FIN)	1	17	32·84
29.	Graeme Ferguson (GB)	1	24	18·09
36.	Malcolm Hirst (GB)	1	25	52·97
39.	Jeffrey Stevens (GB)	1	27	15·87

4 × 7·5 Kilometres

		hr	min	sec
1.	USSR	1	57	55·64
2.	Finland	2	01	45·58
3.	E. Germany	2	04	08·61
4.	W. Germany	2	04	11·86
5.	Norway	2	05	10·28
6.	Italy	2	06	16·55
13.	Great Britain	2	11	54·36

Bob

2-Man

		min	sec
1.	Meinhard Nehmer & Bernard Germeshausen (GDR)	3	44·42
2.	Wolfgang Zimmerer & Manfred Schumann (W. GER)	3	44·99
3.	Erich Schaerer & Josef Benz (SWITZ)	3	45·70
4.	Fritz Sperling & Andreas Schwab (AUT)	3	45·74
5.	Georg Heibl & Fritz Ohlwaerter (W. GER)	3	46·13
6.	Dieter Delle & Franz Koefel (AUT)	3	36·97
18.	Colin Nelson & Jim Lavelley (CAN)	3	52·00
20.	Jackie Price & Malcolm Lloyd (GB)	3	52·10
21.	Mark Agar & William Sweet (GB)	3	52·71
23.	Joseph Kilburn & Brian Vachon (CAN)	3	54·29

4-Man

		min	sec
1.	E. Germany I	3	40·43
2.	Switzerland II	3	40·89
3.	W. Germany I	3	41·37
4.	E. Germany II	3	42·44
5.	W. Germany II	3	42·47
6.	Austria II	3	43·21
13.	GB I (Jackie Price, Colin Campbell, William Sweet, Malcolm Lloyd)	3	46·39
17.	Canada I (Colin Nelson, Thomas Stehr, David Veale, Jim Lavelley)	3	48·02
20.	GB II (Mark Agar, Anthony Norton, Graham Sweet, Andrew Ogilvie-Wedderburn)	3	49·85
21.	Canada II (Chris Frank, William Dunn, Christopher Martin, Brian Vachon)	3	50·86

Luge

Men

		min	sec
1.	Detlef Guenther (GDR)	3	27·688
2.	Josef Fendt (W. GER)	3	28·196
3.	Hans Rinn (GDR)	3	28·574
4.	Hans Winckler (GDR)	3	29·454
5.	Manfred Schmid (AUT)	3	29·511
6.	Anton Winkler (W. GER)	3	29·520
29.	Michel de Carvalho (GB)	3	42·665
30.	Jeremy Palmer Tomkinson (GB)	3	42·724
31.	Larry Arbuthnot (CAN)	3	42·784
33.	Richard Liversedge (GB)	3	44·839
35.	Michael Shragge (CAN)	3	46·292

2-Man

		min	sec
1.	Hans Rinn & Norbert Hahn (GDR)	1	25·604
2.	Hans Brandner & Balthasar Schwarm (W. GER)	1	25·889
3.	Rudolf Schmid & Franz Schachner (W. GER)	1	25·919
4.	Stefan Hoelzlwimmer & Rudolf Groesswang (W. GER)	1	26·238
5.	Manfred Schmid & Reinhold Sulzbacher (AUT)	1	26·424
6.	Jindrich Zeman & Vladimir Resl (CZECH)	1	26·826
17.	Larry Arbuthnot & Doug Hansen (CAN)	1	30·035
20.	Jeremy Palmer Tomkinson & Michel de Carvalho (GB)	1	31·377
22.	David McComb & Michael Shragge (CAN)	1	31·590

Women

		min	sec
1.	Margit Schumann (GDR)	2	50·621
2.	Ute Ruehrold (E. Ger)	2	50·846
3.	Elisabeth Demleitner (W. GER)	2	51·056
4.	Eva Maria Wernicke (GDR)	2	51·262
5.	Antonia Mayr (AUT)	2	51·360
6.	Margit Graf (AUT)	2	51·459
22.	Carole Keyes (CAN)	3	01·883
23.	Mary Bowie (CAN)	3	02·341
26.	Julie Chase (CAN)	3	13·522

Medals Table (Winter Games)

	Gold	Silver	Bronze	Total
USSR	13	6	8	27
E. Germany	7	5	7	19
USA	3	3	4	10
Norway	3	3	1	7
W. Germany	2	5	3	10
Finland	2	4	1	7
Austria	2	2	2	6
Switzerland	1	3	1	5
Netherlands	1	2	3	6
Italy	1	2	1	4
Canada	1	1	1	3
GB	1	0	0	1
Czechoslovakia	0	1	0	1
Sweden	0	0	2	2
Liechtenstein	0	0	2	2
France	0	0	1	1

Medals Table (Summer Games)

	Gold	Silver	Bronze	Total
Soviet Union	47	43	35	125
East Germany	40	25	25	90
U.S.A.	34	35	25	94
West Germany	10	12	17	39
Japan	9	6	10	25
Poland	8	6	11	25
Bulgaria	7	8	9	24
Cuba	6	4	3	13
Rumania	4	9	14	27
Hungary	4	5	12	21
Finland	4	2	0	6
Sweden	4	1	0	5
Great Britain	3	5	5	13
Italy	2	7	4	13
Yugoslavia	2	3	3	8
Czechoslovakia	2	2	4	8
France	2	2	5	9
New Zealand	2	1	1	4
South Korea	1	1	4	6
Switzerland	1	1	2	4
Jamaica	1	1	0	2
North Korea	1	1	0	2
Norway	1	1	0	2
Denmark	1	0	2	3
Mexico	1	0	1	2
Trinidad	1	0	0	1
Canada	0	5	6	11
Belgium	0	3	3	6
Holland	0	2	3	5
Portugal	0	2	0	2
Spain	0	2	0	2
Australia	0	1	4	5
Iran	0	1	1	2
Mongolia	0	1	0	1
Venezuela	0	1	0	1
Brazil	0	0	2	2
Austria	0	0	1	1
Bermuda	0	0	1	1
Pakistan	0	0	1	1
Puerto Rico	0	0	1	1
Thailand	0	0	1	1

N.B. The medals table is liable to alteration as details of drug tests are revealed.